A GUIDE TO

THE HISTORIC BUILDING... OF MILTON KEYNES

Paul Woodfield

INDEX

INTRODUCTION

i.

In 1971 Milton Keynes Development Corporation published a book called 'BUILDING CONSERVATION—A PHOTOGRAPHIC INDEX'. This was a survey of the significant historic buildings of the area with short notes to each photograph, and served the purpose of reminding the relatively young Corporation of what buildings were worthy of notice during the planning of the City. This has long been out of print, and indeed out of date. It is the purpose of this volume to revise that early book in the light of the greater knowledge acquired over the intervening years; both of buildings in which the Corporation had a direct involvement and those remaining in other hands. The presentation remains on the same format, the old parishes are treated one by one, all buildings and monuments of any significance briefly described, and in most cases, accompanied by a photograph. A note of their present listing is given, and additionally, a map giving their location.

This compilation is the result of two activities: on one hand the interpretation of the surviving structure by an architect specialising in historic buildings, and secondly a sifting of the 'lore of the fathers' as already available in written form, leavened with local knowledge. A list of the more important published works used appears in the bibliography. This book makes no special claims to pure and original research in archives although some research has in fact been done by an architectural historian and colleagues in the archaeological world. Not being an academic work the statements are not backed by footnotes giving sources; this would have made the work unnecessarily cumbersome. This work then incorporates a selection of information accumulated by the Conservation Section of the Development Corporation over the 10 years 1973–1984.

The text is in abbreviated form similar to that used to describe Listed Buildings. No apology is offered for this, as the statutory lists are not (astonishingly) obtainable by the general public. These lists, however, are drawn up within certain guidelines, which exclude many buildings of character and interest, as a glance at the entries for Wolverton or Fenny Stratford will show. Time has shown that the guidelines are arbitrary and change with time, and more importantly, with public taste. Thus this present work is more comprehensive and catholic in its choice of entries. Age is not a criterion of quality or interest in itself. Significant buildings therefore, up to 1967 when the Development Corporation started, have been included where they have a particular contribution to make to the environment in the special context of the new city. An exception has been made for demolished buildings. Although no really significant building has been lost since 1973 (in the circumstances of building a city, a record of no mean accomplishment), records show a fair number of losses earlier, particularly in the infamous 1950's. Where these buildings are of interest to us today they have been included, named within brackets, so to complete a picture of the architecture of the area.

The opportunity has been taken on the maps to record the Conservation Areas and to show scheduled archaeological monuments. Again both suffer the same defects as listing, in that the boundaries are necessarily arbitrary and time often shows that the more significant lies outside the drawn line.

To give a historical summary of all buildings within the compass of the space available is a thankless task, and one incapable ever of completion. There will never be agreement that any one building has been adequately covered, and there will be a constant flow of new titbits of information as further research is done, and buildings are investigated in greater detail. For this reason it is suggested that comments and information that readers may wish to make available are sent to the author, or to the Planning Department of the Development Corporation at Saxon Court, Central Milton Keynes. Should a further edition be published in the future it can thus be made more accurate and up to date.

Since the article published by David Anstis and reproduced at length in the 1971 INDEX, the approach to building conservation has moved a long way. His approach was defensive, almost an apology. Now, by contrast the advantages have become well embedded in the consciousness of a more environmentally aware public. People have learned to be suspicious of the dogma of the modern movement in architecture, as a result of much urban re-development, and, at the same time, have been made more aware of the profligate use of raw materials that underlies the practice of the Western economies. This has been accompanied with a growing awareness that tailor-made buildings become the sooner obsolete. Our stock of older buildings not only contains a large investment in energy and natural resources: think for a moment of the energy that goes to make one brick—but are often a sufficiently 'loose-fit', thus adaptable to accommodate a whole variety of new uses.

But there is more to it. Not only do historic buildings often show an awareness of human scale and condition which is immediately acceptable, but they do provide an intangible link with time past, and with geographical identity. Research has shown that this link seems to be an important factor in the stability of the social fabric of human communities. Lack of this framework, linking both geography and history, seems to create, at least in Western societies, an increase in dissatisfaction and consequent instability. Beyond the simple leavening of the environment with colour and meaningful structure, which is normally thought of as the role of the past environment today, there seems to be an immeasurable and uncostable benefit to be derived from retaining some presence of the past, both the recent past and the more removed periods of history, just as much as it is equally necessary to retain a contact with the natural environment. Perhaps it is all part of the creation of a group-identity that we, who often cannot recite even the names of our immediate ancestors as do many people's throughout the world, use in its place. If this makes sense, and is then hitched to the purely pragmatic attitude of making best use of what is re-useable, then, far from being just romantic escapism, the arguments for the conservation of buildings are overwhelming.

THE HISTORICAL ARCHITECTURE OF THE MILTON KEYNES AREA

ii.

Although not noted for its wealth of historical architecture, with a little perseverance and selection, the main elements of the story of English architecture can be discovered in the historic buildings of Milton Keynes.

The earliest upstanding structures are, as is usual, the churches. The medieval churches of the area are, in many cases, the only places where the early history of the peoples of the area can be read, thus are monuments of irreplaceable value. Although there is no indisputably Anglo Saxon work to be seen, it is clear from records and excavation that some churches have such early origins. The earliest work, probably eleventh century, is to be seen at Shenley (K1), where the transepts are almost late Saxon in character, followed by the not inconsiderable Norman chancel. Late Norman work is well illustrated at Bletchley (A1) and Stantonbury, both having been reset, the latter in St. James, New Bradwell (M16). This is robust chevron work, with the less common beak-head ornament on Bletchley's south door. Simple Norman fonts occur at Little Woolstone (G19) and one was found under the floor at Walton (Q1). C13 construction is to be seen in the tower of Great Linford, perhaps a remodelling of an earlier structure, and some interesting work on the chancel arch at Bradwell (B25). The C14 was a period of great expansion in the building of churches, and much work of this period survives. One of the most complete is All Saints, Milton Keynes, perhaps owing its completeness to manorial privilege. Of special interest is the small pilgrimage chapel at Bradwell Abbey (C2), complete of its date c.1350 including roof and outstanding wallpaintings, an unexpected treasure that survived as a stable. Late medieval church work is less common, memorable being the timber roof of Simpson (L1) and the series of important wallpaintings surviving at Broughton (D1).

Of memorials, there is little of special note. Shenley has some fine monuments of 1577 and 1607, other C17 monuments occur at Walton (Q1) where a Nollekins sculpture of 1701 is also to be found. Two later interesting C18 monuments appear at Simpson.

The earliest traces of domestic buildings are now only represented by a series of moats that once surrounded, and to some extent, defended the early manor houses. The best are to be seen in Little Woolstone, Loughton, Simpson and Tattenhoe. As early, if not earlier are the three mottes or castle mounds thrown up to support wooden look-out towers as necessary adjuncts of buildings within the attached moated area or bailey. It is usually assumed that these are of the C12. The most conspicuous is that called 'The Toot' at Shenley, but others occur at Old Wolverton, and Bradwell.

The earliest surviving vernacular buildings, other than churches, are those employing timber frames in their construction. Cruck framing, which is clearly identifiable as an early form of frame supporting the roof, appears to have generally been obsolete by the C17. It was noted in the excavation of a modest dwelling on the southern Green at Great Linford, and is found upstanding in four places in Milton Keynes, in Simpson (L12), two in Milton Keynes, (J3 and J13), and in the priory barn at Bradwell Abbey (C4), there scientifically dated to ± 1320. Immediately around the city, crucks were used in the C14 in Haversham, at Husborne Crawley, and an interesting group of them at Newton Longville. These, together with sub-cruck forms as at Bradwell (B3), suggest that, even though on the eastern fringe of the geographical distribution, nationwide, this form of construction was widespread in the medieval period. Of particular significance is the recent appearance in Milton Keynes (J3) of a base cruck form supporting a two-bay open hall which has at the centre truss a primitive crown post. The crucks support a tie beam over which is mounted arcade-type plates square to the ground and supported by brackets to end posts. This building is of much more than local significance in that it illustrates a point of conflation of the aisled structural system with the cruck form and at the same time the absorbtion of the crown post roof of eastern Britain into the traditional midland constructional forms.

It is more than possible that regular box frames could also be mid-late medieval in date, for those few outside the area that have been checked by dendrochronology have on occasion been shown to be substantially earlier than normal typological dating would have attributed to them. This then may be termed the 'type immobilisée' of architecture and remained constant over some centuries, there being no readily discernable difference in form or method of assembly. Although some non-cruck buildings are doubtlessly medieval, e.g. Simpson (L4) there is no doubt however that most timber framed buildings surviving were the result of the extensive reconstruction of buildings in more permanent and lasting form that took place in the period 1680–1720, known as the Great Rebuilding, and particularly in the 40 years after the Restoration, 1660–1700. This was a time of some material prosperity, and more importantly, of settled times in the rural areas, when surpluses were being made by the more modest farmers and landowners, who were sufficiently confident of the future to expend their wealth in permanent structures, not only for the lifetime of the man himself, but for his heirs and successors. This was also the time when the smaller man could aspire to a chimney to carry away the smoke from his living room through the roof, making upper floors not only tolerable but good sense. Smoke bays, recalling pre-flue days, survive in later structures at Bradwell (B3 and B10) and Milton Keynes. A good example of the new fangled Elizabethan fireplace with a chimney occurs at Loughton Manor Farm (H5). Structural timber was, in early times, readily available, by leave of the landowner or crown, in surrounding forest lands, Whittlebury, Salcey, Whaddon, or Bromswold, as well, no doubt, in the parish woodland and hedgerows. The framing would generally be professionally made at the 'framying place', numbered and delivered to site. You, the recipient, arranged the erection, thatched the roof, and infilled the panels with staves, woven withies and daubed with a clay-lime mix. The celebration after the communal effort of erecting the frame survives in the barn dance. The frame stood on a low wall or groundsill of stone, later brick, to lift it out of the wet. Wheatstraw thatch seems to be the universal roofing material of this area for the smaller house until the C18, when it was gradually replaced by the more fireproof but less insulating plain tiles. Stone slates were probably used to some extent from local quarries, such as had the Romans at the Bancroft and Stanton Low villas, but these perished with time and none now survives. Welsh slates come with the introduction of bulk transport, first by canal, and later by the railways in the mid C19. Leicestershire slate was used at the Bancroft villa.

For the large buildings the story is not much different, for the distinction in style between fashionable architecture of the rich and the vernacular was not made until the C16–C17. Unfortunately major houses of the great period of English timber construction, the C14, or anything earlier, have not survived, the nearest being the Grange at Haversham and the Monastery, Shutlanger. Late medieval timber framed buildings of substance occur at Fenny Stratford (Chantry House E47) and in Bletchley (Rectory Cottages A11), the former being the standardised construction typical of the C16 including a jettied first floor, the only one in the area, and suppressed tension braces. It has an elemental hammer beam roof truss which also appears in the roof of Simpson Church (L1) and in a more developed form in the impressive domestic hall at Rectory Cottages. Both these buildings were no doubt tiled from the start.

Unfortunately the larger houses of the later period have suffered a similar fate to the medieval ones. The De Grey houses at Simpson and Shenley, the Longueville House at Wolverton, the Mallets, Stony Stratford and Water Hall, Bletchley, amongst others less known, would have together added much to the historic architecture of Milton Keynes. These have gone with the viccisitudes of time and the fortunes of the owners.

With the C17 came a re-evaluation of the mode of living in buildings and a consequential break with traditional house planning. The two- and three-part medieval plans such as survive in altered form at Church Farm, Little Woolstone (G17) give way, in our area as in many others to the lobby entry plan with a central door to a lobby against a large central stack, inglenook fireplaces backing on to each other to two rooms, one being a kitchen, the other a more polite room. A stair wound round the back of the stack. Examples occur at Lodge Farm, Great Linford (F46) and The Manor House, Little Woolstone (G16). Attached to the rear a dairy is usually to be found and such rooms are added to earlier buildings at the same period.

Along the northern margin of Milton Keynes, the Great Ouse has recut through the glacial clays and underlying rocks of Liassic and Jurassic age revealing the oolitic limestones which in places can provide a passable building stone. Villages like Stony Stratford, Bradwell, Stantonbury and Great Linford thus had a natural advantage, and appear to have used stone for walling from earliest times. Cartage made stone construction expensive at any real distance from the source, thus it was not until the C16 and the improvement of roads that there is any overtaking of timber construction by stone.

In the C17 farms usually appear within the villages, not out in their fields as they did in the C19. The farm buildings reflect the same pattern of building materials as do the houses, timber framing clad in boarding for ventilation, and raised on low stone walls, and thatched roofs. Examples exist at Manor Farm, Shenley Church End (K8), or in stone at Warren Old Farm, Wolverton (T13). The buildings generally range round a yard for convenience and shelter, the largest, the corn barn, on the north side. Cattle sheds or, in local terminology, hovels, do not survive well but examples appear at Shenley Common Farm South (K25), and converted at Linford (F39) and Hill Farm, Great Woolstone (G2). The barns are frequently replaced by stronger handsome brick structures for loose grain in the C19, such as Downs Barn (F44) or Red Barn, Great Linford (F13). The grain, earlier, was stored in framed buildings raised off the ground on stone staddles to frustrate access by vermin. Examples survive at Shenley Valley Farm (K22), Manor Farm, Willen (S5) and Southside Farm, Milton Keynes (J17).

The C17 saw the increase in construction in brickwork. Stantonbury Manor was using locally burnt bricks in 1655, and Sir William Pritchard at Linford was buying bricks and tiles in 1688 from a widow at Newport Pagnell. Early brickwork can be seen at Bradwell Abbey Farm, Linford Almshouses and elsewhere, sometimes incised with initials and dates (G7, G17, E40). By the C18 brick construction was becoming universal in the Milton Keynes area and some splendid examples of it survive, as at Milton Keynes Rectory (J20), in Water Eaton (R1, R2) and in towns, as in the inns of Stony Stratford (N75, N85). This brickwork, due to the method of firing, often had the ends of the bricks burnt to a vitrified state, producing a blue colour, which was utilized to advantage in laying them in Flemish bond. In Woolstone (G17, G18) we find the curious use of unburnt bricks for internal construction. Only later, in the C19, were the other clays used to produce a pale tan coloured brick at Simpson and Fenny Stratford and laid to the same effect.

Houses of the C18 still by and large retain the single room deep plan inherited from the medieval past but by now usually with a central through stair hall, the chimney stacks being placed at the gable ends. The double pile plan which was introduced to the country c.1650, first appears in our area in sophisticated buildings such as Milton Keynes Rectory in the early-mid C18.

Of the works of the C17 and C18 architectural establishment, we have three important examples, all churches. Perhaps the greatest is the church of Willen 1680, (S1), by Robert Hooke, the great scientist and occasional builder (The Monument, London; Ragley Hall, Ramsbury Manor). The Church of Fenny Stratford (E44) by Edward Wing is interesting as being a particularly early use of the Gothic Revival (as opposed to survival) of 1728, and at St Giles', Stony Stratford, (N21) the rather impressive later Gothic work of David Hiorne of 1777, the nave only now surviving later alterations.

The organised reconstruction of the roads, once notorious through this area, started with the Stony to Hockcliffe turnpike in 1706, followed by other turnpikes on the Buckingham to Newport Road, and the Newport to Leighton Buzzard roads, each with their own distinctive milestones. This began the era of better communications, to be followed by the canals, the Grand Junction with its Newport and Buckingham arms, then the railways from 1833 with their profound influence on the economy and building form of the area. The London and North Western did not reach the architectural heights of the Great Western and its own early architecture has barely survived the frequent alterations and policy changes that overtook the company. However, the design and planning of New Wolverton and New Bradwell are of great interest.

Of industrial monuments, outstanding is the Iron Trunk at Wolverton, 1809 (T19), engineered by the Ketley ironworks. The brick industry was widespread wherever suitable clays were found, but the only upstanding structures are the two kilns at Great Linford (F45) of the late C19. Unique also is the windmill of c.1816 at New Bradwell, old fashioned even for its day.

Two churches of the early C19 are worthy of mention. The little Commissioner's Gothic church of 1833 at Great Woolstone (G3), and the more significant and unusually early essay of 1809 in the Romanesque revival style at Old Wolverton (T1), by the architect Henry Hakewill. Later in the C19 we can demonstrate the work of a number of famous architects. G. E. Street, as well as being diocesan adviser, was architect for the development of New Bradwell 1850–53, and the School, Church and Vicarage are interesting and contrasting examples of his Gothic style. The other favourite of the mid-Victorian establishment, William Butterfield, built the Rectory at Great Woolstone (G5), 1851, later altered, while, at the same time, George Gilbert Scott inevitably appears at the new church of Wolverton End, Stony Stratford (N133), 1863. A little later John Oldrid Scott altered Brandon and Wyatt's St. George's, Wolverton Station (T35), and William White, that curious man of the Victorian scene, extended St. Martin's, Fenny Stratford and built, in 1865, the parish school at Loughton (H14). Of local men, the more outstanding are Edward Swinfen Harris, who did much work around his home in Stony Stratford from the 1870's, Richard Sheppard, architect and builder of Newport Pagnell, and John Chadwick, surveyor of Bletchley.

Later architectural styles are not well represented. Suggestions of both the Art Nouveau and the Art Deco styles occur at New Bradwell (M18 and M9) but by now the fashionable had moved to the larger centres of population and the early moderns are not represented any nearer than Northampton (New Ways, Behrens, 1926) or Rugby (Chermeyeff, 1933).

In the following pages, buildings which have a protected status under the law are noted in the right margin. This is by way of explanation of what the meanings and implications of the symbols are.

The origin of the listing of buildings.

The wish to protect historic monuments from senseless destruction was first brought to the attention of the reading public by a clergyman, William Stukeley, in the mid C18, who had witnessed the superstitious destruction of the stones of Avebury, and the neglect of a Wiltshire church. Later that century, over-zealous restoration and unfettered improvements of cathedrals by Wyatt and others created a climate in which some legal constraint was seen to be essential. Such a move had already taken place in Italy in the mid C18 and France in 1840, but the sacrosanct position held by private property in England delayed the introduction of any proper measures until 1882. Then the tide of public concern was moving under the influence of William Morris, and tentative steps were at last taken to protect a few outstanding prehistoric monuments. The imminent export of Tattershall Castle, Lincs in 1911 finally drew attention to the need to protect buildings. Provision to allow the Minister, later the Secretary of State, to compile a list of buildings of importance to the national heritage was finally made in 1947, and has been amended and re-enacted since.

The present position.

Buildings included in the List of Buildings of Outstanding Architectural or Historical Importance are of two types, Grade I being buildings of outstanding importance to the nation as a whole, and Grade II, buildings of special architectural or historical quality sufficient to merit special care and protection. In the following pages NL means Not Listed.

This simple scheme has been modified in certain ways:

Churches in use by the Church of England are exempt by reason of the established church's special relationship with the state, and by virtue of their own faculty procedure designed to the same ends. These buildings were nevertheless classed A, B or C, depending on their architectural interest, but are now being Graded on the standard system without it having legal status. In Milton Keynes both systems co-exist at present.

Buildings belonging to the Crown, i.e. Ministry of Defence, are graded, but they are exempt from the legal requirements, the naive assumption being that the agents of the Crown are above reproach. The position of privatised national institutions remains (1985) unclear.

Certain Grade II buildings with significantly fine interiors are awarded a star. This does no more than to alert those concerned to this fact, but it does in practice enable owners to apply with some confidence for nationally available grant aid.

Grade III, a non-statutory list called the Supplementary List and included buildings claimed to be of local interest, no longer exists.

The criteria for listing a building are as follows. There is no appeal (the architectural/historical value being a matter of fact). Listing can cover walls, street furniture, minor structures, even dog kennels, milestones and urinoirs.

a. Buildings built before 1700 surviving in anything like their original condition.
b. Most buildings 1700–1840 remaining substantially unaltered.
c. Buildings built 1840–1914 selected as having definite quality, or by principal architects.
d. Important representative buildings built 1914–1939.
e. Buildings specially illustrative of social history or planning.
f. Buildings exhibiting technological innovation or virtuosity.
g. Buildings associated with significant persons or historical events.
h. Buildings important by virtue of being in a special context or group.

It should be emphasised that listing is not designed to preserve the status quo. It is designed to ensure that alterations, when proposed, do no harm to the historical value of the building, but, if possible, improve it. To make this judgement, the local planning authority, who are charged with implementing this legislation, are to obtain the advice of specialists in architectural-historical matters before making their decision.

Grant Aid

As the position varies at regular intervals, this cannot be more than a broad outline. There are no as-of-right grants available to owners or occupiers of listed buildings. However, local authorities, both County and District Council are empowered to make grants on terms they choose to make, it being deemed to be in the public interest that such buildings are preserved from decay or neglect. Not all make these grants, and where they are offered, they are usually not large, and can be assessed on the basis of the calculated increment in cost resulting from the building being a listed building over and above the cost if it were not. Grade I and II* buildings have, in addition, access to funds distributed through the Historic Buildings Council. It may be a condition of grant-aid that public access at certain times should be allowed.

CONSERVATION AREAS

The 1968 Civic Amenities Act allows for areas of particular visual attractiveness to be designated Conservation Areas, introducing measures to prevent harmful alteration such as demolition of unlisted buildings and the destruction of trees, walls and other elements of the built environment. Conservation Areas usually contain a number of older buildings which may also be listed, and schemes can be drawn up for the general improvement of the visual amenities of the zone.

SCHEDULED MONUMENTS

Areas of known archaeological significance can be Scheduled under the various Ancient Monuments Acts. This is designed to afford protection of the remains above or below ground from damage by unauthorised works such as building, fencing, metal detecting and, in some cases, a change in agricultural practices which would endanger hitherto undisturbed land. These are administered by the Department of the Environment through the local planning authority.

ACKNOWLEDGEMENTS

iv.

Firstly, it should be recorded that the initiative to bring this work into print is due to the efforts of Peter Waterman and John Hilton, who acted in the role of publisher. I would also like to thank Janice Walker of MKDC Planning Directorate who has provided the essential links.

This is the opportunity to thank members of MKDC Conservation Section who have each made their special contribution to the large amount of information assembled over the years. These are John Crooks, Iain Cawthorne, Caron Rollins (now Higgins), and Debbie Faulkner, and especially Brian Giggins whose researches and analyses of buildings have been particularly valuable.

The researches and knowledge possessed by others have kindly been put at my disposal, in particular Bob Croft of MKDC Archaeology Unit, Ray Bellchambers of Bradwell, Ted Legg of Fenny Stratford, and I am equally in their debt for the valuable time they have afforded me in checking the text. Others too have helped in this task, including Peter Hall of Woughton, Pat Mortimer of Wolverton, and Robert Ayers of Stony Stratford.

Not least, thanks are due to the numerous householders and owners of property for allowing access where appropriate and for discussing their buildings, for it is from such information this collection is made more valuable.

The photographs have been taken by Paul Woodfield and Brian Giggins. M3 was taken by Tom Jones. It will be seen that whereas some photographs were taken in July–September 1985, some have been selected from earlier years where these show buildings more visible than today, or before certain alterations have taken place. Some of these were taken by Ray Bailey for the Milton Keynes Research Committee. Aerial photographs were taken by John Hilton and cover design was by Bernard Madden of MKDC Commerce Directorate.

BIBLIOGRAPHY

The following list represents a selection of published sources from which further information may be obtained. It does not include many early publications, now more difficult to get outside public libraries, and where the information is repeated in later works, nor does it include the many minor publications such as church guides and ephemera where these are of a general unscholarly nature.

BARLEY, R. E.	Romance around Stony Stratford	Barley	1928
CALVOCORESSI, P.	Top Secret Ultra	Cassell	1980
CROFT, R. & MYNARD	The medieval Landscape of Milton Keynes	MK Arch. Unit	1984
CROFT, R. A. (Ed)	Victorian and Edwardian Milton Keynes	White Crescent	1984
FAULKNER, A. H.	The Grand Junction Canal	David & Charles	1972
FISHER, I.	Old Bletchley Remembered	People's Press	1979
GRIGG, A.	Town of Trains	Barracuda	19
HYDE, F. E.	History of Wolverton		1943
KELLY'S	Directories		
LIPSCOMB, G.	The History and Antiquities of the County of Bucks. IV		1847
LISTER, N.	Building Conservation in Milton Keynes	MKDC	1971
MARKHAM, S. F.	The Nineteen Hundreds	Hillier	1951
MARKHAM, S. F. and HYDE	History of Stony Stratford		
MARKHAM, Sir F.	History of Milton Keynes: Vol. I	White Crescent Press	1973
	History of Milton Keynes: Vol. II		1975
MKDC Arch. Unit	Milton Keynes Archaeology News		1978-1983
MYNARD, D.	St. Lawrence's Church, Old Bradwell		
MYNARD, D. *et al*	Bradwell Abbey, in M.K. Journal III	MKDC	1974
PEDLEY, D. & S.	St. George the Martyr, Wolverton	Stantonbury P.P.	1985
PEVSNER, Sir N.	Buildings of England: Buckinghamshire	Penguin	1960
RATCLIFFE, O.	History of the Newport Hundreds		1900
REED, M.	The Buckinghamshire Landscape	Hodder & Stoughton	1979
R.Comm.Hist.Mons.	Buckinghamshire (North)	RCHM	1913
SIDNEY, S.	Rides on Railways	(Reprint Phillimore 1973)	1851
SIMPSON, B.	Oxford to Cambridge Railway. Vol. I	Oxford	1981
	Oxford to Cambridge Railway. Vol II	Oxford	1983
SIMPSON, F. D.	The Wolverton and Stony Stratford Steam Train	Omnibus Soc.	1981
TAYLOR, J.	Tale of Two Cities		1979
Various	Records of Bucks. XIV, XIX, XX	Bucks. Arch. Soc.	
VICTORIA COUNTY HISTORY	Buckinghamshire. Vol. IV etc		
WEST, W. S. Y.	The Trainmakers	Barracuda	1982
WILLIAMS, R.	St. Andrew's Church, Great Linford	MKDC	1981
WOODFIELD, P.	Bradwell Windmill	MKDC	1976
WRIGHT, Canon K. *et. al.*	Fenny Stratford Album	People's Press	1979

GLOSSARY

V.

Although specialist words have been avoided as far as possible, it is impossible to avoid some terms specific to the study of historic architecture; to avoid these would have involved long circumlocutions. For those not familiar with them, a short glossary of the more specialised words follows.

ABACUS	In a column, the pad between the capital and the superstructure.
AEDICULE	A panel with side columns and a pediment in correct architectural form.
AUMBRY	Cupboard for holy vessels, usually left of the altar.
BALUSTER	A lathe-turned support for a handrail, or a column so shaped.
BARGEBOARD	A board running up the face of a gable to finish the roof tiles.
BAY	(a) A structural division of a building. (b) A window projecting on the ground floor.
BRATTISHED	A decoration in the form of miniature crenellations.
BRESSAMUR	A horizontal timber in a frame, usually mid-way up a wall.
CANTED	Projecting, with sloping sides, as in a bay window.
CAPITAL	The top member of a column.
CHAMFER	A 45 degree splay on the corner of wood or stone members.
CHEST TOMB	A graveyard tomb in the shape of a chest.
CORBEL	A projection from a wall on which a roof member or a figure sits. CORBEL TABLE. A line of corbels at eaves level carrying a parapet.
COGGED	At the eaves, bricks set cornerwise in a projecting row.
CONSOLE	A scrolled bracket longer vertically than horizontally.
CORNICE	The projecting top mouldings of any feature.
CRENELLATED	A parapet with raised and dropped sections, as on a castle.
CRUCK	Large curved timbers carrying the roof load well down in the wall.
DENTILLED	In classical architecture, a row of small square projections. BRICK DENTILS where the brick ends project in a similar manner.
DOUBLE PILE	A house two rooms deep with the stair off at the side at the back.
ENTABLATURE	In Classical architecture, all that happens above a column.
FIRE-MARK	A C18 and later Insurance sign fixed conspicuously to a building.
FLEURON	A stylised flower, usually square, in Gothic mouldings.
FLUTED	On columns, etc. parallel rounded grooves.
FRIEZE	Strictly, the upper decorated band above a line of columns.
GADROONING	The raised decoration of classical type, often round a panel.
GAUGED	Of a brick lintel, special fine density bricks which can be rubbed to a precise shape, as radial bricks in a lintel.
GLOVER	On a dovecote, a roof structure allowing the birds to fly out.
HOOD MOULD	A projecting detail to prevent rain running down over the opening.
HOVEL	A local non-perjorative term for a beast shelter.
IONIC	Classical column with flutes and scrolled capital.
KEYSTONE	A tapered stone, or imitation of such, above an opening.
LABEL	A square hood-mould with ends turned down.
LANCET	A tall narrow window with a pointed head.
LIGHTS	Vertical divisions of a window.
LINTEL	A horizontal member supporting a wall over an opening.
LOBBY ENTRY	A form of house plan where the door faces the side of an internal stack forming a small lobby.
MARGIN GLAZING	Glazing bars of a window placed near the sides like margins.
MODILLION	Small brackets, particularly those supporting the eaves in Regency houses.
NOGGINGS	Infilling of the panels of a timber frame.
NOOK SHAFT	A small column in a recess at the side of a window or door.
OGEE	An arched shape curving back on itself and coming to a point.
PARAPET	The wall extended up beyond the seating of the roof.
PARVISE	An enclosure within the aisle of a church.
PANE	Division of glazing; A classification of window types, sash windows with 12 panes being generally C18, 16 or more being later.
PEDIMENT	An architectural gable feature with the cornice forming a triangle. OPEN PEDIMENT is where the bottom member of the triangle is absent. BROKEN PEDIMENT is where the sloping sides stop short of the top.
PISCINA	A recess in the chancel of a church where holy vessels are rinsed.
PILASTER	A flat column attached to a wall or other surface.
PLAT BAND	A projecting band at floor level formed by the provision for seating the joists.
PLATE	A horizontal member in a timber frame, particularly the one at the top of a wall.
PORTICO	Generally, a porch supported on free standing columns.
PULPIT	A raised platform for preaching in a church.
PURLIN	Horizontal members of a roof supporting rafters along their span.
QUEEN POST	Two vertical posts in a roof supporting the purlins in a truss.
QUOIN	Specially formed corner stones or bricks, often raised above the face of the wall.
RE-ORDER	Of churches, adaptation of part of the church to secular use.

RUSTICATION	Treatment of stonework, occasionally brickwork, to emphasise the joints.
SEGMENTAL	Of an arch, a curved form being a segment of a circle.
SHOULDERED	Of an opening, where the top of the sides project inwards to carry the lintel.
SILL	(a) At the bottom of a window, to cast the water away from the wall. (b) The lowest horizontal member of a timber frame. SILL WALL, a dwarf wall on which the sill is set.
SEDILIA	Seats for the priest etc. in the church, usually on the south of the altar.
SPINE BEAM	A beam running lengthways in a house, i.e. from gable to gable.
STACK	The structure of a chimney. SHAFT: a separate structure for individual flues at the top.
STADDLE	A stone mushroom shaped support for a structure so shaped to prevent vermin entering.
STRING	A horizontal projecting member, usually decorative.
STUD	A vertical member in a timber frame.
TACK-ROOM	A room where leathers, harness etc. are kept.
TERRACE	A line of buildings designed as a group, as opposed to a ROW.
TESTER	The sounding board above a pulpit.
TRIGLYPH	In classical architecture a triple feature on an entablature.
TRIPARTITE	A window divided into three parts, the centre part wider.
TRANSEPT	The cross spaces in a church, usually by a central tower.
TUSCAN	A Roman Order with unfluted columns, and simple capitals and bases.
TYMPANUM	That part within a pediment or arch.
WATTLE & DAUB	Infilling of a timber frame, using stakes, woven hazel, and clay.
WINDBRACE	In a roof, a timber between a truss and purlins to keep it square.

ABBREVIATIONS

In the text, the initial part of a description has been set out in note form to save space and to avoid needless repetition. Numerals are often used instead of spelling out the number in full. Throughout, for the same reasons, the following standard abbreviations have been adopted. Brackets around the name of a building indicate that it no longer exists.

C19	=	Nineteenth century
c.1900	=	About (circa) 1900

BLETCHLEY
Bletchley Station
Bletchley Grammar School
Bletchley Park
Police Station
Fire Station
Tennis Courts
Car Park
Playing Field
Viaduct
QUEENSWAY
BUCKINGHAM ROAD
DUNCOMBE STREET
PARK STREET
SOUTH TERRACE
SHERWOOD DRIVE
WILTON AVENUE
CHURCH GREEN ROAD
COTTINGHAM GROVE
BROWNING CRESCENT
CHAUCER ROAD
ROCHE GARDENS
WHALLEY DRIVE
RICKLEY LANE
THE GROVE
The Coppice
Cemetery
St Mary's Church
Rectory
Wilton Hall
Works
Music Centre
Methodist Church
Hostel
T A Centre
Recreation Ground
Holne Chase County Infants School
Holne Chase County Junior School
Signal Box
Coal Yard
Track
5290 Pond 3·12ha ·77
0150 198·587ha 490·72
B 4034

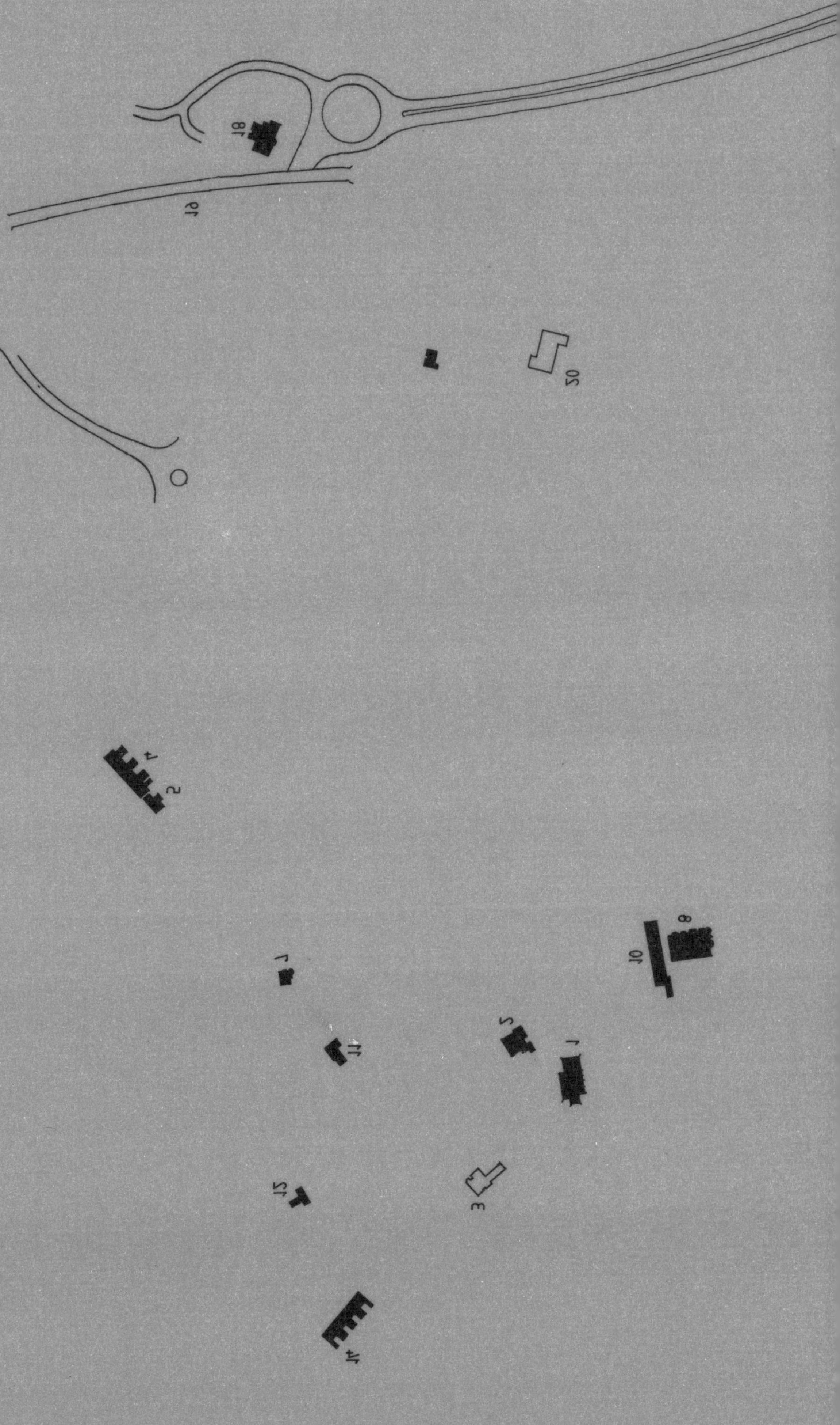

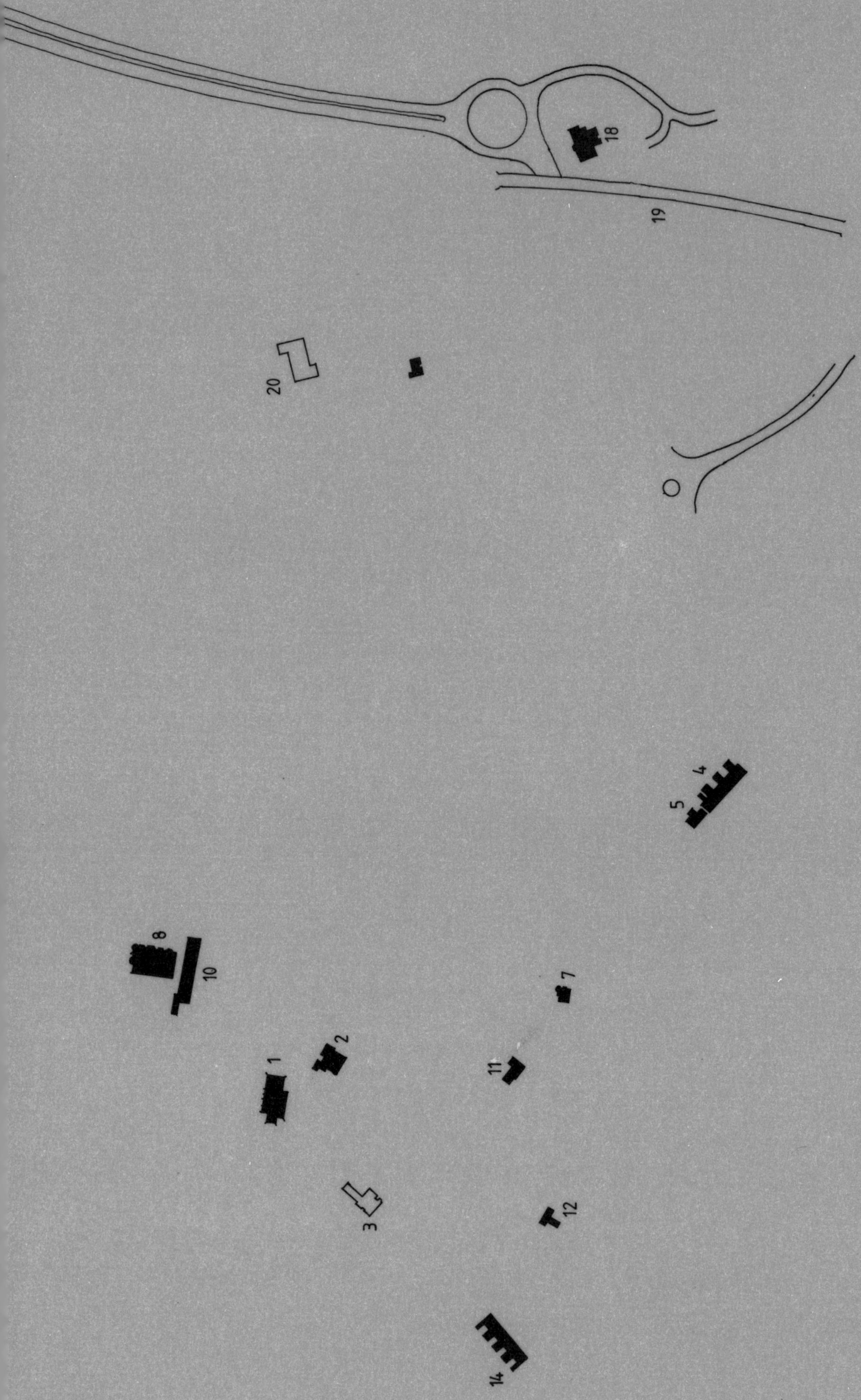
18
19
20
4
5
8
10
7
2
1
11
3
12
14

A

BLETCHLEY

BLETCHLEY

It comes as something of a surprise to many that Bletchley is one of the oldest established settlements in the Milton Keynes area. Although described by Sheahan (1861) as 'scattered and mean looking' it cannot always have been so, for the church is large and imposing. Before the railways came in 1838, it was renowned for its pillow lace, November 30th being Tandering Day (St. Andrewing—the patron saint) and a public holiday. It was also known for the longevity of its inhabitants. In history it became the property of the De Grey family from c.1200 who held it until 1603, when it was confiscated and passed to George Villiers, later Duke of Buckingham. In 1674 it came to the grandfather of the eminent historian and antiquary Browne Willis, benefactor to the town and perhaps its most famous son, who installed the well-known diarist William Cole to the living in 1753–68. The railway junction between the old London and North Western Railway, the Bedford and Cambridge Branch line and the Banbury and Oxford Branch put Bletchley at a railway crossroads, a fact which contributed to its hasty growth in the late C19, and a brickworks on a modest scale was established in Duncombe Street to supply this demand.

1 Church of St. Mary B

Anglican parish church, and one of the finest in the area. C12, C14, C15. Restored in 1705–10 and in the C19. Limestone, patched with Brickhill ironstone, and lead roofs. Nave with aisles partly clasping the west tower, on the south. Chancel and north chapel. Probably in origin a two-cell Romanesque building of which only the finely carved south door remains, reset to a pointed arch in the south aisle. It has beak-head decoration. Late C15 square-headed windows replacing earlier Gothic windows and C15 clerestory replacing an earlier one. Three-stage C15 tower with twinned belfry openings. Low porch with moulded ceiling beams. The chancel restored in the C19. The north chapel is built as one with the north aisle, all late C15. Internally, nave arcade of four bays, late C13–early C14, on octagonal columns. The roofs of the south aisle and north chapel are of the C15 while the nave has a C16 roof.

A1

Font, probably C17 tub, with a contemporary spire cover.

Monuments: In the arch between chancel and north chapel an alabaster recumbent knight in plate armour on a panelled chest, c.1442, to Richard, 6th Baron Grey of Wilton. On the north wall an alabaster slab with an unusually fine brass to the protestant Rev. Thomas Sparke, died 1616. Under the north-east window a C13 slab with a foliated cross and, curiously, a suspended hunting horn. There are remains of other effigies of c.1600 and various small wall tablets. These are described in detail in Records of Bucks IX No. 3.

In the churchyard there are many well-lettered head-stones of the C18 including, close to the south porch, a group of five. Noteworthy are a stone to William Cooke, 1761; Mary Souster of Water Eaton, 17??; and two other groups of three, fortunately left in position.

A1

2 The Old Rectory II

Parsonage house of 1834, built for the Rev. T. D. Broughton. Of stone and brick, in a simplified Gothic style, with central door and slightly set forward gabled wing to the right, bay window to the left. It replaces a more extensive building with a central hall, a parlour wing, kitchen and brewhouse, and another range parallel with stables and barns. Brown Willis used some bricks from Salden House, Mursley, one of the great Elizabethan mansions of the Country, demolished mid C18, for the repair of the south side. A keystone from the 1754 rectory is set over a door in the stable range, and internally it has some panelling also taken from this house.

A2

3 (The Elmers)

This was a house of the Selby Lowndes family, tall late Victorian and slightly Gothic. It was demolished c.1980 after damage by fire.

CHURCH GREEN ROAD (East side)

The Green on Church Green Road is the old centre of Bletchley. There were up to the First World War, a number of timber framed cottages here and extending down Church Green Road, only one of which survives.

4 Nos. 1 to 13 NL

A terrace of brick estate cottages 1889 for H. S. Leon. Two storeys with tile hanging and timber framed gables. The entrance porches are combined under a hipped roof. Cogged floor band, wavy bargeboards and ribbed stacks.

A5

5 No. 15 Rose Cottage NL

A single storey cottage, formerly the estate laundry, 1888 for the Leon Estate. Timber framed gable and ribbed chimney stack. The datestone is of terracotta and similar to that of the Lodge.

6 (Water Hall)

Located in Bletchley Park, and built in 1710 in what was becoming a slightly dated Artisan Mannerist style, three storeys, apparently with giant pilasters and string courses at floor levels, and with steps up to the central door. The approach was flanked by rounded walls linking to two-storey terminal pavilions. It was demolished c.1760 but had not this happened, it would have been one of the outstanding architectural monuments of Milton Keynes area. Cole's drawing of it appears in Markham, The History of Milton Keynes and District, Vol. I, p.149. Browne Willis built in the grounds various garden structures, a Gothic temple and a Chinese Gothic pavilion. Sadly these fun buildings no longer survive.

A6

7 Lodge to Bletchley Park NL

Driveway Lodge of 1886, for H. S. Leon. Brick with tile hanging and timber framed gable. Moulded brick around the arched entrance in the two-storey buttressed porch. Large round living room projects as a bay with a wood balustrade on its flat roof. Dormer to rear. Moulded terracotta datestone.

By the lodge, fine iron entrance gates on sandstone Gothic piers, curved to provide a recessed entrance. There was when built another lodge on the other side of the entrance gates.

8 Bletchley Park II

Large house, built 1860, extended in 1883 and further extended in c.1906 for Herbert Samuel Leon, born in Hamburg, and became a rich London financier, newspaper proprietor and Liberal MP for Bletchley 1891–1895. He gave the recreation ground to the town in 1898 and was knighted in 1908. Foreign Office communications centre from 1939. A building in a robust Victorian style, brick with stone dressings, gables and a large two-storey angled bay with a lead roof. The architect is not recorded. It was here, during the 1939–45 war, at Bletchley Park that the wartime government's operation to decode the Nazi Enigma code was set up that played so large and effective a part in counterintelligence. Hut 3 (decoding) and Hut 6 (information action) still exist. Many famous people were to work here almost anonymously and during their little spare time, discover the treasures of the district.

A8

9 *Ice House* NL

Close to one end of the house is an underground ice house.

10 *Stables to Bletchley Park* NL

1883, by E. Swinfen Harris, for H. S. Leon. Rendered brick with a tiled roof. Stair tower to attic.

11 Rectory Cottages II*

A house of the late C16–C17, timber framed, the wattle and daub replaced with brick, and tiled roof. 'L'-plan with central C17 brick stack extended through the roof and ribbed in the C18, when the house was also extended to abut the hall, and divided into two cottages. The east room has moulded ceiling beams, and, on the first floor, a three-centred stone fireplace. A large open fireplace also exists on the ground floor level, and a dragon beam suggests it once had jetties on at least one side.

Attached to the north end, a timber framed hall, traditionally dated to 1447. It is a medieval building of manorial status, and probably erected by the De Greys, Lords of the Manors of Bletchley and Simpson, at their seat of Water Hall, 500 yards from the church, later to be used as a barn after the demolition of that building by Earl Spencer in 1620. It is of three bays, with hammer-beam trusses and arch braces with arched and pierced panel infilling supporting a double purlin roof. The ends of the hammer-beam have carved masks. The posts and wallplates are moulded. It is a curious instance of the total re-use of a timber framed building. The building was carefully restored and conserved under the direction of Janet Frost, 1972–3.

A11

CHURCH GREEN ROAD (West side)

12 No. 60 Freefolk Cottage II

Cottage of late C16-early C17. Timber framed with corner braces, one panel high to the ground floor. Two bays, with the major stack to the left gable, and a clasped purlin roof with queen strut trusses and windbraces. It has a large open fireplace at the east end. C20 extensions to the rear.

A12

13 The Old School House NL

A brick school of 1854, and extended in 1885 to take 93 children. A further room was added in 1912. Converted 1982 to two houses using characterful details.

CHURCH GREEN ROAD (North side)

14 Noel Cottages NL

A terrace of estate cottages, 1904, for H. S. Leon. Vigorously detailed with Gothic porches and gables.
There were at one time over 200 staff employed on the estate, including eight specifically allocated to the orchid house.

A14

CHURCH GREEN ROAD (South side)

Two cottages either side of the path to Church Walk.

15 No. 14 Well Cottage II

A C17 timber framed cottage of two bays, one storey and attic, with a thatched roof. Four panelled door and windows renewed. Large open fireplace in the room to the west.

A15

16 No. 15 Walnut Tree Cottage II

A C17 timber framed cottage with a thatched roof. Two bays, the framing two panels high to the ground floor, one panel to attic floor, and tension bracing. Collar beam trusses, and chamfered spine beams.

A16

CHURCH WALK

17 Yew Tree Cottage II

A late C16–C17 timber framed cottage with a thatched roof. Two bays, with a north wing and extended both ends in the C18 and C19. The house may have had an open late medieval hall with purlins and collar trusses to the roof. Chamfered timber fire lintels to the ground floor fireplaces with bread ovens. It was the dwelling of a bootmaker in the early C20.

CHANDOS PLACE

18 The Park NL

Hotel, 1869. Three storeys, three bays with a central recessed entrance flanked by canted bay windows and with paired plate glass sash windows above. The cèntre bay is slightly recessed. Paired modillion eaves.

A18

19 Railway Viaduct NL

A rather monstrous concrete viaduct dwarfing the area around, with a concrete balustrade typical of engineering design of the 1930's, but in fact built 1956–57.

20 (Bletchley Station)

The present station replaces a station of c.1860 by J. W. Livock, in a Jacobean gabled style. This had replaced the original LNWR station of 1838. The Oxford Line was opened in 1851. A terrace of 20 railways cottages, known as Company's, or alternatively, Driver's Cottages stood where Telephone Rentals now stands. They were demolished in 1972. One house remains from the 1860 period lost in undergrowth. Just to the rear, behind the fire station is the rather ridiculous standby wartime HQ bunker for the County Council and senior officials.

QUEENSWAY (Formerly Bletchley Road)

Formerly the Buckingham Road, much improved since Milton Keynes and now quite animated. There are few buildings of any architectural or historical interest.

21 Conservative Club NL

1891, built as a school for a Mr. Holloway. A robust design using strong stone details in its windows and terracotta panels on two of the three gables below the windows. Recently extended on both ends.

22 No. 122 NL

Now a shop with similar details. Canted and turreted bays with fishtail tiles to the roof and terracotta balls on its gable kneelers.

23 The Elms II

A Regency villa, the first house on Queensway, probably built for a doctor. Two storeys, three by two bays, stucco with a hipped slate roof and wide bracketed eaves. The door has a round fanlight with curvilinear glazing. Margin glazed sash windows. The roof has king post trusses.

24 Bletchley U.D.C. Offices NL

Offices. 1909, by John Chadwick, a Neo-Elizabethan design with a gabled wing having stone pilasters and exuberant terracotta foliage in the shaped gable. It has the entrance under an elliptical arch, and a balcony immediately over. Sash windows, with top lights.

25 Fenny Stratford Board Schools NL

Now the Knowles First School, 1890, Neo-Elizabethan, and adjacent, the Boys School, 1897, both by John Chadwick, M.S.A. Red brick on a blue brick plinth. Stone and terracotta details. Timber windows with large panes. Internally open trusses on corbels. The Schoolmaster's House is of the same date.

26 Methodist Church NL

A brick chapel of 1910–11. Four bay nave with lobby and ante-rooms on the gable end facing the street. Large window with intricate tracery surrounded by tile hanging. Some of the bricks are stamped with the benefactors' names. Art Nouveau railings to the front garden.

A23

A24

A25

A26

FAR BLETCHLEY

Far Bletchley developed along the Buckingham Road on a ridge east of the Newton Longville crossroads. Until the early C19 it was little more than a clustering of timber framed and thatched farmhouses. By c.1830 however the gaps between the buildings were being filled in with yellow brick cottages, and slightly later, with short terraces of diaper red and yellow brick houses, mostly for agricultural workers. Now many of these have been altered almost beyond recognition and as a result of fires the thatch of the older properties has been replaced with tiles. Diaper façades survive on No. 184, Nos. 198–200, and No. 210, the only one retaining its original well-proportioned sash windows and door. Nos. 218–222 have been much altered. This cluster of buildings extended as far as Shenley Road, and turned the corner into Newton Road where Nos. 2–6 are of similar early Victorian date.

BUCKINGHAM ROAD (South side)

27 Grange Lodge **NL**

A late C19 lodge, later than Far Bletchley as a separate settlement. Brick, timber framing and tile hanging, a well modelled example of late Victorian picturesque vernacular style. It has pierced ridge tiles, a dominant ribbed and chamfered brick stack, and large leaded windows.

A27

28 No. 128 **II**

House of the early–mid C18 on earlier brick foundations.

29 No. 135 Brooklands Farmhouse **II**

Farmhouse, originally a single bay building with external gable stack, to which a second timber framed room was added in the C17, forming a lobby entry plan. It was extended in the C19 by one two-storey bay on the east and the door blocked, although a rear door survives under a lean-to porch. It is timber framed, now roughcast on all but the end gable, and has a thatched roof. There is a stable wing of c.1900. The west bay has chamfered ceiling beam and joists, and windbraces in the roof.

A28

30 No. 139 **II**

House of the early–mid C19, more substantial than others of this period. Three bays, built of buff brick and slated roof. The two left bays are symmetrical with central three-panelled door and decorative fanlight, the third bay is beyond the main chimney stack to the right. 16-pane sashes with rendered wedge lintels. It is a comely building which has escaped rewindowing and other alterations.

A30

31 No. 141 **II**

A house of the C17, timber framed and tiles replacing a thatched roof. The earlier section is that with the gable to the road and having a southern wing, the re-entrant angle being filled with a two-storey block in the C19. 12-pane sashes to the earlier section. Internally it has a dog-leg stair and ceiling beams.

32 No. 143 Elm Farmhouse **II**

A C17 farmhouse, timber framed with a half hipped thatched roof, now roughcast externally. The door leads to the central living room which is divided by a timber framed partition from the parlour on the east. The main stack separates the third, western, room which has a large fireplace with chamfered lintel and Coalbrookdale iron oven door. The building was renovated and extended to the rear in 1981–2, when a C17 three-light gable window was uncovered. The western end outbuilding, originally thatched with the house, now has its independent roof.

A32

BUCKINGHAM ROAD (North side)

33 No. 170 Bengal Farm II

The farmhouse has been replaced in the C19, but there remains a timber framed building of 1½ storeys, and four narrow bays, originally thatched but with a half-hipped tiled roof, at one time a cottage, and with dormer windows, now all storehouse and workshop with two doors. It has a storeroom to the west, also timber framed but much mutilated, and a small one-bay timber framed extension to the rear. Outbuildings are an unusual survival, particularly those retaining some wattle and daub infilling as this does on the rear. The timbers are two panels high with jowled posts carrying a clasped purlin truss.

A33

34 Nos. 180 and 184 NL

Formerly three cottages, now one, brick with a slate roof, c.1840. The entrance on the right still has a Victorian porch.

SHENLEY ROAD (West side)

35 No. 15 Melville Farmhouse II

A C17 farmhouse at right angles to the road, now much altered. Timber framed, roughcast to the front and some brick. One storey and attic, 3½ bays but originally longer. Lobby entry plan with the left end rebuilt in C19 with stacks. C18 leaded windows to attic rooms and C19 casement windows to the ground floor. A smaller timber framed house stood in the garden to the east.

A35

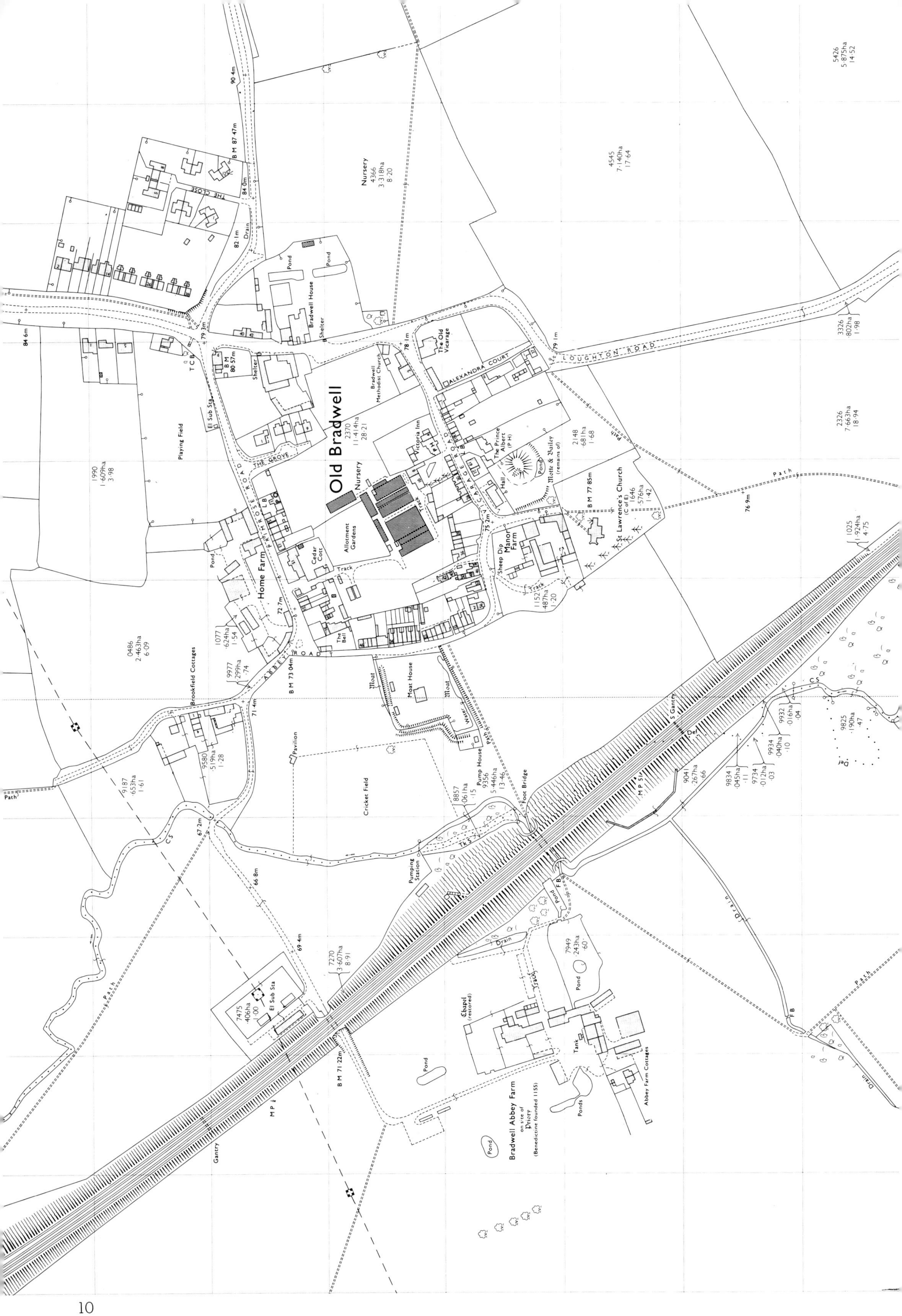

Old Bradwell
Nursery
4366
3·318ha
8·20
4545
7·140ha
17·64
5426
5·875ha
14·52
THE CLOSE
B M 87·47m
90·4m
84·0m
82·1m
Drain
Pond
Bradwell House
Shelter
The Old Vicarage
ALEXANDRA COURT
LOUGHTON ROAD
79·1m
78·1m
79·3m
84·6m
3326
·802ha
1·98
B M 80·57m
T C B
El Sub Sta
Bradwell Methodist Church
2370
11·414ha
28·21
Nursery
Victoria Inn
The Prince Albert (P H)
Motte & Bailey (remains of)
2148
·681ha
1·68
2326
7·663ha
18·94
Path
76·9m
B M 77·85m
St Lawrence's Church (C of E)
1646
·576ha
1·42
Hall
VICARAGE ROAD
THE GROVE
PRIMROSE ROAD
Playing Field
1990
1·609ha
3·98
Allotment Gardens
Cedar Cott
Track
Home Farm
Manor Farm
Sheep Dip
1152
·487ha
1·20
1025
1·924ha
4·75
75·2m
72·7m
1077
·624ha
1·54
The Bell
ABBEY ROAD
0486
2·463ha
6·09
9977
·299ha
·74
B M 73·04m
Moat
Moat House
Brookfield Cottages
71·4m
Pavilion
Cricket Field
9580
·519ha
1·28
9187
·653ha
1·61
Path
8857
·061ha
·15
Pump House
9356
5·446ha
13·46
Foot Bridge
S Gantry
MP 51
9041
·267ha
·66
9834
·045ha
·11
9734
·012ha
·03
9934
·040ha
·10
9932
·016ha
·04
9825
·190ha
·47
C S
67·2m
66·8m
Pumping Station
Pond
F B
Drain
7949
·243ha
·60
69·4m
7270
3·607ha
8·91
7475
·406ha
1·00
El Sub Sta
Chapel (restored)
Tank
Abbey Farm Cottages
B M 71·22m
Pond
Ponds
Bradwell Abbey Farm
on site of Priory (Benedictine founded 1155)
Pond
Gantry
MP 51/2
F B
Drain
Path

B

OLD BRADWELL

BRADWELL

Bradwell, or as it has been known since 1840, Old Bradwell, is a small parish of some 917 acres, lying on the higher glacial deposits overlooking, to the west, the valley of the Loughton Brook. The parish is irregular in shape as it extended to contain a share of the common to the south east, where the City Centre now stands. Bradwell Abbey is an extra-parochial area lying west of the parish of Bradwell, an arrangement surviving from the medieval period when the Benedictine priory fell outside normal parish arrangements. Bradwell village has traces of an early origin surviving in the small motte castle in Church Lane, unrecorded in history and assumed by some by virtue of its small size to be an adulturine or unlicenced castle built during the unrest in the mid C12. It probably originally supported a wooden tower or refuge, and has a fairly large bailey, the ditches of which can only now be clearly seen against Church Lane, but once extended from the back of the pasture to Vicarage Road. Many pottery fragments have frequently been found around the Memorial Hall. West of this lies the church, and to its north, the manor site within its moat, perhaps the successor of the motte in more settled times.

ABBEY ROAD

Nos. 4–46 are a series of short terraces of cottages looking out to the west. The two end blocks were built in the 1870's and the centre block after 1881 replacing an earlier building which had long been demolished. The village stocks stood until the end of the C19 on the small godcake or green at the end of Primrose Road, opposite the last house on the south, once The Bell Inn.

1 The Moat House II

House of 1784 incorporating a wall from an earlier timber-framed building. It is on the site of the Manor House and lying within a square moat of medieval date. The present building is of limestone with a machine made tile roof and gable stacks. There are two parallel blocks, the north one narrower. three bays, C19 casement windows. The house once owned a large barn and some smaller farm buildings where the cricket field now stands.

During the construction of the playing fields to the north, excavations revealed a building of medieval date, probably a substantial outbuilding of the manor, which had within it a large limekiln. This was carefully preserved below the top of the bank.

B1

2 Tunnel under the Railway Embankment NL

The Loughton Brook had to be diverted when the railway embankment was built in 1838 and conduited through a completely oval tunnel of seven rings of half-bricks. Blue brick wing walls and stream revetments with large copings and stone cappings. A timber footbridge suspended halfway up the tunnel maintains the ancient footpath that led eventually to Watling Street.

3 Brookfield Cottages, Nos 1 to 4 II

Farmhouse, now 4 cottages, C16 and C17. Rendered rubble stonework with thatched roof. Four bays, the easternmost bay retaining a quasi-cruck roof truss which had elsewhere in the building been replaced in the C17. The original plan is obscure but it has a large central stack inserted into an original smoke bay, a bay of the roof which lay directly over an open ground floor fireplace in the medieval manner. A further stack appears on the east gable, serving a large inglenook fireplace also at ground floor level, no doubt the parlour of the original C16 house. The western bay was originally a single storey lean-to, rebuilt to two storeys in the C17. Before major renovation and conversion in 1975–6 the roofspace was insulated by hand-made hurdles. The rear garden of No. 1 has the original well.

B3

LOUGHTON ROAD (EAST SIDE)

4 Nos 40 and 42 II

Two limestone cottages with thatched roof, No. 42 being the earlier. Late C17—early C18, each having a central door and flanking casement windows, one dormer. The major chimney stack is at the south end, possibly originally the kitchen, and other stacks to reception rooms. Brick outbuilding at the north end.

B4

5 Bradwell House II*

A large house of the C18, of two storeys and five bays, originally a C17 stone building to which the fine front block was added. This is of two storeys and five bays with a symmetrical central door and end brick pilasters supporting an entablature and cornice, with a panelled brick parapet over. In the early C19 the building was extended by two bays to the east, in a matching style accommodating the library on the ground floor. The roof is hipped with three pedimented dormers and gable stacks. The west gable has a gault brick and flat roofed entrance building, also early C19 with recessed arcades and double panelled doors. Internally the building has a fine staircase in a central stair hall and good period doors and fireplaces.

B5

6 Garden Wall to Bradwell House II

The wall fronting Loughton Road is a fine diaper brick wall of the C18 with traditional pitched brick copings and stretcher course apex, some 3m high. The wall ramps down to meet the street entrance of the house, but originally had a central opening to the garden front.

LOUGHTON ROAD (WEST SIDE)

7 Village School NL

A red brick primary school of 1891, built by the London and North West Railway Co. and now much altered.

8 Stables to Bradwell House II

Directly opposite the house entrance, a range of stables of the early C19 with a hipped slate roof. Two carriage doors with segmental arches are set towards the centre, flanked by stable doors with round arch heads. The building, which is still used as stables, has a low walled forecourt.

B8

9 Methodist Chapel II

Chapel of 1823, of stone rubble, now rendered and painted. It has a central round headed door on to the road and graded round headed windows with 'Y' tracery in the fanlights.

PRIMROSE ROAD (North side)

10 Home Farm II

Farmhouse. C16–C17. Limestone rubble with a patterned tile roof. Lobby entry plan, the entrance to the east facing the former farmyard. The south end has a large stack with inglenook internally, and a timber framed partition to the central room. On the west front there is a timber three-light mullioned window probably C17. To the west a small projecting building originally independent is now attached to the house as a kitchen. The roof has curved principals with some smoke blackening in the centre, suggesting, like Brookfield Cottages, it incorporated an earlier C16 building.

B10

11 Barn to Home Farm II

A large C16 or C17 stone built barn backing on to the lane. Five bays, with a half-hipped roof and a midstrey in the centre bay on the north side, the opposing door to the lane now blocked. It originally had ventilation slots and a roof with windbraces, now much altered.

B11

12 Stables to Home Farm II

Range of stables with a pond to the rear. Late C18 or C19, six bays, with timber roof trusses supporting a tiled roof.

PRIMROSE ROAD (South side)

13 No. 15 NL

House of the mid C19, of two storeys, three bays, extended at both ends in single storeys. It has a central door and gable stacks, and brick modillion eaves. The windows are C20 multi-paned, sometimes called 'Georgian'.

VICARAGE ROAD (South side)

14 The Old Vicarage II

Vicarage of 1870. A rather plain Victorian building of limestone rubble consisting of two parallel blocks incorporating part of an older building now indistinguishable.

The coachhouse immediately to the west has been converted to a dwelling house. It once served as the first schoolroom in the village.

B14

15 No. 1 The Old Sugar Loaf II

Cottage of the late C17 or early C18. Limestone with thatched roof. Two bays, with the entrance in the upper, parlour bay and the major stack to the original service room opposite. To the right, a thatched timber framed and weatherboarded outbuilding, now a garage, with braced chamfered purlin roof. The roof extends down at rear forming a rear service extension, probably originally a dairy.

B15

16 Prince Albert P.H. II

Public house, Mid C19. A symmetrical two-storey building with a recent central porch, and 12-pane sashes. Gable stacks on front slope of roof.

B16

17 Memorial Hall NL

Erected 1924, as a memorial to the fallen of World War I. The iron gates were designed by a local artist of note, H. Stammers of Bradwell House, well known for his stained glass work.

VICARAGE ROAD (North side)

18 No. 2

Stone cottage, C17, remodelled later, with external stack at the west end. Originally timber framed, single storey with attic and thatched roof. Extensively reworked in 1970's. The lower east end was once a butcher's shop.

B19

19 No. 4 II

House, an early C18 rebuild of the upper parlour end of the Victoria PH. Stone, faced with diaper brick and having an attic floor. 16-pane sash windows with gauged brick heads and a fine six-panelled door within a fluted pilastered doorcase having a triangular pediment. Eared architrave around the door, which is said to have been originally the central door to Bradwell House. The tiled roof has a central hipped dormer and is quarter hipped left, with gable stack to the right.

The front garden wall of local stone adds to the building's setting and is separately listed. II

B20

20 Victoria P.H. II

Public House, formerly a farmhouse. Late C17 or early C18. Limestone with a tiled roof. It has a lobby entry plan, with central later C20 hipped porch. Timber casement windows with radial flat stone lintels. The building was extended by one bay to the left in the C19.

21 Turner's Farmhouse II

Farmhouse set back from the road. C17 or early C18. Limestone rubble with a thatched roof now clad in iron. The building is believed to have been the original barn of the farm, and has been extensively altered through the centuries, including conversion to separate cottages.

B22

22 No. 36 II

Cottage, Late C18. Timber framing with brick infilling and stone. Thatched roof. Two bays, with entrance in recent porch to the right bay. Clasped purlin roof. The rear wall has slender timber framing two panels high, probably the last in a long tradition of framed buildings. The interior has chamfered spine beams. Plan altered and extensively reworked in 1984–5.

The cottages to the right, Nos. 26 and 34, were probably originally single storey farm buildings, converted and raised to two storeys in the C19.

CHURCH LANE

B23

23 Manor Farmhouse II

Farmhouse, now a Youth Hostel. C17, a three-bay baffle entry building gable to the road, to which was added, in 1790 (date stone over the doorcase), a large block on the north side. The first building was originally thatched. The newer block has a central hall with large flanking reception rooms with panelled shutters. The central stair reconciles the two builds. The door within the 1790 doorcase has a radial fanlight and open timber pediment. Tripartite 12-pane sashes to main rooms. This building may be Over House recorded in C18 documents. In 1902 the insurance policy for the farm covered such items as a nag house, a gig house, pig house and hen house, a carthorse stable and adjacent chaff house and a granary with a drying kiln. Conversion to a Youth Hostel was completed in 1981, at which time the range of stables was converted to the warden's lodge. The C18 steep pitched barn in the south-west corner of the yard was demolished after storm damage in 1973.

A fine stone wall with part tiled copings runs from the side of the house enclosing the north garden. II

24 Gates to Churchyard II

Mid C19, cast iron gates by E. & H. Roberts of Deanshanger, perhaps the finest extant specimen of gates by this widely reputed firm of agricultural engineers. Fleur terminals to rails and braced dog rails. Stanchions have ball and spike terminals.

B24

25 Church of St. Lawrence II*

Parish Church of Old Bradwell, C13, C14, C15 and C19. Limestone, comprising nave with a wide south aisle, and north porch. Chancel on a different alignment to the nave, and a C15 west tower. The earliest work is to be found in the chancel arch and arcade, the former with a most unusual C13 inscription, fragmentary, but sufficient survives to discover that it firstly confirms the dedication of the church to St. Lawrence, the date which should follow has been tantalisingly lost, and secondly, opposite, and also reset, an inscription awards VIGINTI : DIES : RELAXIONIS . . . (20 days remissions of sins) but for what? Perhaps a visit to Our Lady of Bradwell. The west column of the arcade is richly carved, and the eastern column has a waterleaf capital, and the east window has C13 nail head decoration internally, placed there in 1867–8. Some fragments of medieval glass are retained in the head of the east window. The east end of the south aisle must be the Stafford chapel referred to in the will of William Wogan of Bradwell Abbey wherein he willed to be buried. Externally the church can be seen to be considerably restored in 1867–8 and in 1904, most windows, except the small chancel north window, replaced, the nave heightened when the clerestory was added, the sanctus bellcote replaced with a cross. This work was done by E. Swinfen Harris of Stony Stratford, who probably also provided the robust rainwater fittings. The modest two-stage tower, partly C14 or early C15, and restored in the C16, has a saddleback roof similar to that of St. Mary Magdalen, Stony Stratford. The treble and second bell are early C13, cast by Michael de Wymbis, the third is by Chandler, and the fourth by Walgrove, early C15. The early bells probably came from the demolition of the priory church.

B25

The Graveyard has few items of interest, one C17 headstone with a pierced heart and crown, and some early C19 stones, including three chest tombs formerly in a railed enclosure against the south chancel wall. They have fine lettering, commemorating Joseph Key Baily, who died 1817, and John Baily, died 1816. A more distant enclosure contains later tombs of the Chetwode Baily's, one, it records, 'went about doing good' for 65 years! Until a few years ago there was a row of gravestones simply inscribed with initials only. These were known locally as 'railway row' and reputed to be the memorials of men killed building the railway.

26 Alexandra Terrace II

The court development, of which Alexandra Terrace is the best surviving example is a system of alleyways or jetties leading off the main roads. It apparently originates in the early C19 when the long plots of the houses on Vicarage Road, in this instance, were divided off and built upon, access being by means of a narrow walled footpath between plots. Alexandra Court has three dwellings ranged along the court between Vicarage Road and Bradwell Road, all of c. 1820–40.

The brick walls, with round and stepped copings running back some 25m from Vicarage Road are listed as being of interest.

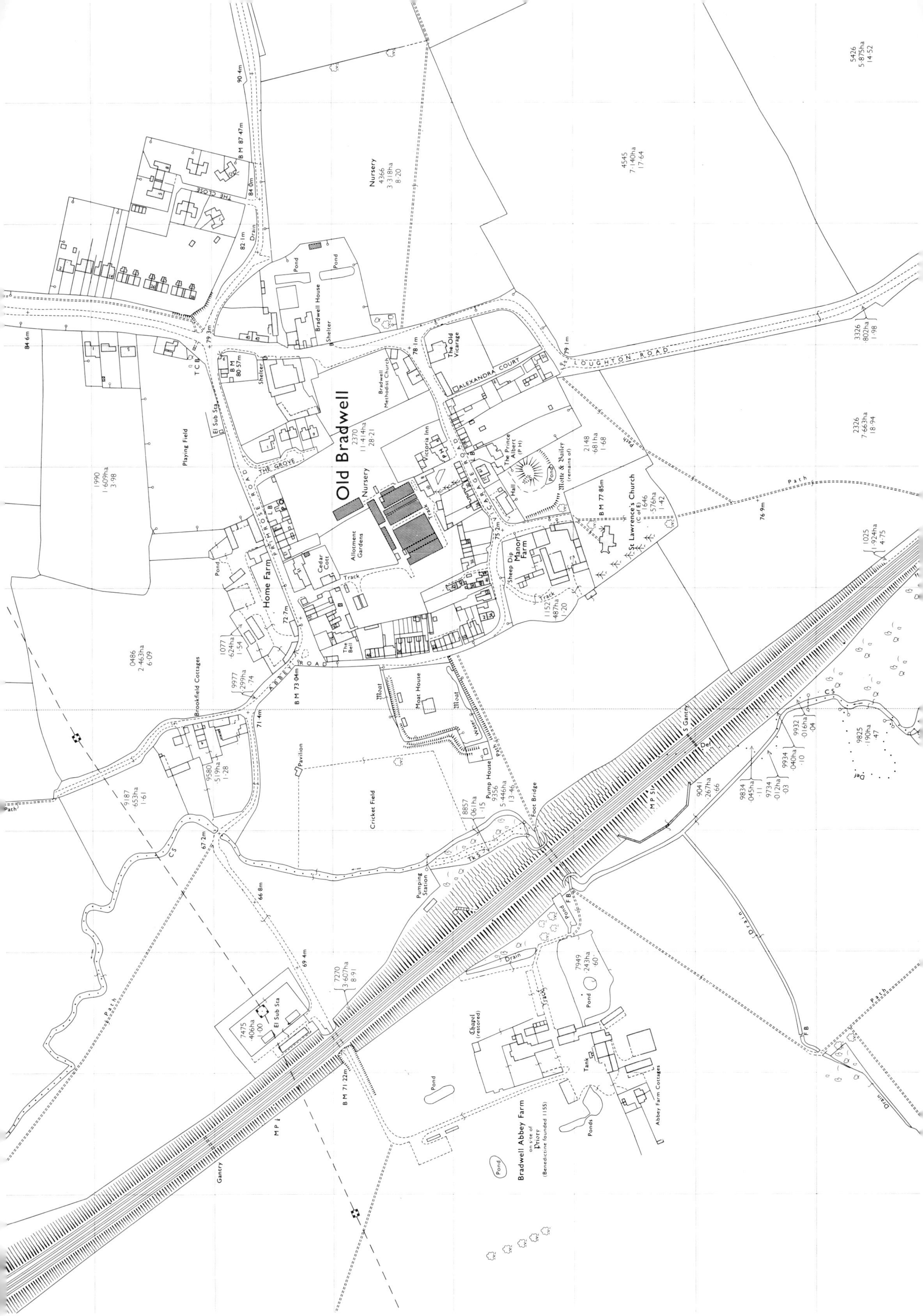
Old Bradwell
Nursery
Bradwell House
Bradwell Methodist Church
The Old Vicarage
Alexandra Court
Loughton Road
Victoria Inn
The Prince Albert (PH)
Motte & Bailey (remains of)
St Lawrence's Church (C of E)
Manor Farm
Sheep Dip
Allotment Gardens
Cedar Cott
Home Farm
Primrose Road
The Grove
The Close
Playing Field
The Bell
Abbey Road
Moat House
Moat
Pavilion
Cricket Field
Pump House
Foot Bridge
Pumping Station
Brookfield Cottages
El Sub Sta
Chapel (restored)
Bradwell Abbey Farm
on site of Priory (Benedictine founded 1155)
Abbey Farm Cottages
Pond
Ponds
Tank
Gantry
Path
Drain
Track

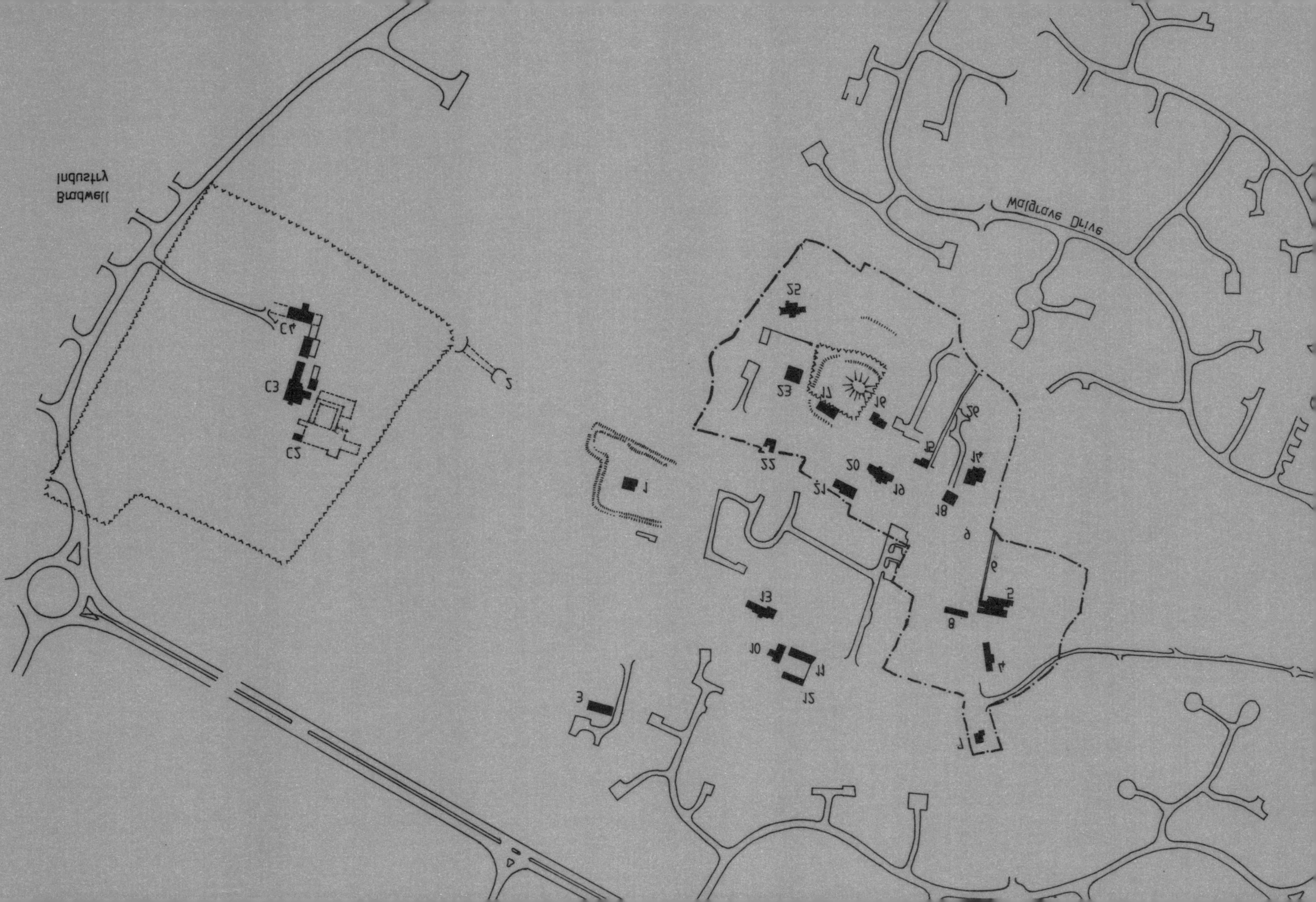
Bradwell
Industry
Walgrave Drive
C2
C3
C4
1
2
3
4
5
6
7
8
9
10
11
12
13
14
15
16
17
18
19
20
21
22
23
25
26

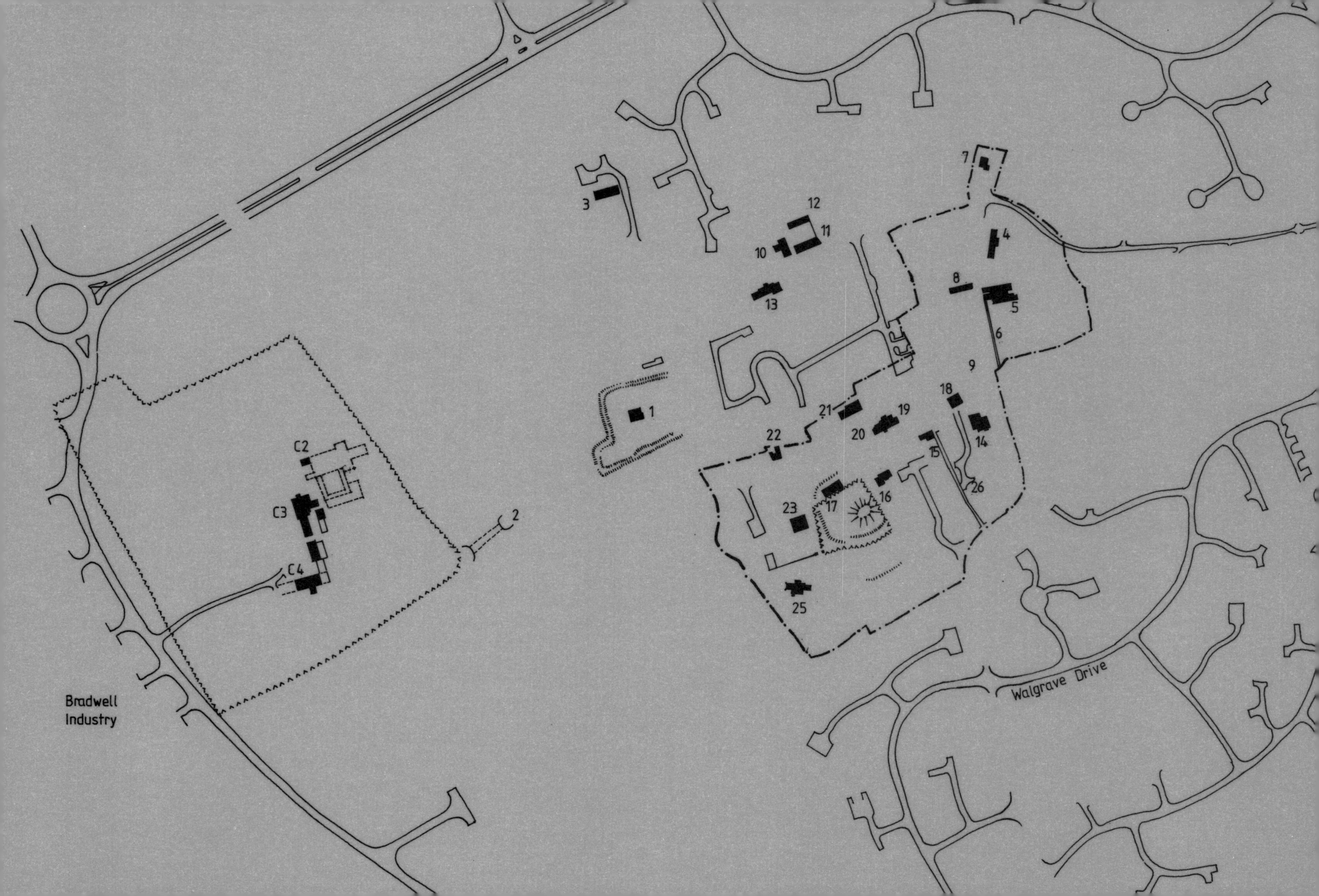
1
2
3
4
5
6
7
8
9
10
11
12
13
14
15
16
17
18
19
20
21
22
23
25
26
C2
C3
C4
Walgrave Drive
Bradwell
Industry

BRADWELL ABBEY

BRADWELL ABBEY

Bradwell Abbey is a small extra-parochial area on the west side of Bradwell Parish. This anomalous arrangement derives from the existance of a small Benedictine Priory with its endowment of lands in the southernmost corner of the old Parish of Wolverton. Although in the C16 and C17 it had a closer association with Bradwell, it has never lost its independent status. It consists of the farm which replaced the priory after the reformation, and an arm of land extending westwards to Watling Street.

1 Priory of St Mary Bradwell

A Benedictine priory was founded in Wolverton by Meinfelin, Lord of Wolverton in 1154, on his own lands, initially as a dependency of Luffield Priory, Newport Pagnell, but independent by 1189–90. The layout of the priory is not known in detail, but it appears to follow the normal monastic form with a church and the secular buildings laid out around the cloister on its south side. Evidence from the surviving chapel and excavation has determined the position of the church but as yet the claustral arrangements remain undiscovered in detail. It appears the main buildings were erected in the C12 and C13 and the priory flourished in a small way up to the Black Death in 1348. The prior died of the plague in 1349 and by 1361 the then prior was charged for allowing the buildings to fall into disrepair, a situation he probably was not able to avoid. The priory however struggled on until it came into the hands of Cardinal Wolsey in 1524, when, in common with a number of other small and unprofitable religious houses, it was legally suppressed and its funds diverted to the support of his new educational foundations of New College, Oxford, and at Ipswich, his home town. Before transferring the ownership to Oxford, Wolsey had the place surveyed by one, William Brabazon, who was later to return to complete the survey of the buildings for Thomas Cromwell, Henry VIII's agent. It is fortunate that this survey survives, describing the buildings as he found them, and from this a reconstruction of the medieval layout has been suggested by Brian Giggins and drawn by Dylan Roberts.

C3

C1

2 Chapel of Our Lady of Bradwell I

Around 1350, at the height of their troubles, it seems that the black monks made a significant discovery—a figure of the Virgin Mary in a niche on the west front of their church had miraculous healing qualities. As her fame grew, so the need arose to enclose within a protective building the figure and the devotional offerings acquired. This building was of necessity butted against the front of the church, but avoided the central west door. When the Suppression came, Brabazon's survey recommended the retention of the chapel whereas the church had to be demolished, either by the Crown, who held the estate from 1539 to 1543 or by Sir Arthur Longueville to whom it subsequently passed. The chapel as it now stands is a unique survival and thus a building of national significance. The fabric is wholly of the mid C14, including the roof and Little Brickhill floor tiles. Recent restoration included some patches of the floor, new doors, glazing and reroofing, including pinning up the internal vault.

Externally the thick east wall of the church can still be clearly seen and on the east face, a column represents the west respond of the north aisle arcade of the priory church. Above the string, the jamb of a lancet window of the aisle can be seen. Around the column there are a number of small drillings which still remain a mystery. Perhaps they survive from the fixing of some wall covering?

The greatest significance lies in the wall paintings. They are of three periods: the side walls are of the C14 and display a number of themes, including scenes from the life of the Virgin (the Teaching of the Virgin and the Annunciation in the north window reveals) and a unique scene of pilgrims with their staffs visiting a shrine, no doubt this one, bringing with them tokens of their afflictions, a diseased head, a child and other less discernable problems. It is highly probable that these scenes had been whitewashed over at the Dissolution, for the next period comprises a Royal coat of arms of James I high on the east wall, evidence that the Lonqueville's were maintaining it as a private chapel, to which was added, after the Civil War, the rather naive ceiling paintings of cherubs amongst clouds. This scheme tells us that the building once again was in use as a chapel by the new residents, the Alston family. Later this use lapsed and over a period of time its glory was forgotten, to become a mean stable only to be rediscovered after 1950, when a hole appeared in the roof allowing the rain to wash the limewash off the wall paintings, proving that the building was indeed genuine and not a rebuild of old fragments as was the current belief.

Around the chapel some walls of the former church have been laid out in gravel.

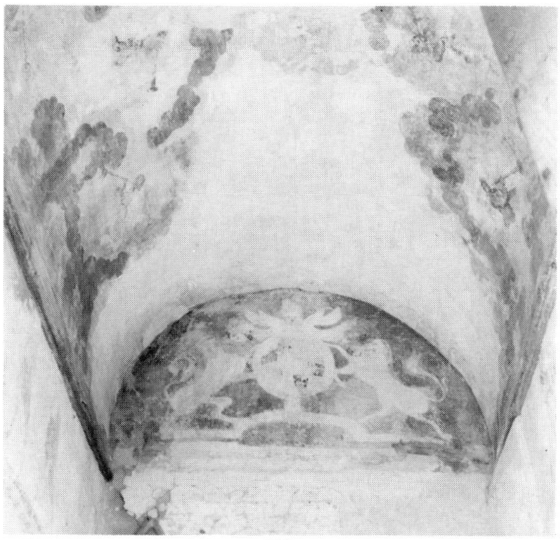

C2

C2

C2

3 Bradwell Abbey Farm II

Farmhouse on the site of the Prior's lodgings of the Benedictine Priory of St. Mary, Bradwell. Built c.1600 and comprising an 'L'-shaped block, the west facing arm was remodelled in the mid C18 and provided with a symmetrical elevation with four sash windows and a mid-wall stone cornice. The windows were again altered in the early C19 when they were changed to 16-pane sashes, and altered again later in Victorian times. It has a steep pitched roof, with double purlin trusses and boot shaped struts. When re-roofed in 1981 a window transome was found reused, this was from a large eight-light window, probably indicating an earlier phase of fenestration of the building. It has a large central stack and a second stack at the south end having an early brick base. A scratch inscription on an east quoin reads PH..MANCASELE 1650. and, high on the stack, the inscription A.B.1829. A porch was added on the north front, probably in the C19. The house is extended to the south in a long single storey range with attics; this is largely medieval work in small rubble. An original two-light hollow chamfered window, partly boarded over, survives and the two most southerly bays have been extended in width in the C17 and a new west frontage built with a central door and ovolo moulded windows, probably as a stable. This medieval range originally continued further south at the same width, the timber framed attic space spanning the present long standing entry to the rear yard. Beyond the entry, the medieval structure has been rebuilt in the C17 as a corn barn of four bays with owl holes in the gables and a simple window at the south end. This barn seems again to have been refurbished and the gables carried up in stone in the later C18 and reroofed with patterned clay tiles.

C3b

4 Cruck Barn II

Beyond, to the south, a range of C19 brick hovels connects to the Cruck Barn, the remains of the medieval corn barn described by Brabazon as being of nine bays. Now, the building is of five bays, with a two-bay midstrey to the south facing the fields. It is of prime interest in that embedded in the walls internally are the remains of a pair of heavy raised crucks, the date of which has been confirmed by tree-ring dating to $\pm$ 1320 AD. The walling of the barn shows many phases of rebuilding and alteration, including, to the rear, the remains of a buttress. This rebuilding included shortening the barn to the more modest needs of a post-Reformation farm, and left the original gable wall overlooking the monastic ponds incorporated in the cow sheds. The present roof is probably C19 in date and was restored in 1983.

C4

C4

WATLING STREET (East side)

5 Milestone NL

Milestone, sandstone, probably erected c.1830 by the Turnpike Trust after the re-engineering of the road by Thomas Telford. The iron plate giving the distances has been recently stolen.

C5

Broughton
Brooklands Farm
LONDON ROAD
A 50
Manor House
The Rectory
The Old Rectory
St Lawrence's Church (C of E)
The Haven
The Cottage
Hall
Hazeldene
Sunny Mead
Anscott House
Southview
Allot Gdns
Allotment Gardens
Foot Bridge
Shelter
Refuse Tip
Pond
Ponds
Track
Path
Posts
Drain
Water
Gravel Pit (disused)
Hopper
Conveyor
Silo
Manor
CS
GP
FB
LB
60·0m
61·9m
63·1m
62·8m
B M 64·78m
B M 65·78m
0024 3·776ha 9·33
6822 5·777ha 14·28
5519 1·256ha 3·10
4226 1·532ha 3·78
4711 5·255ha 12·99
3536 1·463ha 3·61
3224 ·997ha 2·46
2521 2·272ha 5·62
2516 ·032ha ·08
2905 ·170ha ·42
1722 3·662ha 9·05
1230 ·388ha ·96
0124 3·970ha 9·81
7600 ·129ha ·32
6900 1·483ha 3·66
6900 ·210ha ·52
5400 10·265ha 25·37
4496 1·149ha 2·84
6296 ·550ha 1·36
2900 ·267ha ·66
2900 ·826ha 2·04
2200 ·393ha ·97
2200 1·372ha 3·39
0005 2·998ha 7·41
0005 ·380ha ·94
1100 ·073ha ·18
0600 ·057ha ·14
0005 ·320ha ·79
1100 1·619ha 4·00
0002 2·884ha 7·13
0002 2·041ha 5·05
7600 ·546ha 1·35
8386 ·858ha 2·12
9184 ·259ha ·64
7785 1·732ha 4·28
0084 ·850ha 2·10
7867 6·075ha 15·02
4371 3·109ha 7·68
3166 4·343ha 10·73
2280 1·817ha 4·49
0070 ·113ha ·28
0063 1·473ha

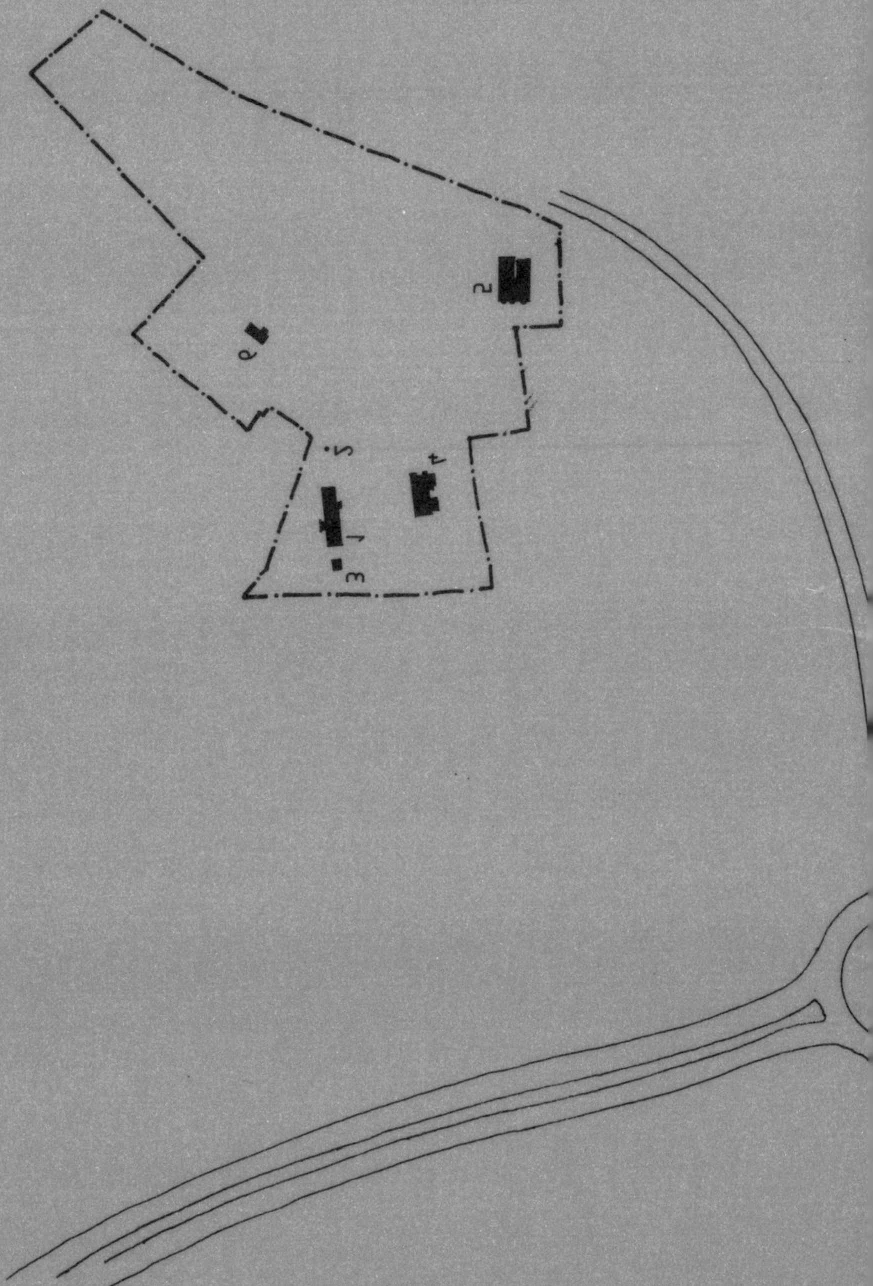

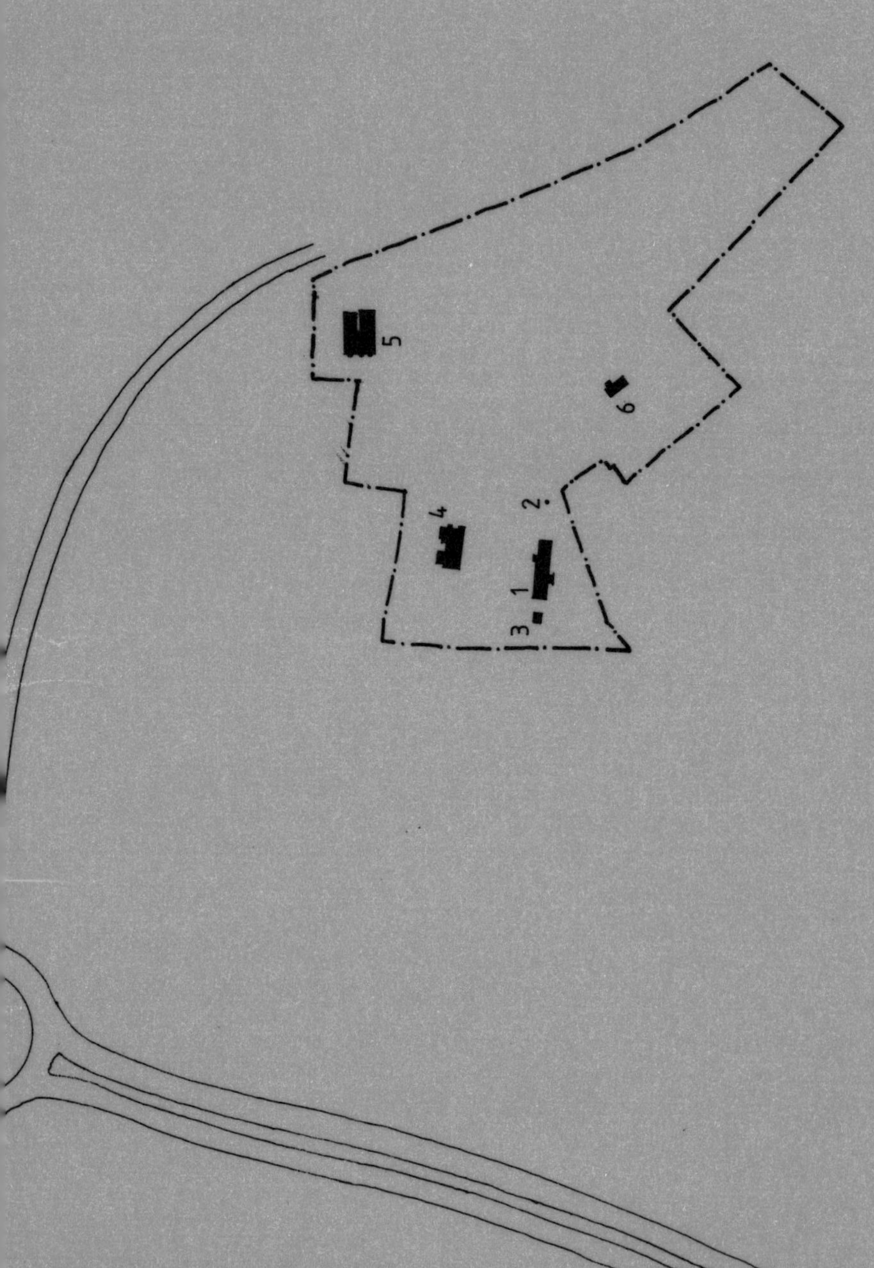
5
6
4
2
1
3

BROUGHTON

BROUGHTON

Broughton is one of the smallest villages of Milton Keynes, much of its acreage lying outside the designated boundary of the city. It appears in Domesday Book, and later a water mill on the Ousel is mentioned in the early C13. A younger branch of the Duncombes of Great Brickhill acquired the manor in 1573. The population however has always remained small, dropping by one third between 1851 and 1901.

1 Church of St. Lawrence I

Anglican parish church, early C14. Nave with south porch, chancel and west tower. Restored 1880–81. Limestone with ashlar quoins, and lead roofs. The building seems to be a major rebuild of c.1300–1320, the time when it is recorded that three new altars were dedicated here. The windows of the north wall are a little later, as is the inserted rood stair, now obscured by the organ. There is evidence that the chancel was extended to the east. The tower was added in the C15 and has the stair embedded in the thickness of the walls. The south door is also of this date and is an interesting survival of medieval carpentry, complete with its iron sanctuary ring. The porch is late C14 and the corresponding north door blocked. The chancel roof is C15 while the nave was re-roofed in c.1850.

D1

The church has some fittings of interest. The pulpit is an C18 one while chained to C17 bookstands either side of the chancel arch are copies of two important works which had, by law, to be installed in post-Reformation churches. These are, on the north, The 'Defence of the Apologie of the Church of England' by Bishop Jewell, dated 1567, and on the south, 'Paraphrases' by Erasmus, c.1550, installed in 1632, both interesting examples of black-letter printing. In the chancel is a brass of John of Broughton, who died in 1403, and his wife Agnes, who died in 1399. On the north wall there is a tablet to Thomas Duncombe, died 1672, whose wife has a brass in the chancel.

St. Lawrence's has two medieval bells by Henry Jordan, c.1460–70 one called John, the other calling upon St. Crispin's intercession, and two C17 bells by Anthony Chandler and John Keene. There is also a sanctus bell.

D1a

The great feature of St. Lawrence is the splendid array of later medieval wallpaintings, a collection rare in its completeness with yet more to be discovered. They are mostly of the C15, and comprise:

North side.
The Last Judgement, St. Michael weighing the souls, the balance being tipped in the soul's favour by Our Lady placing her rosary on the pan, whilst sheltering a host of souls under her cloak. This 'La vierge de Misericorde' survives at only a few other places in Britain, one being Bradwell Abbey chapel. The Warning to Blasphemers shows a collection of fashionable young men dismembering the body of Christ by their words and actions as described in Chaucer's Pardoner's Tale. Again a rare subject graphically illustrated, within a nebuly border.

South side.
Princess in the background with animals around. St. George has unfortunately lost his head, and the dragon much of its body. East of this, St. Helena, mother of Constantine I with a bishop, thought to be St. Eloi, patron saint of blacksmiths. St. Helena holds the Holy Tau Cross.
Below, a most interesting collection of blacksmith's tools; chains, locks, keys, a quenching trough and a shoeing frame. St. Eloi had the sense to remove the leg from an obstreperous horse before shoeing it, and fixing it back with the aid of a miracle afterwards.

D2

The paintings are unified by a mid-C15 scheme of red curtaining painted at low level around the walls, some panels bearing the letters I H U. In the C17 the paintings were obliterated and black-letter texts superimposed, traces of these can be seen all round the nave.

2 Sundial in Churchyard **NL**

A sundial by H. Sutton, dated 1657, formed from the bowl of an C18 lobed font, filled in, itself supported on the upturned bowl of a medieval font with shield panels on its eight sides. The font in the church is a plain Victorian one.

3 Old Schoolroom **NL**

Directly west of the church lies the old schoolroom, now a rabbit-house. C18, red brick with a hipped roof. Square on plan with two windows to the south, now blocked.

4 The Old Rectory **II**

House of C18, altered c.1860, stone, of two bays with central through hall and flanking reception rooms, each with a hipped canted bay window. It has a large brick rear wing, and gable stacks.
A parsonage terrier of 1605 describes an earlier rectory as of 5 bays, timber framed and tiled, with four rooms on each of two floors, together with various thatched outbuildings.

5 Manor House **NL**

A large house, 1875 for R. W. G. Tyringham. Brick with tiled roof, the bargeboards supported on stepped brackets to the two gables facing the road. Central door and hallway, and canted sashed bays to the flanking reception rooms.

6 School Room **NL**

A small brick schoolroom of 1864 built by William Backwell Tyringham, Lord of the Manor. It has pale brick quoins and an arched doorway in a gabled porch. The date is inset in the chimney.

There are two or three early C19 cottages opposite the church drive, including Church View and Fea Cottage. The other houses are semi-detached villas built by Roger Tyringham, all of red brick, the earliest, City View and South View with stone dressings, and later pairs with yellow brick dressings or with the harsher blue bricks and yellow dog-tooth decoration (1878 and 1885).

7 (Pinchcote Farm barn)

A late C17 or early C18 timber framed barn of three bays survived from Pinchcote Farm until fairly recently. It had angle braces to the ties. The outside walls were apparently rebuilt in the C18.

D5

D4

D6

River Ouzel
Grand Union Canal
Belvedere Farm
Belvedere
Pond
Pump House
Football Ground
Stand
Printing Works
Chemical Works
Gasholder
HIGH STREET
WATLING TERRACE
Sugar Refinery
PINEWOOD DRIVE
Joinery Works
Timber Yard
FENNY STRATFORD
ALYESBURY STREET
AYLESBURY STREET
CHURCH STREET
GEORGE STREET
DENMARK STREET
VICTORIA ROAD
VICARAGE ROAD
Brush Factory
Engineering Works
STAPLE HALL ROAD
THE LAURELS
BILTON ROAD
DENBIGH ROAD
Vehicle Works
Prefabricated Building Works
TAVISTOCK STREET
WESTERN ROAD
NAPIER STREET
Stag Bridge
Methodist Church
St Martin's Hall
Leon County Junior School
Leon County Secondary School
War Memorial
Almshouses
Corporation Yard
Fenny Stratford Station
Police Station
Depot
Warehouse
Telephone Exchange
Tudor House
Bowling Green

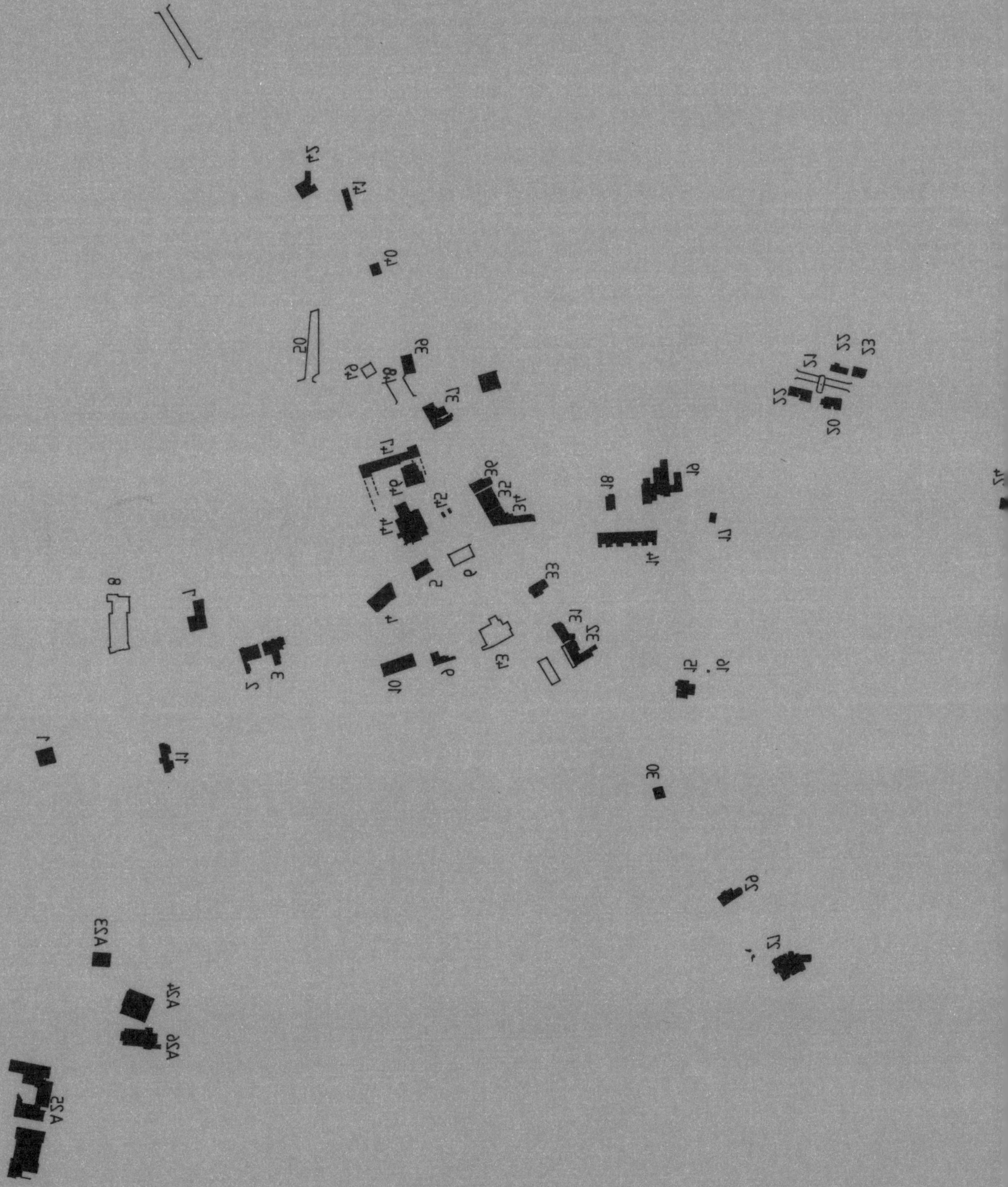

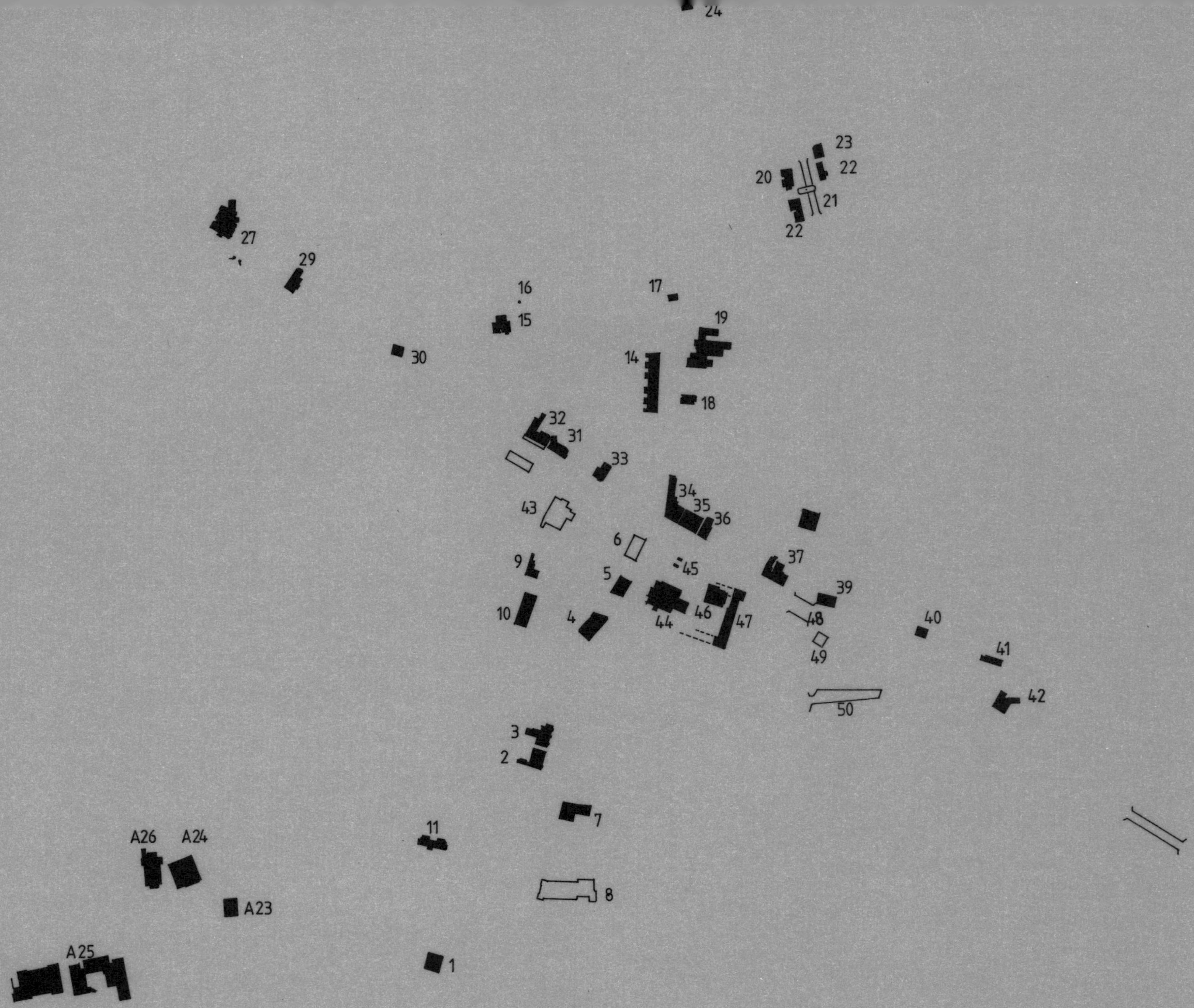
24
23
22
20
21
22
27
29
16
15
17
19
30
14
18
32
31
33
34
35
36
43
6
45
9
5
37
39
10
4
44
46
47
48
40
49
41
50
42
3
2
7
11
A26
A24
8
A23
A25
1

FENNY STRATFORD

FENNY STRATFORD

Fenny Stratford is located as a node of communications, the Roman Watling Street from Dover to Wroxeter, later one of the few medieval arterial roads, and later the first turnpike highway; the Grand Junction Canal of 1800, and later again, the Bedford to Oxford railway of 1846. It is therefore no wonder it is a town of service to travellers. It appears to be the natural successor to the Iron Age settlement at Danesborough followed by the Roman town of Magiovinium, a trading settlement, initially an adjunct to a military fort, but later a posting station on the main Roman road to the north-west. This Roman town lay a little to the south, beyond the crossing of the Ouzel, and slight traces of its enclosing bank can be seen. Why it was not succeeded on the same site is not known; perhaps the ground became too waterlogged in the deteriorating climate of early Anglo-Saxon times. It cannot yet be shown that Fenny Stratford was indeed a transfer to a drier site on raised terrace gravels, but this would seem probable, and it did have the advantage of being on the left bank route along the Ouzel and thus easily linked to its neighbouring villages. Watling Street was in regular use in the early medieval period, for it clearly appears on the Gough Map of c.1360 and appears to be the route followed by John and succeeding kings in their perambulations around the kingdom.

Lack of aristocratic or monastic patronage ensured Fenny Stratford did not develop into more than a traveller's resting place and local market. The only significant building surviving from before the C18 is the Guildhall indicating that needs were generally met by relatively insubstantial buildings. In 1651–1656 three local traders issued tokens, one bearing the Grocer's Arms. Prosperity however accelerated with the construction of the canal c.1792–1800, and many of the surviving buildings were built in the early decades of the C19 using a yellow coloured brick. With the rise of Bletchley as a railway junction, Fenny Stratford was again eclipsed but benefited from the construction of the Bedford Railway in 1846 which brought trade to its wharf and station. Its fate in the third quarter of the century is closely linked with Bletchley, and the development north of Aylesbury Street commenced in 1863. Fenny Stratford continued as a small town of hotels and wayside inns (some 15 different names have been recorded), until the M1 redirected much of its through traffic. Now, with a second by-pass, it is seeking a new role as the southern gateway to Milton Keynes as well as a local specialist shopping place.

AYLESBURY STREET (North Side)

Aylesbury Street is a continuation of the valley road from Newport Pagnell to Leighton Buzzard. It shows a distinct widening indicating that here was held the market, perhaps the Monday Market granted in 1204 renewed in 1608 and held up to the time of the plague, and again revived by Browne Willis. In the early C18 the Butchers' Shambles was held here and a sheep market into living memory. Photographs of the turn of the century show much of Aylesbury Street lined with terraces of single storey timber framed and thatched cottages, none of which has survived.

E1

1 Bracknell House II

A dignified house of the mid C19. Yellow brick, two storeys with a recently altered portico. Margin glazed sash windows.

2 No. 43

Butcher's shop and house, 1898, by John Chadwick, local surveyor. An interesting and well built building of red brick with a tiled roof. The house on the left, and the shop under a large timber framed gable with a terracotta panel and date on the right. The shop window is contemporary with glazed brown brick pilasters and ventilated top appropriate to all butcher's shops. Above there is an oriel window with rounded ends. All openings have arris mouldings and drip moulds.

E2

3 The Maltster's Arms II

A public house, opened in 1842, rendered yellow brick. Four bays with canted bay windows to the ground floor, 16-pane sashes above. Wide door.

E3

4 No. 59 II

One of the few older buildings to survive, the Home Farm, probably of C17 origins which had two groups of tall striking brick chimney stacks removed in 1928. It is basically timber framed with a cellar. It was modernised in the C19 and was given a new shop front in 1883.

5 Church Street Corner NL

A late C19 building with an unusual frieze of moulded flowers, outlined with blue brick.

6 (Rose and Crown Hotel)

This and the adjacent building stood on the north side of Aylesbury Street until demolished for road improvements. They were an interesting group, including the few listed buildings in Fenny Stratford. The Rose and Crown was of brick, with a tiled roof, two storeys and attics, five bays with an altered entrance and a sign board raised above the eaves line.

E6

AYLESBURY STREET (South Side)

Most buildings along this side are small scale commercial premises of the early-mid C19. Of note is No. 84, double fronted with two-storey canted bays and margin glazing, empty and still more or less as re-built. The 'fountain', a horse trough given by Lady Leon in 1913 stood opposite the entrance to the church.

7 Bull and Butcher P.H. II

A good C18 hostelry built by 1753. Rendered brick with tiled roof. Three bays, with central entrance, extended to the right. The name recalls the flesh market once held in the street. Gibbs, the landlord, was also a butcher.

E7

8 (Spurgeon Memorial Hall)

A major baptist chapel and hall, built in 1892 in an Italianate style with a recessed gabled centre section and pediments to end blocks. All openings had alternating brick and stone round arches, and a roundel in the central gable. The main body of the church had a delicate framed iron and wood roof. This building, which formed an important element in the street, is one of the few significant losses of buildings of character (but unlisted) since the advent of Milton Keynes, demolished for car standing space, in1976.

E8

Church Street

Development of Fenny Stratford proceeded with the laying out of New Street (later Denmark Street) in 1863, followed by Church Street and George Street, extending over the farmland once belonging to the Home Farm, now No. 59 Aylesbury Street. Church Street contains little of interest except to note;

9 No. 41 NL

House of c.1883 built by J. Munday for J. Cowlinshaw the schoolmaster. Hipped canopy over a seven-panelled door flanked by canted stone bays with carved capitals. Margin glazed sashes with flashed corners.

10 Salvation Army Citadel **NL**

Built 1887, the foundation stone being laid by Commander H. H. Booth.

DENMARK STREET

Formerly New Street, its claim to fame rests in the long demolished Bletchley Ironworks, located on the corner of Victoria Road and opposite the Foundry P.H. Here is where Charles, and his son Herbert Ackroyd Stuart invented the compression-ignition oil engine in 1886–1890, now known as the Diesel engine. Rudolf Diesel was at the time working on a different fuel system, but eventually patented a similar engine in 1892. Stuart sold out to Hornsby of Grantham, the name now most associated with such machines. A memorial plaque on the Denmark Street corner commemorates this event. The Foundry Inn opposite was a cottage built by Holdom.

11 Rowland Memorial Homes **NL**

Built 1927–8, three simple brick almshouses with large timber framed gables.

MANOR ROAD

12 Manor Farmhouse **II**

Farmhouse, C17, a timber framed building of two storeys, with main elevation to the rear. Central four-panelled door with a fanlight and flanking reception rooms, the central hall leading through to the back. The framed building consists of two main rooms with an intervening central stack, probably originally a lobby entry building, altered in the C18 by the addition of a parallel range at the rear, and the entrance relocated between. The framing is of storey height studding.

E12

13 Cemetery Chapel **NL**

A rather delightful and unaltered building of 1879. Red brick with stone dressings. It consists of a chapel room of two and two half bays and a rather disproportionately large porch and a corner tower with an open spire. Fish-tail Welsh slates on the roof. The interior is now rather plain but no doubt the original decor would have been comfortingly rich.

E13

QUEENSWAY

The schools, council offices and church are considered under Bletchley.

SIMPSON ROAD (North side)

14 Oddfellows Terrace NL

A terrace of ten yellow brick cottages with a central carriage entrance, built by the Oddfellows Lodge, 1858–9. They are well proportioned, and Nos. 11, 15 and 17 retain their original bead-moulded two-panel doors. The windows are sadly being altered.

E14

15 Fenny Stratford Station II

The Bedford Railway Company laid their permanent way in 1846, running from Bletchley to Bedford, part of a larger route that eventually led from Bristol through Oxford, Bletchley and Cambridge, to Norwich and Kings Lynn, thus providing an important cross-country route. The patron of the Bedford Line was the Duke of Bedford, who asserted his rights to insist that the railways stations of Fenny Stratford, Bow Brickhill, and Woburn Sands correspond in design to his estate style. This is a particularly picturesque form of timber framing, one inch thick, applied over timber stud walls. The building is of a 'T' plan, the booking office and waiting room in the front stem of the 'T', and the stationmaster's houses at the rear attached to the Ladies Waiting Room at the north-west end.

The building has a large central diagonal stack and delightful Gothic bargeboarding to the gables and dormers.

16 Signal Post NL

Almost opposite the station building there is an original LMS signal post with upper quadrant home and distant arms. It was re-sited here after the second world war.

17 Signal Box NL

Against the level crossing, a timber weatherboarded signal box of LNWR type 4 of 1884–1903, on a brick footing wall, controlling both the signalling along the line and the manual crossing gates of Simpson Road. These were replaced by automatic gates in c.1978.

E17

SIMPSON ROAD (South side)

18 Benford, Butchers NL

A mid C19 four-bay building with an interesting butcher's shop at one end. This has ventilation over the windows, and outside a poultry rail. At one time all butchers shops displayed poultry and other meats outside, now there are very few of them left.

19 County Police Station and Courtroom NL

A yellow brick building of c.1860 with a slate roof, now containing County Council offices and, at the south-west end, a single storey courtroom added c.1900, with separate public and magistrates' entrances and keyed oculi in the gables.

20 Red Lion P.H. II

A canalside public house, C19, considerably remodelled in 1907, now having a strong hollow moulded string course between the brick lower part and the pebbledashed upper floor. It has shaped gables, and the porch on the corner has turned baluster columns.

E20

21 Fenny Lock No. 22 II

A curiosity of the inland waterways system, with a drop of only 15 inches, due to the accidental leaking of the embankment through Simpson and the failure to maintain a proper level between the previous lock at Stoke Bruerne lowest lock, and the next one at Stoke Hammond. Between the two gates there is a turntable bridge for vehicular access to the lockkeeper's cottage on the south side, and the fields beyond.

22 Waterways Cottage II

There are three cottages associated with the canal. On the north side, Lock View and Pine View with a later extension, recently doubled in width, and on the south a three-bay lock-keepers cottage remodelled in 1911. The first two have been modernised c.1980.

23 Pump House II

A brick pumphouse with a rounded end and hipped slate roof, built c.1841 to contain one of the 'Northern Engines'. There were nine of these extending down the canal from Fenny to Marlsworth locks (Nos. 37–38) recirculating water from one side of the lock to the other as a water conservation method. It is presently being converted to a tearoom.

24 No. 76 Fenny Lodge II

An C18 brick house of two storeys, stone cellars and attics in a gambrel roof. Three bays, with gable stacks, the entrance being against an extension added to the south west side in the early C19.

E24

VICTORIA ROAD (Formerly Back Lane Road, and Stag Street)

Stuart Close occupies the site of the Brush Factory, one of Fenny Stratford's principal industries until recent times.

WATLING STREET (East side)

25 Denbigh Hall Bridge II

Denbigh Hall Bridge was built as a temporary terminal to the London and Birmingham Railway during the construction of the notorious Kilsby tunnel and the Great Ouse viaduct, the two major engineering works on the line. Here passengers disembarked and were carried along the turnpike in carriages to Rugby to rejoin the remaining section of the railway. The bridge is of sandstone, built 1838, by Robert Stephenson, square to the road over which the permanent way passed on the skew. The heavy abutments carry an inscription recording its place in railway history. It was widened on the south side in the 1870's to carry two extra lines.

Close by there were a number of disreputable establishements that had mushroomed to provide for the unfortunate travellers arriving at this spot. These have now all gone.

E25

26 (West Farm)

West Farm stood immediately south of Denbigh Hall Bridge on the east side. The farmhouse disappeared in the 1970's and was a simple brick C19 building with front and back rooms and a recessed side entrance and stair.

The group of farm buildings stood until the 1980's and included a C17 timber framed and weatherboarded barn on brick sill walls, of four bays, with curved braces to the tie beams.

27 Nos. 102–103 Staple Hall, and No. 104 NL

An early C19 building replacing an C18 farmhouse. Three storeys and cellar, three bays, facing Watling Street and with a central entrance, paired doors and wide round fanlight with interesting circles. This has been enclosed in a flat roofed porch with rounded ends. To the rear, at an angle, the building has been extended with an overpowering Victorian elevation with central porch and flanking square two-storey bays, the third floor being gabled. It has mullioned and transomed windows and railings to the roof.

E27

28 Gates and Gatepiers **II**

Erected for Staple Hall, the Portland Stone gatepiers with scrolled tops and cast iron gates by F. Morton & Co. of Liverpool now lead to the Lodge.

29 Staple Lodge **NL**

A most picturesque building splendidly maintained, brick lower storey and the upper with elaborate timber framing. Canted two-storey bay window with small turret, and tiled roofs containing some courses of shaped tiles. Built as a lodge to Staple Hall in 1896.

30 No. 1 **NL**

Once a comely house of c.1840 completely encasing a late C18 timber framed house, now savagely altered with a modern porch and windows. Red brick with a hipped slate roof. Entirely symmetrical, it has much that is Regency in style, with its wide eaves, blind central panel, and 16-pane sash windows around the central entrance.

31 Nos. 17–19 Grade House **NL**

This house, until recently the village shop and now altered almost beyond recognition. It has a fragmentary timber frame and ogee-chamfered ceiling beams, with end stacks, and has been extended at varous times at the rear. In the late C18 it was a wheelwright's and was then converted into a bakery early in the C19.

32 The Red House **II**

A dignified town house appearance disguises a dwelling of the late C18–early C19 at right angles to the road. The front block was built c.1816, three storeys and three bays with a lower annex on the south. The entrance is a fine panelled door within a Tuscan portico, and has a pretty fanlight. This leads to an entrance hall with elegant stairs winding up at the rear, where there is a central round headed stair window. It is of the best brickwork and was finely tuck-pointed, but has been clumsily pointed in recent years. The raised terrace in front with its cast iron bollards is a legacy from the time before the road was re-aligned by Thomas Telford in 1830 who reduced the levels at this spot. Apart from two short breaks The Red House has been the residence of the local doctor since the end of the C18, and is on the site of two earlier inns, the Cock and the White Hart.

33 The Chequers P.H. **II**

Public House, formerly The Bell. A C17 timber framed building, first recorded in 1662, of two bays with a stuccoed front. The C18 sash windows on the upper floor appear to be original, those to the ground floor replaced at different times in the early C19. It has a large fireplace internally.

34 The Swan P.H. **NL**

A handsome hotel and inn, rebuilt in 1879 by E. Gotto of Leighton Buzzard. Three storeys, stucco with a slate roof and moulded architraves to the openings. It forms a satisfactory turn into Simpson Road. An inn was recorded on this site as early as 1474.

35 The Old Town Hall **NL**

Now a building supplier's showroom, it was built as the Town Hall for Fenny Stratford in 1883. Red and blue brickwork with stonework details, it consisted of a spacious entrance hall leading to a wide split stair at the rear, rising to a large meeting hall, the Council Chamber on the first floor. The rest of the ground floor was occupied by offices.

E30

E32

E33

E34

E35

36 No. 39 NL

A private house, c.1883–4, now interconnected with the showroom next door. It was built as a doctor's house, with shopwindows defined by carefully carved stone capitals and cornice. It is a splendid example of Victorian exuberance both in the use of materials and design.

37 The Bridge P.H. NL

Hostelry, 1915, replacing two earlier inns on the same site, The Roebuck and The Navigation. Brick, with stone trimmed bays with window transomes. Central entrance.

38 Canal Stores NL

To the rear, two warehouses owned by the canal company, 1840–50. Both have double pitched roofs and large doors, with lifting beams over the upper openings. At one time the northern one had an iron gantry which has now been taken down and placed inside.

39 Recketts Colours Offices NL

A rather fine house built by Gregory Odell Clarke, brick manufacturer and general factor c.1860. Three bays, rendered with vermiculated quoins and keystones to the moulded window architraves. Those on the upper floor break through the eaves line and have hipped slate roofs. A bay window on the ground floor is a later addition. Heavy eaves brackets. The windows have margin glazing with red and blue flashed glass to the arched stair window to the rear. The offices for the brickworks were probably also here.

To the rear stood some three lime kilns, and opposite, beyond the wharf, was the brickyard, with one square muffle kiln. Clarke's kilns and those of Simpson Road appear to have made the yellow bricks which are the distinctive feature of Fenny Stratford.

OLD WATLING STREET

The old course of Watling Street dipped sharply after crossing the hump-backed canal bridge and curved slightly to the east. From the Bridge Inn this line is still preserved below the present embankment and has two buildings of interest.

40 No. 4 & 5 II

A heavily diapered pair of cottages with 12-pane sashes in segmental headed openings and with brick dentilled eaves. The block was to be extended to the south but apparently this was never carried out. The facade has a number of bricks inscribed with initials, JH, DM, JB, JW, JG, JY and GWG. Who were these people?

41 No. 1 II

Two cottages, now one. Single storey of almost Scottish type. Pale red brick and slate roof. One door is blocked and its windows were replaced later in the C19. Gable stacks. It was at one time known as Gas Cottage, being associated with the gas works built by Gregory Odell Clarke.

42 Green Grass Club NL

A late C19 building, formerly the Saracen's Head from 1753, and until recently known as The King's Head. Now pebbledashed brick with twin gables.

43 (River Ouzel Bridge)

The bridge over the Ouzel and its marshes was, until replaced in 1800, a brick structure 270 ft long carrying a 17 ft carriageway over eight arches, three towards the centre being larger, at 8 ft span. A survey drawing exists in the Grant Collection at Northampton Record Office.

E36

E39

E37

E38

E40

E41

WATLING STREET (West side)

North of Aylesbury Street, the west side was cleared and redeveloped c.1977. It had a few buildings of mild interest, in particular a house with Gothic intersecting glazing bars to the sash windows.

44 (National School)

A simple brick building of two schoolrooms and a schoolmaster's house, by E. G. Burton of London, and built in 1861 to replace an earlier National School some yards further up Watling Street. It was enlarged for the growing population in 1881, the extra accommodation being added on the south side. It was later to become the Freemason's Hall, and was demolished ahead of redevelopment.

45 Church of St. Martin B

This building is a surprise and of considerable interest. The church was built as a chapel for Fenny Stratford in 1724–30 for Browne Willis so that the inhabitants did not have to make the long walk to Bletchley Church. The architect was Edward Wing of Aynhoe, Northants. Browne Willis was probably aware that he was replacing the townspeople's medieval chapel that had fallen on bad times since the suppression of religious houses. Browne Willis was Lord of the Manor 1703–1760, an active patron and a keen antiquarian who later became one of the founders of the Society of Antiquaries of London. The church started as a Georgian preaching nave, wide and rectangular, with a west tower. It is this building that faces Watling Street. To this building was added a second nave in a Gothic style in 1866 by the well-known architect William White, and, to accommodate the growing late Victorian population it was then given a further aisle on the west side by John Chadwick, in 1908. The Georgian work is of locally made brick with some vitrified headers, with windows with pointed heads and a stone crenellated parapet. The tower, not so dissimilar to that of Willen, also has a stone parapet, and is of three stages with a recessed north end entrance with line rustication and, on the keystone, a coat of arms and the inscription 'Ecclesia Sancti Martini 1726' in a cartouche. Of added interest is the fact that the tracery of the side windows is Gothic in style. These were installed at the insistence of Willis, despite, so it seems, the architect's wishes, and as a result we have in Milton Keynes, one of the earliest examples of the Gothic revival in Britain.

Internally, the Georgian building has a splendid flat ceiling of 40 compartments painted with the coats of arms of contributing local families. Dr Browne Willis, who was interred in 1760 under a white marble slab in the chancel, now the north aisle.

In the north-east window there is a fine collection of C17 and C18 stained and painted glass of the Tudor and later periods, collected by Browne Willis from Salden House, and formerly in his east window. Of note are the arms of the Fortescue and Stonor families, and the Boleyn family, descendants of the hapless queen. William White's nave is only slightly less of interest, for it is in the full tradition of contrasting brickwork introduced by Butterfield at All Saints Margaret Street, London in 1851. To our eyes it seems harsh but is true to the confidence and non-accommodating attitude of its age. John Chadwick, the last contributor, was the local versatile surveyor to the Council. The modern porch and ecumenical meeting room completes the picture of this interesting building.

E45

E45a

Monuments NL

In the graveyard against Watling Street are two impressive chest tombs, one to Gregory Odell Clarke, the local brickmaker, who died 1873, and members of his family, and the other to Thomas Holdom, and relatives, together with members of another eminent family, including Thomas Hammond, died 1864.

On St. Martin' Day, 11th November each year a cannonade of six small ordnance, the Fenny Poppers, are fired and a dinner is held in remembrance of the town's benefactor but probably originally started by him in remembrance of his grandfather. Due to safety precautions, the cannonade has recently been removed to Leon Park.

46 Bull Hotel NL

There has been a Bull Hotel in Fenny Stratford since 1609. This is but the last of a long line of buildings, built in 1939, and probably replacing an C18 building with three ground floor bay windows.

47 The Chantry House II*

One of the most important early buildings in Milton Keynes. Built in the C15, it has had a chequered career and is just embarking on a new existance as small workshops and offices.

The Guild of St. Margaret and St. Katherine the Virgins was founded by royal licence of 22nd November 1493 for eminent local citizens to establish a chapel and guild, with an attendant chaplain. It later had two resident priests who were not replaced after 1546, after which it was sold to Lord Grey. It seems as though part became the Bull Inn, and another part was acquired by Browne Willis in 1724, where he later erected his chapel.

The building is timber framed, comprising a front block of at least three bays, only two now surviving, apparently older than the rest in that it had jetties on moulded beams both front and partially at the rear. To this was added a back wing of two bays, and well to the back of the site, a parallel range of at least four bays (only two now survive). Between these two, at a slightly later date a two-storey framed structure of five bays was inserted, in fact a major medieval structure. It has been suggested that the rear block continued to the north-west and returned back to Watling Street completing an enclosed courtyard, thus what we now see is little more than half the original building. The part facing Watling Street appears to have been a dwelling, as it has a large axial stone stack, secret tension and windbraces, and a curved collar although the ground floor is uncommonly high, and may have included a shop. The stack terminates in three diagonal Tudor shafts, now rebuilt. The rear wing also had a stack. The main five-bay range to the rear was originally divided into two rooms, of two and three bays; one was probably the meeting hall for the guild, the other part of the hostelry, since the income to maintain the charity no doubt came in large measure from the facility of food and accommodation it provided for travellers on Watling Street. This range has wind braces and one moulded arch to the tie beam. The shorter room has the tie beams replaced by short hammer beams, an attempt to add greater dignity to the interior. These also occurred in the arch that stood over the opening to the Bull Yard, this range ending to the north in a cross wing extending to the rear. The architectural details of the front range points to a date in the later C14 or C15 for its construction. If the five-bay range is in fact the building for which permission was given in 1493, then the front range must be sufficiently older to have been extended by its back wing before that date. More at present cannot be said. Preserved at Aylesbury Museum is part of a wall-painting showing a standing cat playing a fiddle; no doubt a painting from its secular days. In the C19 the building became a brewery converted from a steam powered corn mill c.1870, and until recently a heavily constructed warehouse rose directly from the canal it served with a steam corn mill. This was then converted into a brewery and later it became a glucose refinery for the brewing trade, with animal feedstuffs as a by-product. The smell and steam that permeated the town from those processes will be long remembered.

E47

E47b

E47c

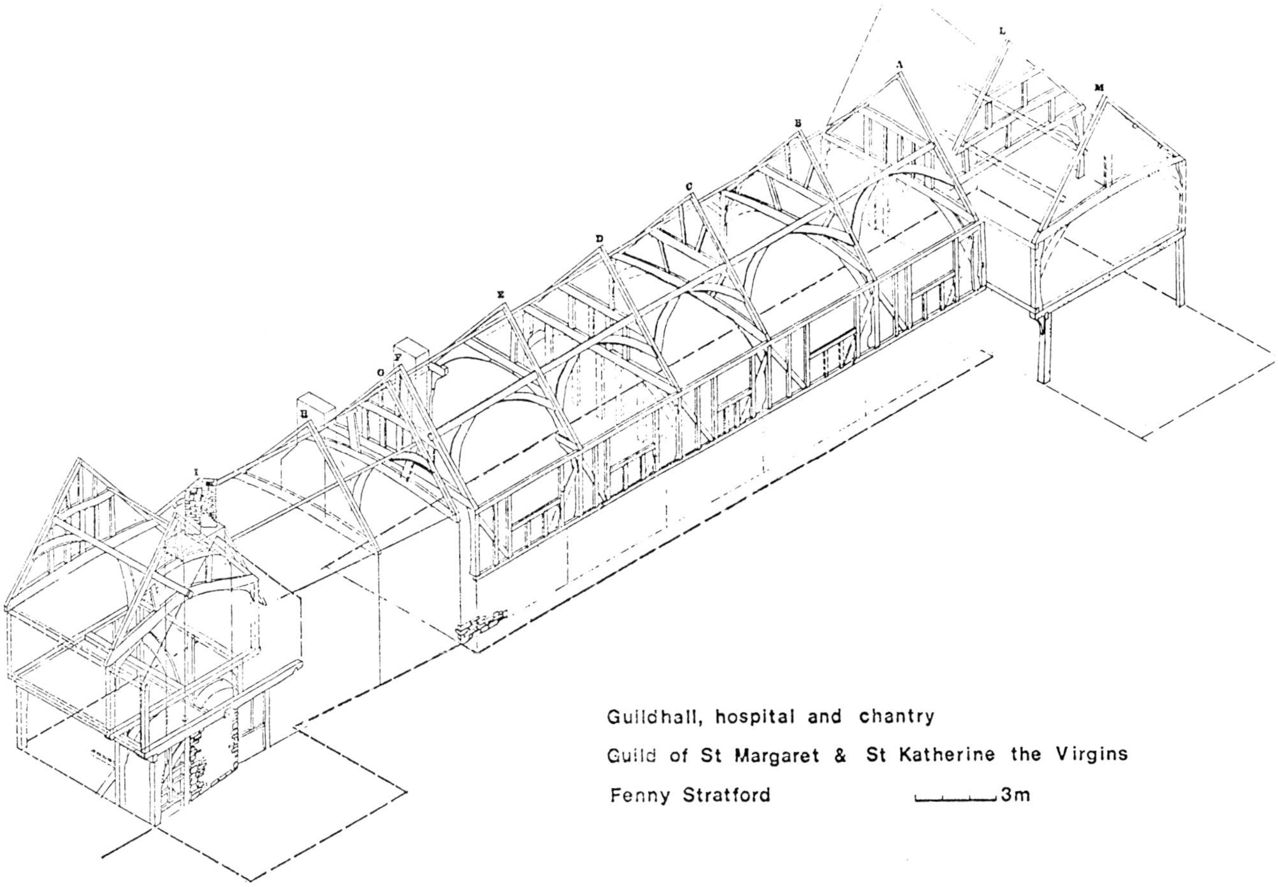

Guildhall, hospital and chantry

Guild of St Margaret & St Katherine the Virgins

Fenny Stratford 3m

48 Canal Bridge No. 96 NL

The original narrow hump-backed bridge was replaced with the present ugly structure in 1927.

49 (Repeater Station) NL

The small GPO building of 1898 with its hipped roof containing the repeater station for the telegraphic signals on the old Holyhead Road was demolished c.1982. In the adjacent building which still stands, was a Ruston & Hornsby Akroyd type Oil Engine, built in 1924.

50 Fenny Stratford Dock NL

To the rear of the GPO exchange lies a wet dock off the Grand Union Canal. Built after 1880.

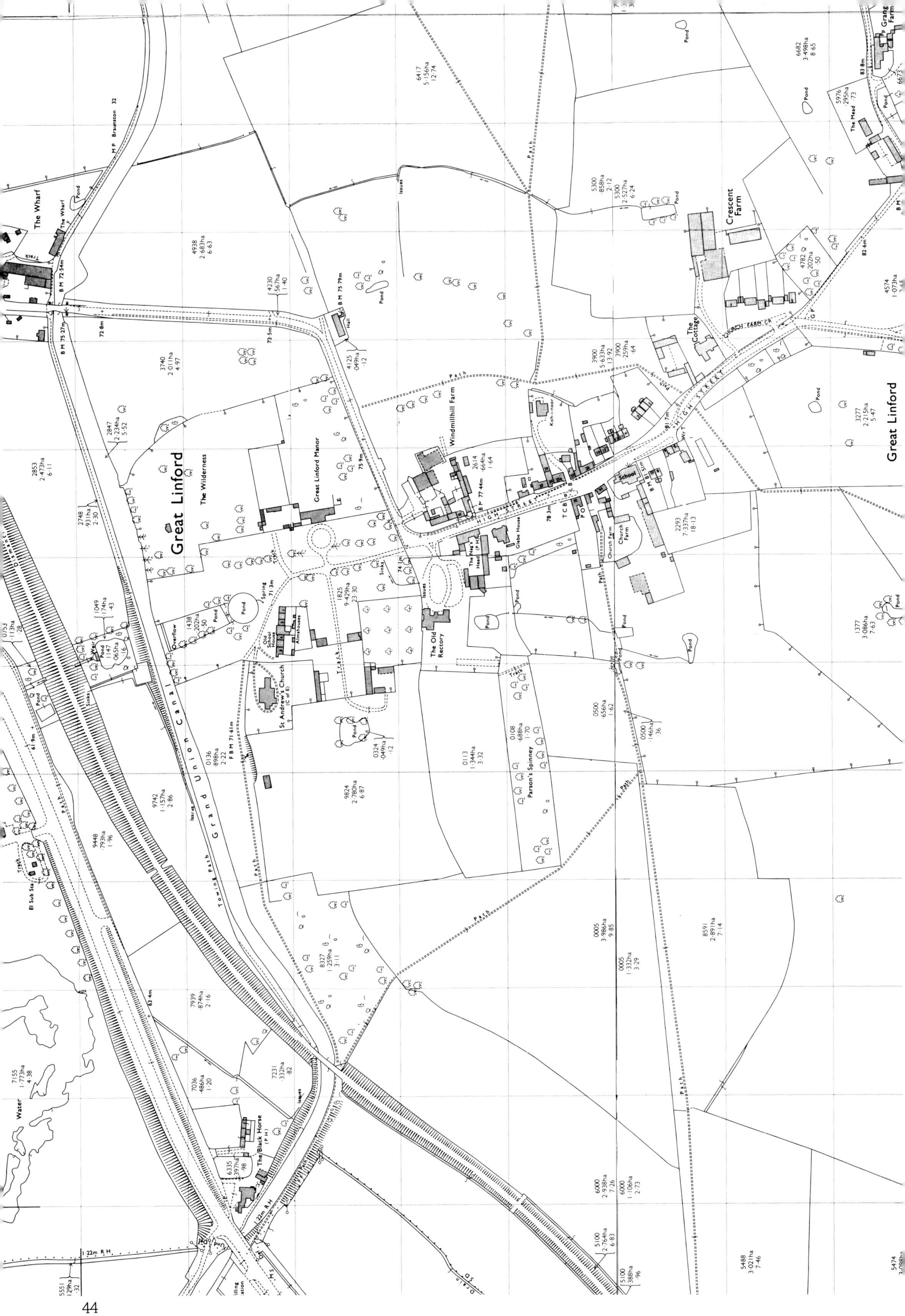
Great Linford
The Wilderness
Great Linford Manor
Windmillhill Farm
Crescent Farm
The Cottage
High Street
School
Church Farm
Glebe House
The Nag's Head (P H)
The Old Rectory
Almshouses
Old School House
St Andrew's Church (C of E)
Parson's Spinney
Grand Union Canal
Towing Path
The Black Horse (P H)
The Wharf
The Mead
Pond
Path
Track
Issues
Sinks
Spring
Overflow
Water
El Sub Sta

Marsh Drive
Hartley
Parklands

Marsh Drive
Parklands
Hartley
Gibbwin
1
3
4
5
6
7
8
9
10
11
12
13
14
15
16
17
18
19
20
22
23
24
25
26
27
28
29
30
31
33
34
36
37
37
38
39
40
41
43

GREAT LINFORD

GREAT LINFORD

Great Linford is one of the more nucleated villages of Milton Keynes. It stands on the southern scarp of the Great Ouse valley on the road from the south to Newport Pagnell. It is unusual in that the parish name extends across the valley to Little Linford, the river having been a boundary for much of history including being the southern march of the Danelaw. The church stands on the edge of the slope, and appears to represent the early nucleus, with a secondary centre developing later in the medieval period around the green at the southern end of the High Street.

The village has been subject to more detailed archaeological investigations than most. They show that there has been late Saxon and C12 settlement in the area of the church, and that the green at the southern end of the High Street was lined with houses in the C15–C16 probably with earlier origins. One apparently was a simple cruck structure. On Willen Lane there were more farmhouses and farm buildings than exist now, and an important result of these investigations is the confirmation that villages up to the C17 contained a large number of relatively flimsy and ephemeral structures, sheds, fences, tenting frames; a conclusion if not unexpected, serves to remind us that what we imagine as England's past is built upon the biased evidence of those more substantial buildings that have managed to survive until today.

It appears that the original structure of the village, consisted of a north-south road with the settlement clustered around the church on the scarp of the Ouse valley. This road, now the High Street descended the hill directly where the Manor ponds now are. Perhaps this became too eroded and wet, as it seems to have fallen out of use in favour of a more direct route back from the brow of the hill to the east, leaving the church in a backwater. The arrangement became fixed by the establishment of the Manor grounds in the late C17-early C18. The road branches at the green, one arm going to Willen, the other to the Woolstones.

Two further events took place in the C19 that altered the geography of the area. Firstly, in May 1800 the Grand Junction Canal was opened which had a wharf on the Newport Road from Linford, destined to become a very busy port. From here a separate arm off the canal was built 1814–1817, descending a flight of seven locks, to Newport Pagnell. This was never popular with the company as water flowing through was lost to the system, and it was eventually closed in 1863.

In 1867 Newport Pagnell was connected to the rail system by the Newport Branch line, which also ran through the Manor park. This is now a public footpath.

1 Church of St. Andrew **II***

Parish church, late C12–C13, C14, C15 and C19. Limestone rubble with a tile roof. It consists of a nave with narrow south aisle and north chapel combined with a porch, chancel and vestry, and a west tower. The earliest work is embodied in the tower, early C13, with lancet lights. This was the west tower of a small Norman church with nave and small square chancel. The nave is a rebuild of the C13, wider than the original, and eccentric to the tower as it used the earlier south wall so as to avoid demolishing the aisle. The aisle was extended to the east in the mid-C14. A north porch was added in the late C14 with a parvise above, shortly followed by the fine north chapel. This has large windows with fleurons as does the internal column. The church as it stands owes much of its appearance to the rebuilding of the chancel and the south aisle in 1706–10, the latter narrower than its C12 predecessor which we must assume was now in poor order. This was probably the work of Sir William's widow, Sarah, through her nephews who had inherited a life interest in the manor. The interior was embellished with panelling, pulpit and the plaster ceiling which appears, from the accounts, to have been painted. The unfortunate stone mullions to the windows are also of this time. This ceiling hides a baroque Royal arms of Charles II high on the nave east wall. The south-east window is of 1904, by Kempe, and the south window by Kempe and Tower, c.1910. The pews were cut down and rearranged in 1884.

F1

In the North Chapel there is a fine wall monument to Sir William Pritchard, died 1705, Lord Mayor of London, describing how, as president of St. Bartholomew's Hospital, he funded the provision of what may be the earliest renal unit, 'for the cutting of the stone'. On the opposite wall, a white and yellow marble tablet to Thomas Uthwatt, died 1754. During renovations of 1978, under the floor of the nave, a large area of medieval encaustic tiles were found to be preserved. They were made in the Little Brickhill kilns in the C15, and were apparently laid with the assistance of the legacy of Roger Hunt whose brass recording the donation still survives. Outside the church an interesting C13 headstone was discovered near where there lay a priest with a pewter chalice and paten.

F1a

2 Linford Manor (formerly Linford Place) II*

Modest as it is, it is the only place approaching a stately home in the Milton Keynes city area, and its development to what we see today is of special interest.

It has already been noted that the road which once ran through the park was cut off, probably early in the middle ages, leaving the church and some surrounding farms and houses somewhat in a backwater. We are most fortunate in having two maps survive, one of 1641 prior to the emparkment and the other 1678, after the land had been enclosed.

The 1641 map shows the High Street extending to the Hine Well, and then swinging to the west to the church. The fact that this well is named shows that it had more than usual significance, and it may have had special properties or dedication. It now supplies the ornamental ponds.

F2

The medieval Manor House

The Manor House, shown on the 1641 estate map, stood between the Old Rectory and the Church, more or less where the south pavilion now stands. This house, the manor of Sir Richard Napier from 1633–1676, proved on excavation, to be a fairly large medieval hall house with service rooms, to which, late in the middle ages, a stone wing was added on its north side. To the rear there were various yards and outbuildings. This house may be the one modified to take Jacobean moulded timber windows, and which was bought in 1682 by Sir William Pritchard, merchant tailor of London, as a country house, in addition to his seat at Lauderdale House on Highgate Hill. He was a man of substance and standing, and had been Lord Mayor of London on various occasions between 1682 and 1688 and MP for London in 1685, 1690 and 1702. He had been knighted for his services in 1672.

3 The Manor House II*

Sir William decided to rebuild the manor in a more convenient and contemporary style, and selected a new site on the opposite side of the road, facing west. For the house he built over the years 1688–9, he used amongst others, the same builder, Atterbury, as did Dr. Busby and Robert Hooke at Willen Church. Sir William carefully reused what materials he could salvage from the old house. What the new house looked like is now difficult to disentangle from the many later alterations. It was probably of two storeys and attics, one room deep, with cross windows, and a steep pitched hipped roof. The front doorcase of the present house, with its rather over correct detail and broken pediment may well be his, otherwise there is little to see externally.

Sir William Pritchard died in 1705, and his estate was left to nephews of a family from Scotland, the Uthwatts, who held it until the advent of Milton Keynes. Unfortunately the family papers are mostly missing, and we cannot now know when the Manor House was remodelled, but it was drastically altered between c.1720 and 1740, probably in two phases by Thomas Uthwatt, and the ballroom wing added c.1740–50 by Henry Uthwatt. In 1758 an inventory describes 21 rooms, including cellars and the garrets where the manservants and maids slept. The main rooms seem to be the Great Room, the Stone Hall, the Brown Parlour and a drawing room with bedrooms on the first floor. The house had considerable outbuildings and a large service yard built on the north side probably utilizing some earlier works there. The two added wings contained the kitchens and a ballroom in the full mid-C18 fashion. At the same time the house was panelled throughout, and Sir William's fine stair with its turned balusters reset in a rear hall (although here it is possible that it occupied the same position in a C17 rear wing). Later in the C18 probably c.1780, the house was refronted and the roof lowered and slated at the front to keep abreast of fashion. The next phase of alterations took place in Victorian times, and fortunately these were not radical, the roofs were again altered and a curious panelled box eaves carried across the back. Further panelling and fireplaces were inserted, but on the whole the building remained much as it was in the mid C18. Internally, the main features are the C17 stair, the fireplaces on the first floor, and the ballroom. The latter has caused some controversy, for it is so like the C18 pattern books of such men as William Halfpenny that it has been suggested that it is a re-creation of the later Victorian period. With the documents gone, we shall never know. The Carrara marble fire surround looks, as does the main entrance door, late C17, the overmantel C19, while the fibrous plaster cornice is newly inserted in 1979. As many buildings it has its ghost, a desperate mother and child in one of the first floor rooms, but she has not been seen for sometime.

F3a

F3b

F3c

F3d

4 The Pavilions II*

Facing the Manor House across the old road stand two pavilions. They are substantial two-storey three bay buildings of ashlar limestone, mid C18, with fiendishly complicated tiled roofs. The north one was fitted out in the C19 as stabling, the other a barn. Whether these were the originally intended uses is not so clear, for it would be customary amongst the wealthy gentry to build one as a chapel and the other a library, as for instance at Stoke Bruerne. However if ever buildings had Mary Ann backs these do, as they have pitching doors to the loft floors.

The placing of pavilions facing the main house instead of on wings to the sides is very rare. One other place is Ragley Hall, Worcestershire, built for Sir Edward Seymour by, significantly, Robert Hooke. Could it be that Hooke himself suggested a plan that was not to be implemented for 50 years?

F4

5 The Great Barn II

Behind the pavilions lies the Manor courtyard, apparently just a barn and kennels opposite, now replaced with craft workshops by Donald Insall in 1979. On the gable end of the barn there are however traces of three large oval openings of a type popular in the later C17. Perhaps the barn is a survivor of the early manor, adapted as a more lowly barn when the present manor was built. It was burnt out on the day the thatching was completed in 1976, but the roof was totally rebuilt as it was.

Forming the other side of the courtyard was a long range of stone kennels for the Uthwatt's otterhounds. The Great Linford Otterhounds were famous throughout the neighbouring counties and photographs have survived of this barbarous sport.

II

The carriage yard is defined by stone walls and low stone piers. Between these piers new iron railings and gates of a design appropriate to the period have been erected.

F5

6 The Almshouses II*

Sir William Pritchard, as was expected of the landed gentry of the time, built in 1696–7 for the benefit of the village a range of six almshouses with a schoolmaster's house in the centre. This philanthropic gesture was converted in 1975 for craft workshops and a dwelling. They are built of local stone and tiles from Newport Pagnell, William Atterbury again being the main builder. The cost was kept down to £151.15s.0d. as Sir William directed that materials from the old house were to be reused. Each poor person had one room, with a fireplace flanked by ventilated cupboards, and a through corridor with a washstand. At the end of the small garden were the privies. They remained in use as they were intended until the 1960's. The schoolmaster, as well as his scholastic duties, was to undertake the duties of a warden for the old folk. He admitted village children to his living room, to which was added, shortly after, a general purpose washroom at the rear. The house has two attic bedrooms, and a fine stair as well as the handsome shell canopy over the front door.

F6

7 The Kitchen Garden NL

East of the service yard is a rectangular kitchen garden enclosed with a fine stone wall, faced in brick on the inner side to conserve the sun's heat to bring the plants on. Part of the wall had patterned bricks, possibly of the C17, but it was clearly rebuilt in the C18. The lining of brick became standard practice and was recommended by J. C. Loudon in his book on horticulture in 1822.

8 High Street Gates NL

Cast iron gates and railings of the C19, the stanchions recast by Tattershall Foundry, Towcester in 1983.

F8

9 (Gazebo)

The grounds north of the manor house are described in the C19 as a Wilderness. This is clearly not the C18 concept of a wilderness, which consisted of straight avenues through controlled banks of trees but is a more informal area, possibly created in the later C18 or early C19. In the centre, lay a Doric gazebo consisting of a central gabled pediment and flanking side arches, all of wood with brick and stone rear walls. Local lore relates how it was built for an unhappy wife of a later Uthwatt to sit and gaze upon her former family home at Little Linford (the canal was not yet built), but this story has not been confirmed. This wilderness area is bounded on the east by a ha-ha, now little more than a dip in the ground, but which appears to follow the line of the early medieval back lane, a feature which until recent development, could be traced on both sides of the High Street.

F9

10 The Ornamental Ponds NL

The remodelling of the manor grounds in the early-mid C18 converted the outfall of the old spring to ornamental pools. The Hine well fed, at the top, a large circular pool, which overflowed into a long rectangular pond. This in turn flowed down into a lower pond, which in turn flowed down a picturesque cascade into a yet lower pond. This arrangement was brutally curtailed first by the construction of the Canal in 1800, and later by the Newport Branch Railway, leaving the lower ponds practically inaccessible. The use of water and formal ponds in this manner had been demonstrated by William Kent and others at Rousham and Stowe, not far away, before the mid C18.

HIGH STREET (East side)

11 The Cottage NL

The core of this building is a two-bay two-storey timber framed cottage of the C17, to which has been added extensive wings, one bay to the south in the C18 and later, one bay to the north end. Both then received rear outbuildings and a forward wing in the mid-late C19. Late C19 porch. Tiled roofs with six gabled dormers with diamond lattice glazing in cross windows. Refurbished in c.1977.

F11

12 Stables to The Cottage NL

Against the road, a timber framed building with a thatched roof, probably late C17-early C18. It returns at the north end and is continued in later brickwork. Re-thatched with an inappropriately decorative ridge about 1984. Internally four loose boxes with iron mangers.

13 The Red Barn NL

A substantial brick barn of the late C18-early C19, formerly with Crescent Farm and now discreetly converted to a house. It is of five bays with central opposed cart doors and slit vents to the west side and an owl hole to the gable. The walls are of 450mm brickwork suggesting it was intended for storing threshed grain rather than corn on the ear. Double purlin roof with collar and raking struts.

F13

14 Cottages Nos. 21–27 II

A row of farm workers cottages of the C18, of stone, originally thatched but now having tiled roofs. They appear to have been built as one-storey dwellings and raised to two storeys in the late C18-early C19. No. 23, Forge End, has a Sun firemark No. 404788 of 1778. No. 25, Old Bakery, C19, with rendered lintels and four panel doors, incorporating earlier work internally, and a rear wing with a bakehouse and large oven. A deep well was discovered at the rear during the construction of the large modern extension. No. 27, now colourwashed, has a modern tiled roof. The row was thatched until the 1920's.

F14

15 No. 29 Rivet's Yard II

Cottage, probably C18, roughcast stone with thatch. Three bays with gable stack. Late C20 windows and four-panel door.

16 Nos. 35 and 35A NL

Brick cottages, late C18 or early C19, originally one storey and later raised to two, the thatched roof being replaced in recent times. No. 35A has been rendered, with a stone gable onto the street.

A probate inventory of Edward Harris dated 1694 is in existence but this must refer to an earlier building on the same site.

17 Windmill Farm House NL

A stone built cottage, not the original farmhouse, C17–C18, also raised to two storeys in brick about the mid C19. Brick dentilled eaves and three partly raised flush dormers. There are two stacks, one between bays one and two.

F16–17

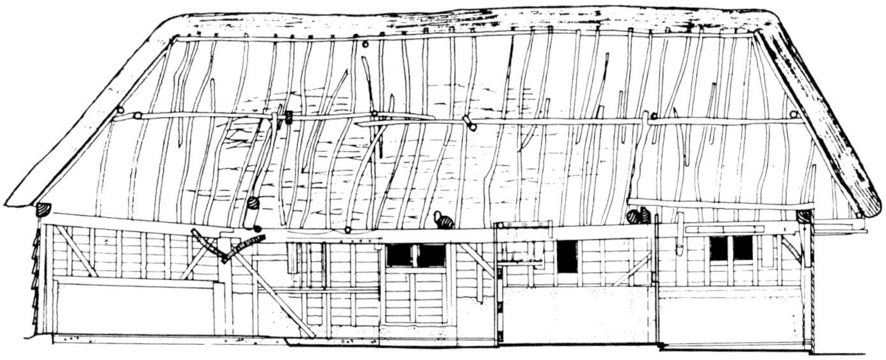

F18a

18 Cricket Store II

Originally a stable and store for Windmill Farm. Undateable but probably C18. Timber weatherboarding and a thatched roof. A very rare survival of an ephemeral building such as is encountered in almost all medieval village excavations. It has no regular framing, the posts miscellaneous and set into the ground, and propped with other timbers on the south side when it took up a rhomboid shape. The roof was of round poles as cut from the hedgerow, with a variety of props and stays. The thatch was roped on and patched over many a year. Hurdling and gates have been used as internal partitions, and a variety of hooks and nails fixed to the walls. It is this sort of building that is an essential element of the true village and distinguishes it from the commuter village. Very sadly, the building was partly destroyed by fire in 1985, and now has a new roof, removing much of its interest.

F18b

F18c

19 No. 41 NL

House, c.1870–90, neat and well proportioned, two bays, with central stair hall. Four-pane sash windows and four-panelled door. Gable stacks. It has a new rear wing.

20 Windmill Hill Farm Barn II

A range of limestone stables and shelter sheds, once small cottages and now (August 1985) once again being converted to a dwelling. Probably C19, the foundations standing on land occupied in the C14.

21 (Windmill)

Archaeological excavation has revealed the cross trees of a post mill east of the village High Street. Scientific evidence obtained from the traces of wood preserved suggest that it was erected sometime after the late C13, thus must be one of the earliest windmills to be erected in Britain. The mound was surrounded by a ditch 40m in diameter.

F19

LINFORD WHARF

22 The Wharf House II

An inn of the last years of the C18 built to serve canal traffic. Colourwashed stone and a tiled roof. Three storeys but two facing the canal. Three bays, with central door to hallway, and 16-pane sashes. Lean-to against the west gable.

23 Canal Bridge NL

Brick hump-backed bridge over the Grand Junction Canal, built c.1800 and refurbished c.1975.

24 No. 6 The Wharf NL

An interesting brick building at the head of the former flight of seven locks that gave entry to the Newport Arm. Early-mid C19. Two storeys one side, one the other with the main central door. It probably housed the lock-keeper.

F22

HIGH STREET (West side)

25 No. 2 and the Baptist Chapel — NL

Brick cottage, c.1830–40, with stone hoods to ground floor door and window. Concrete pantile roof. To the rear, Baptist Chapel, 1833, the central gable door and porch replaced with a window. The gable is treated as a simple brick pediment.

F25

26 Rose Cottage — NL

Stone cottage, possibly of C17 origin. One storey and attic, two bays, its historical origins now entirely disguised by recent alterations.

27 Primary School — NL

The first school room is of 1874, brick stone quoins and a slate roof, gable to the street, for 71 day pupils and 18 evening students. This was greatly extended in 1905 and provided with a slightly canted gable against the footpath. There have been a number of further single storey extensions with flat roofs in the last two decades.

F27

28 School Barn — NL

A thatched stone barn to rear, formerly with Church Farm, was converted for school use in July 1975.

29 No. 12 Church Farmhouse — II

Farmhouse of the C17, stone built with a tiled roof. Three bays with a cross passage between the left two bays, to the rear of the stack. The right end bay may be an addition beyond a second gable stack. Modern panelled door and windows. Three rendered brick buttresses have been added to the front.

F29

30 No. 14 — NL

Colourwashed stone cottage prominent in the street. Of two bays, corrugated asbestos replacing thatch of a steeper pitch. The entrance is in the gable at the side of the major stack, and a further stack to the opposite gable.

F30

31 Post Office and Stores — NL

Shop of the early C19. Three narrow bays, with a panelled shop door and modest canopy flanked by paned windows, all nicely in scale with the village.

32 Nos. 24 and 26 — NL

Two cottages in one build, C17, originally one storey and attic, and raised to two storeys in brick in the C19. The recessed central door leads to both front doors either side. No. 24 has a chamfered spine beam internally. Gable stacks. Re-windowed 1985, but preserving the original chamfered and stopped timber lintels.

In front of No. 24 is an iron standpipe, probably mid-late C19.

F31

F32

33 No. 28 The Glebe House — II

House of the late C17–early C18, of ashlar limestone with a platband and timber dentilled eaves. Two storeys and attics, the roof hipped with dormers and gable stacks. 'L' plan with central stair hall and chamfered ceiling beam in rear wing room. The front has mid C19 two-storey canted bay windows added, and a doorcase with an elegant fanlight, possibly early C19. A late C19 excrescence has been added to the roof to extend the central attic. Rear wing and a further extension on the north side. The drawing room and one room on the first floor has painted panelling, and some Delft tiles around the fireplaces of the main reception rooms.

F33

34 Carriage House and Stables to Glebe House — II

An C18 building with an arched carriage door and stables. The roof is hipped and has a late C19 pitching door to the loft space. The yard has patterned cobbles.

35 Wall to High Street — II

A fine brick wall in English garden wall bond, with a weathered course and brick on edge coping, apparently raised by a number of further courses. Probably late C18–early C19.

36 No. 30 The Nag's Head — II

An inn, later C17, of colourwashed stone with a thatched roof. It has two storeys and an attic still lit by the original C17 wood mullioned and diamond paned windows. The other windows have been replaced in the C19 and C20. The building is of four bays, with a rear wing, also thatched, extending back along the High Street.

F36

37 The Old Rectory

A large house of C17 origin, extensively modernised by E. Swinfen Harris in 1876–8. It is 'E' shaped on plan, but with a long rear wing. The forward wings have two-storey bay windows, that to the left raised on an open framed ground floor. Central gabled porch, and massive decorated chimney stacks, including a twisted brick stack on the rear gable of the right wing. The interior has an early C18 stair with turned balusters and some panelling of the early C17.

The rector from 1590–1634 was the Rev. Richard Napier, astrologer, whose fame for his medical abilities had wide repute. He was something of an eccentric, claiming continual dialogue with the angel Raphael. In c.1630 he bought the manor of Great Linford for his son, Sir Richard Napier, one of the first members of the Royal Society, who also practised medicine. The Napier papers were left to Elias Ashmole and are now in the Bodleian collection.

Edward Bury, locomotive superintendent of the London & Birmingham Railway and designer of the Bury class locomotives, lived here c.1840–1850.

F37

38 Dovecote to the Old Rectory — II

Square limestone dovecote, since 1970 without its roof. Early C17. It originally had a square glover. 600 'L' shaped nesting boxes are still to be seen in the walls.

F38

HARPER'S LANE

The original lane to Willen, now a footpath.

39 Farm buildings formerly with The Mead NL

An early C19 barn and farm buildings, of stone and slate roof, carefully converted to a dwelling in 1974, retaining the original sliding doors to the cartway. To the rear, a former animal house built in stone in 1887 and lengthened in brick.

40 The Mead II

Farmhouse. C17. A substantial stone building of two storeys, three bays with a lobby entry plan. The windows have timber lintels. Two gable stacks, one having been added at a later date.

41 Grange Farmhouse (formerly, Green Farm) II

An extensive building along the south side of the road, of the C18 and with a central wing to the south, probably C17. Colourwashed with slate roof over older roof structure. The upper floor of the roadside wing is claimed to have been a wool store. Internally there is an inglenook fireplace with an oven projecting on the south side. The farm buildings stood a short way to the south and were demolished in 1976.

WOOD LANE

42 Linford Lodge (formerly Ivy House) II

Restaurant, formerly a farmhouse. C18 with some earlier work in the west wing. Limestone. Tiled roof. 'L' plan with three bay elevation to road having a central door and slender Doric porch. Sash windows.

NEWPORT ROAD (South side)

43 Black Horse Inn II

Early C19 canalside building considerably enlarged in the C20.

F40

F41

F42

DOWN'S BARN

44 Barn — NL

A good early-mid C19 brick barn with a slate roof on the north side of an outfield farmyard flanked with cow hovels. The barn has perforated brickwork to sides and gable ends, and a pitching door at high level in addition to the major opposed cartways.

NICHOLAS MEAD

45 Brick Kilns — SCHED MON

Brickworks owned and operated by George Price, c.1880–1900 probably the same yard as was owned earlier by R. Sheppard. Originally comprising three down-draught muffle kilns of which only two survive. One is domed with a large top vent, the other with a saucer dome and both had 12 firing ports around the perimeter. The hot gases were drawn down through the bottom of the kiln and away along a duct to a tall brick stack to create a strong pull. After 36 hours of firing the kiln would be shut down for two days before unloading, and the bricks barrowed to stacks. The moulding sheds were flimsy structures and the drying clamps long stacks with temporary roofs outside. Near the kilns the old clay pits have been landscaped. Of the many brickworks in the area, in Loughton, Wolverton, Fenny Stratford, Simpson and Bletchley these are the only kilns remaining. The kilns were sited here primarily because the canal offered transport for fuel coming in, and for the finished products to be shipped out. The foreman's cottage once occupied by John Read still stands against the old lane.

F45a

F45

WOOLSTONE LANE

46 Lodge Farmhouse — II

Farmhouse. C17, brick on stone footings and quarter hipped tiled roof. Classic lobby entry plan, with stair in lobby and doors to flanking reception rooms. Rear wing containing kitchen and brewhouse widened in the later C19. Double purlin roof with struts. A tile bearing the date 1667 was found on the roof; this may well be the date of the building. Internally there are chamfered ceiling beams and a good lattice food cupboard of the C17.

To the rear of the farmhouse stood a smoke house presumably for the curing of bacon.

47 Lodge Farm buildings — NL

The farmyard stood between the farmhouse and the lane, and was later extended c.1897 on the other side of the lane. The brick barn on the north side, early C19, of six bays, double purlin roof with collar and struts, and with attached cow hovels. A C17–C18 stone barn raised in early C19 brickwork stands on the south side of the yard.

F46

LINFORD WOOD

48 Wood Farmhouse

A C19 farmhouse and outbuildings demolished c.1974. Brick, of two bays, two storeys with tiled roof.

Little Woolstone
Great Woolstone
Red House
Cloebury House
Church Farm
Holy Trinity Church (C of E)
Mill Lodge
Well
Foot Bridge
Manor Farm
The Barge Inn (P H)
Filling Station
Village Hall
The School House
Silos
Ponds
Pond
Mill Lane
Filter Bed
Moat
Manor Farm Cottages
Clarkes Cottage
The Cross Keys (P H)
Manor Farm Cottage
Hill Farm
Issues
Track
Path
Drain
River Ouzel
River Ouzel or Lovat
Fish Ponds
The Rectory
Holy Trinity Church (C of E)
B 488
65·5m
63·0m
60·3m
71·9m
B M 62·83m
B M 72·16m
B M 62·86m
61·8m
60·8m
64·7m
72·1m
M P 35
B M 63·22m
B M 72·12m
62·2m
72·0m
61·7m
B M 72·87m
62·7m
5546 7·041ha 17·40
7443 ·902ha 2·23
2343 ·073ha ·18
2940 1·206ha 2·98
3442 ·097ha ·24
7538 ·012ha ·03
4037 ·308ha ·76
1435 3·072ha 7·59
2433 ·243ha ·60
4134 ·478ha 1·18
4831 ·291ha ·72
5330 ·486ha 1·20
4330 ·227ha ·56
6231 ·567ha 1·40
6729 ·093ha ·23
2225 2·141ha 5·29
4923 ·785ha 1·94
5628 ·154ha ·38
5922 ·813ha 2·01
6728 ·712ha 1·76
3222 ·097ha ·24
3723 ·178ha ·44
6617 ·040ha ·10
6941 ·809ha 2·00
2614 2·558ha 6·32
6108 ·081ha ·20
1000 ·473ha 1·17
1000 6·526ha 16·13
2900 1·076ha 2·66
2900 3·829ha 9·46
5000 5·018ha 12·40
5000 ·882ha 2·18
6700 3·043ha 7·52
6700 6·437ha 15·91
3990 ·243ha ·60
5184 2·008ha 4·96
4584 ·308ha ·76
4179 ·478ha 1·18
2673 4·396ha 10·86
5774 1·153ha 2·85
4772 ·291ha ·72
4269 ·542ha 1·34
4563 ·117ha ·29
5161 ·178ha ·44
4759 ·121ha ·30
6266 ·417ha 1·03
6960 ·526ha 1·30
6357 ·065ha ·16
5861 2·251ha 5·56
5054 ·219ha ·54
0656 1·457ha 3·60
0755 ·299ha ·74
2053 6·971ha 17·22
4449 3·967ha 9·80
7044

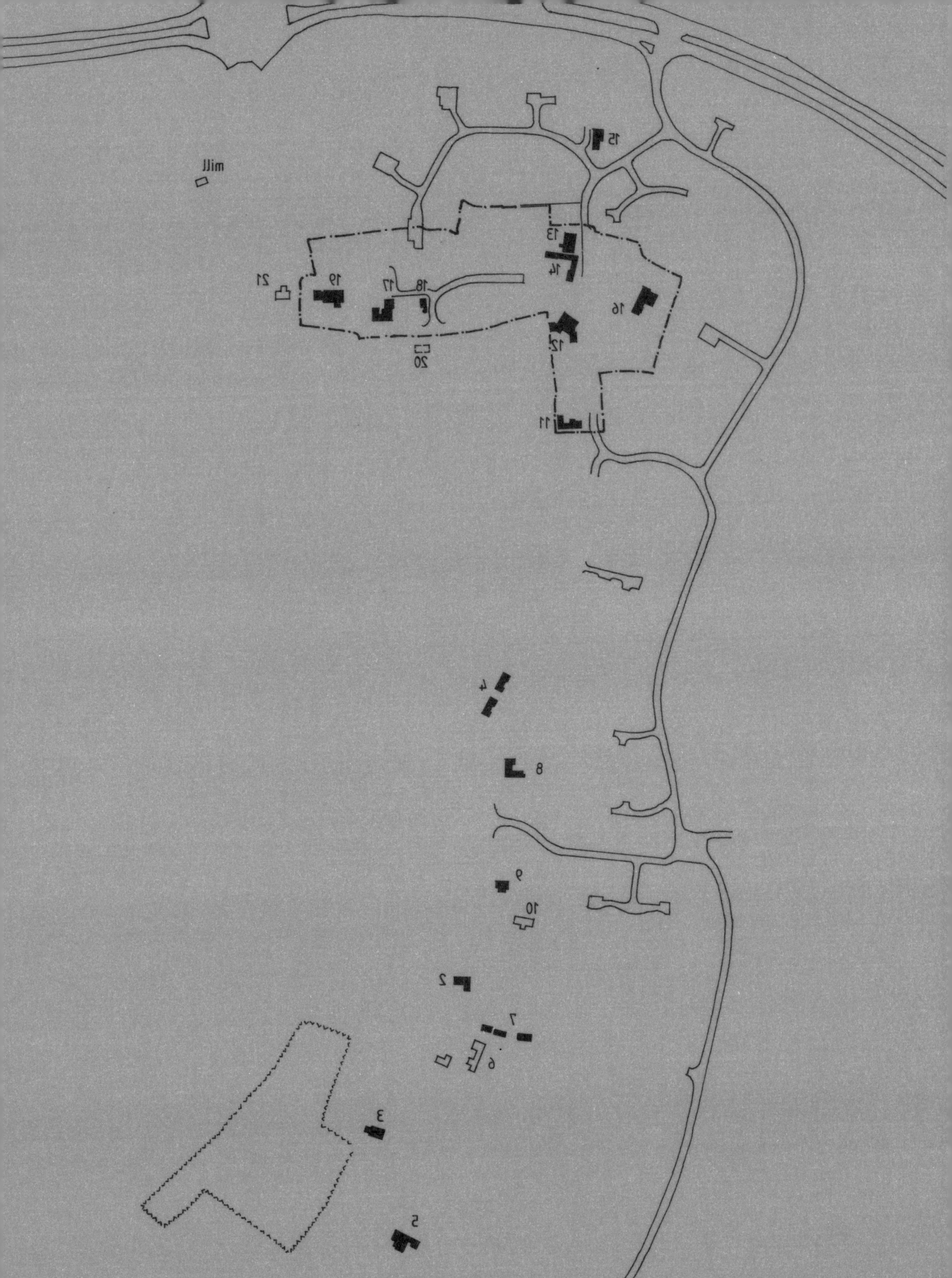

mill
2
3
4
5
6
7
8
9
10
11
12
13
14
15
16
17
18
19
20
21

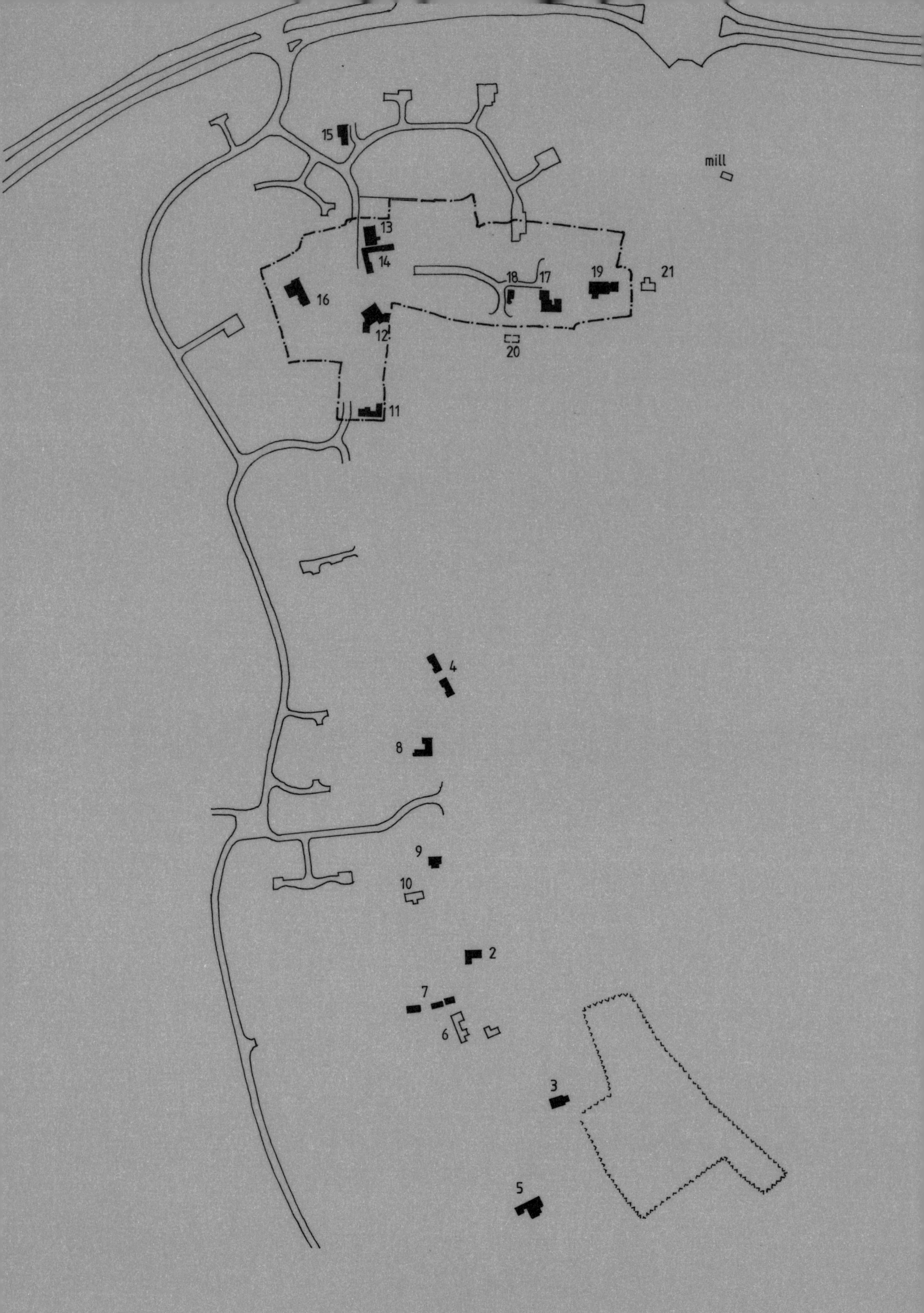
mill
15
13
14
16
12
11
18
17
19
21
20
4
8
9
10
2
7
6
3
5

GREAT and LITTLE WOOLSTONE

GREAT AND LITTLE WOOLSTONE

The name Woolstone and its variants is not an uncommon name in England. Here the original medieval parish had two centres, Great and Little Woolstone, presumably so named in regard to their relative importance. Up to the establishment of Milton Keynes city both were merely hamlets, Great Woolstone being the smaller and consisting of no more than a small church and a few farm buildings strung out along the old lane meandering along the left bank of the Ouzel just above flood level on its way from Fenny Stratford to Newport Pagnell. The parishes were united in 1855. The parish runs from the Ouzel back on to the boulder clay topped common land near the present city centre. There are a number of archaeological sites, a moat around the Cross Keys Inn, and, across the road, a number of different earthworks including another moat and some fishponds, and against the river in the southernmost corner of Little Woolstone parish, a finely preserved moat. These have been surveyed but not explored underground. In the C20 the combined parishes of Great and Little Woolstone were joined to that of Willen, and later, with Woughton.

GREAT WOOLSTONE

NEWPORT ROAD (East side)

1 Cottages Braemar and Sunset NL

A pair of cottages, c.1840, brick with slate roofs, both symmetrical with central panelled doors and casement windows. The chimneys are in buff bricks. At each end there is a washhouse with door and gable stack, that to Braemar having been altered.

G1

2 Hill Farmhouse II

An unusual farmhouse, c.1720 and fashionable in its day. Diaper brick with stone footings and raised quoins. Two storeys, three bays long, built close to the road. The central door leads to a stair hall with access to a back wing which was replaced in the C19, probably at the time the original cross windows were replaced with the present windows. Either side of the door the windows are set in raised panels meeting the original plat band. The five upper windows were reduced to two. It has a fine timber moulded and dentilled eaves and a hipped roof. A firemark of the Sun Company No. 67653 establishes the owner in 1735 was a Thomas Smith of Holborn, and it was in the occupation of John Allen. Internally the house has some original joinery, including a fine baluster stair, a shouldered doorcase and a moulded fire surround. The stacks are set at an angle on the rear wall, that on the right containing an oven served from the rear room.

G2

3 Rosebery Music Room, formerly Holy Trinity Church II

Parish church of 1832–3, replacing a small two-cell medieval building on the same site, which appear for a time in the C16 to be dedicated to the unknown St. Bartanus. The church was made redundant and has been converted as a base for a local orchestra. This building is also of two cells, a three-bay nave and raised chancel, and a west door. It is in what is called a 'Commissioner's Gothic' style after the 1818 Act of Parliament which made provision for Commissioners to build inexpensive churches as the state of faith and its buildings was then fairly abject. This church cost £1,100. It is of ashlar limestone, although the chancel is, curiously, in rubble. The broad west front has terminal towers with pinnacles, and a deeply moulded generous door with hood mould, and above, a large roundel which presumably once had a painted inscription. There is a string at the low-pitched roof level, originally lead and now slate, and a parapet terminating in a bellcote with a bell of 1689 by Anthony Chandler. The side windows are handsomely moulded

G3

with 'Y' tracery and transomes, repeated at a smaller scale in the chancel. Internally the church had delightfully simple painted furniture, including pulpit and sanctuary screen. There is one late medieval oak pew with a panelled end, temporarily at Bradwell Abbey, and a portable organ. The interior was reordered in an appropriately simple style in 1976 and WCs included, partly with the help of the dowager Countess of Rosebery (of Mentmore).

The extent of the medieval graveyard is not known but probably ran a little further to the east. It now contains a few C19 and C20 monuments.

G3b

4 Two Pairs of Cottages, including No. 29 and Ousel End — NL

Two separate blocks of cottages, c.1870, each with end gables and a recessed central section having a raised dormer. Excellent brickwork and blending tile roofs, but having unfortunate recent lean-to's and porches and inappropriate window changes.

NEWPORT ROAD (West side)

G5

5 The Rectory — II

Great Woolstone rectory, designed 1851 by William Butterfield, the hero of mid-Victorian architectural establishment, and built by James Rose, builder of Newport Pagnell at the cost of £611. Unfortunately much altered 1871, and a porch added 1879, using the proceeds of the sale of Little Woolstone rectory. Red brick of the best quality and tiled roof, and casement windows set within slightly recessed arches, that to the south wall with tumbled brickwork. Tall brick chimneys. The first building comprised a central dining room with study and parlour in a wing to the east, and kitchen and single storey service rooms to the west.

The Woolstone living has attracted more than its usual share of eminent rectors, amongst them Weedon Butler, political writer and poet, Dr. Henry Tattam, the Egyptologist and Coptic grammarian 1831–49, followed by the Rev. Edward Hill, 1860–61, patron and friend of Sister Dora in her formative years.

G6

6 (Rectory Farmhouse)

One of the more interesting buildings in the village, sadly demolished many years ago without more than a photograph and a few notes. Timber framed, probably C16, a long range with a large central stack and two forward wings in the form of an 'F'. The building was altered about 1700 and a new door and stair provided.

7 Farm Buildings for Rectory Farm — NL

A range of three buildings running end to end from the road.

Next to the road, an equipment store, 1789, most unusually built in header bond (the ends of the bricks only showing) but with a top course incised with the date and initials IG, TP, WA, and EH, probably the initials of the bricklayers or farmhands rather than the owning family. It has offset eaves and a hipped tile roof.

At its rear, modern Fletton walls contain timber trusses of C17 type. It is probably a small barn totally refaced.

Again to the rear, a curious two-storey building, now without its intermediate floor, and open to the west end. It possibly started as a granary in the C18, and adapted in the C19, the date of its roof structure.

G7

8 No. 34, Cross Keys P.H. II

A C17 building, now an inn, colourwashed local stone and thatch. The early building is of three bays, with a cross passage between first and second bays, behind the stack, turning across the back to the right end bay. The room to the south was presumably a service room extended later to the rear. It has a timber framed gable and has received extensive alterations and extensions.

G8

9 No. 36, Manor Farm Cottage II

A C17 timber framed building with brick noggings, lobby entry plan with a small lean-to room at the front and a recent kitchen to the back. The interior has a fine moulded spine beam and corner braces to the tie beam. The stack is also C17, and ribbed.

G9

10 No. 1 Newport road NL

Two brick cottages of c.1880. Panelled door and three paned fanlight. Sash windows and a brick dentilled eaves course. On its north side a ventilated farm building with a loft.

The north end now has an addition in a matching style.

LITTLE WOOLSTONE

NEWPORT ROAD (East side)

11 School House NL

A modest village school room and teacher's house, c.1860. Red brick with yellow brick decoration, the house lying to the back of the site and an infant's wing attached later to the north side where it could share the main chimney stack. The building is famed for being where Dorothy Pattison was schoolmistress for the years 1861–1864 and discovered her independence of spirit and vocation. She was born in Hauxwell, Lincolnshire in 1832 and devoted her later life, as 'Sister Dora' to the care of the sick and elderly, in admiration and emulation of Florence Nightingale. A brass memorial appears in the church.

G11

12 The Barge Inn NL

Public House, originally a building of the early C19 to serve the newly constructed canal, to which has been added the c.1900 wing on the left with its gable facing the street. At the same time the building was re-windowed with the small panes on the upper sash, a favourite device of the late Victorian period.

G12

13 Cloebury Farmhouse II

The house is a symmetrical brick building of c.1850, three bays with a good central panelled door in a fluted case and segmental hood. The windows have wedge lintels to later frames. The house has a parallel rear wing also with gable stacks.

The paddock behind has, on the south side, a stone herringbone coursed wall, also being the outer wall of a barn. This is a method of using irregular stone, of great antiquity, being particularly favoured at the turn of the Norman conquest and in the Roman period. It's appearance here at Woolstone is a surprise.

G13

14 Cloebury Farm Buildings NL

The farmyard occupied the whole corner with Church Lane consisting of a well built brick stable with hay loft against the road, the back wall once continued with cattle shelter sheds, returning against the substantial stone wall backing on the farmhouse. There used to be a further brick building at the end, with a curious low wide arch of unknown purpose, and a large shed on the east side where housing now stands.

NEWPORT ROAD (West side)

15 The Red House NL

A row of two cottages, later C19. Red brick, hence the name, and tiled roof. Now one dwelling.

LINFORD LANE

16 Manor House and Manor Farm Cottage II

Farmhouse of the C17, altered in the late C18 or early C19. Lobby entry plan and a classic example of its sort. Half hipped slate roof. Central entrance opposite the stack, with a C20 door with a bracketed canopy. Large casement windows of the C19 replacing the original and a plat band at first floor level. The stack has four flues, by the later C17 both upper chambers being heated as well as those on the ground floor.

The farmhouse was extended to the right in the early–mid C19 in two-storey brickwork with iron framed windows. This has now been converted to Manor House Cottage.

G16

MILL LANE

17 Church Farm II

One of the more interesting buildings of Milton Keynes. Originally a farmhouse of the later C16 or early C17, timber framed, comprising a one bay central hall section with a large axial stone stack, and either side end rooms originally two storeys with gables to the front. The room to the left of the centre bay has a large stone fire surround with brick herringbone backing to the fireplace, and two similar but smaller ones survive on the first floor. To the rear of the main stack was the original stair, of which the upper section only now survives. The original entrance faced the side of the stack in what is now known as the lobby entry plan—an early example of this. In the later C18 the house was refurbished and given a new fashionable brick frontage, and the gables removed. The new brick front only just wraps round the ends leaving the original framing showing. The date of this is recorded in a number of incised bricks giving a date of 1773 and various initials, TS, IR, WE, AW, WH, WL, perhaps members of Smith's wider family or less likely, the bricklayers of the time. In the early part of this century the front door was taken out and reset at the other end of the central hall, and in 1924, what was originally a long wing at the rear containing the dairy and cellar was replaced in part by an extension with pseudo-framing and modern bricks. In 1981 the building was refurbished as an expensive private house. The three C16 stacks, some rebuilt to the old form, still form one of its most dominant features.

G17

Church Farm is known to history as being the farm of the agricultural pioneer and innovator, William Smith, whose best known contribution was developing the use of steam traction engines for cultivation in 1855, he being aware of the damage to fertility often occasioned by deep ploughing, a conclusion rediscovered again in recent years. His famous plough was walled up in a barn after he had trouble with his labourers after a visit of Joseph Arch. Smith's solution to the problem of organised labour was to convert from arable to pasture. The Smith family had interests in the Woolstones from 1642 up to recent times.

G17a

18 **Gazebo and Dovecote to Church Farm with No. 20 The Cottage** II

An octagonal structure at the end of the former garden of Church Farm and attached to a farmworker's cottage on the north side out of sight behind the cattle hovels. Probably built c.1870, of brick with sliding doors with pointed heads facing the garden, and above, a dovehouse for 400 birds, but at this stage probably for decorative doves rather than food, and crowned by what is known as a glover, a gabled flight platform for the birds. The house attached to the gazebo is also of interest, built c.1789 (date on bricks with initials AS, MS, WS, and WS 1839 added surely by William Smith), of two bays, divided internally by a timber framed partition and with the central chimney built of unburned clay bricks. This internal use of such bricks (they could not of course be used externally) is rare in this area, but also occurred in the former rear wing of farmbuildings of the house itself. Perhaps we have here an experiment in economy by the resourceful William Smith himself.

G18

20 **(Rectory)**

The Rectory for Little Woolstone stood almost opposite the church, and was demolished in 1879, being redundant after the parishes were combined in 1855. In a glebe terrier of 1607 this was recorded as being of four bays with a lean-to buttery, timber framed and thatched. It also had a four bay barn and some stables with a hay loft. It must have decayed badly for it was rebuilt c.1830, and called c.1860 as a poor glebe house.

21 **(Woolstone Mill Cottage)**

At the end of Mill Lane stood, until earlier this century, Woolstone Mill Cottage, a C17 building with a stone built ground floor, and a timber framed upper floor. It had a lobby entry plan with a large central stack including an oven. It also had a one-bay wing to the rear.

The mill itself stood a little to the north, astride the mill race off the river. It was a timber framed and weatherboarded building in two parts, with a pitched roof. It was demolished about 1940. A photograph appears in Record of Bucks. Vol. 24 (1982) Plate 1a.

G19

19 Church of The Holy Trinity now the Woolstones Community Centre II*

The parish church for Little Woolstone, now a local meeting place with the chancel reserved for religious use, in fact something of a reversion to the pattern of use familiar when the building was first built. It consists of a Nave with south porch, a chancel with a north vestry, and over the nave, a belltower.

Archaeological excavation has shown it is not the first building on the site, for during works of conversion to its present use not only were signs of Roman occupation found, but the foundations of a smaller, earlier church of Anglo Norman date. It was not possible to prove it was earlier than the Norman conquest but must have followed shortly after. This little building had foundations of gravel. The present building is as always a result of change and addition over the years. The earliest section is now demonstrated by the chancel arch, of the late C13, to be followed by the early C14 windows, now much renewed to their original design, these may be part of the same building phase rather than replacement of earlier windows. To this phase also belongs the fine crown post roof, the trussed rafters and braces hidden behind later plasterwork. This building had at one time a chapel on the north side, the jamb of the arch thereto can still be seen. Next was added the porch, late C15 or early C16, with one terminal of the label mould over the arch set sideways, surely only an error although other more covert explanations have been offered. The next event in its history was the erection of the belltower, sometime in the middle C17, probably to carry the new bells, one dated 1662. Timber framed, with its spindly legs carried down into the nave. It was always weatherboarded with a flat roof, a characteristic feature if unprepossessing. When this was done the large west window was obstructed, and the builders replaced it with a smaller window similar to those in the nave. Some two hundred years passed before it was decided, in 1861, to rebuild the chancel entirely, exactly on the old foundations and include a small vestry. This vestry had at one time a small piece of medieval glass in its window, and the west window of the nave had further pieces, almost opaque with age but including a nice fish. The church had a good limestone and marble reredos by J. S. Westmacott the central panel of which has been retained and built into the east chancel wall and the remainder stored at Bradwell Abbey. In 1982 the church, which was made redundant in 1970, was converted to its present use. The arcaded Norman font, which had survived all these changes, was reset in the chancel, as were a number of encaustic tiles made at Little Brickhill in the C15. These are placed against the walls to minimise further wear and the brass plate to Sister Dora refixed to the wall. Also during these alterations, a large limestone sarcophagus was discovered. This was carefully recorded, and covered below the present floor, and a cast of the various graffiti on the lid taken, which has now been set on the north wall of the nave. These included what would now be called board games, suggesting the coffin had at one time been accessible to idle hands.

Loughton
Manor Farm
Sheep Dip
The Green
Council Bungalows
Church Farm
All Saints' Ch (C of E)
Church Lane
Beech Cott
Elm House
Rectory Farm
Grave Yard
Rectory
School Lane
Pitcher Lane
Leys Road
Leys Court
Manor Cottage
Bradwell Road
The Meadway
Hall
Ashbourne House
Loughton Baptist Church
Moat
Fish Pond
Tel Ex
The Talbot (P H)
London Road
Guide Post
Shenley Road
Bridge House
The Fountain (P H)
Drain
Pond
Path
F B
L B
T C B
G P
B M 87·55m
B M 77·57m
B M 74·18m
B M 75·65m
B M 79·84m
84·4m
85·1m
86·5m
73·2m
73·1m
73·3m
75·8m
77·4m
78·8m
83·3m
83·1m
3200 1·570ha 3·88
4500 ·728ha 1·80
5300 ·024ha ·06
5800 ·077ha ·19
7900 1·263ha 3·12
9100 ·032ha ·08
5187 2·130ha 5·26
2279 5·740ha 14·18
4275 3·222ha 7·96
8779 ·275ha ·68
5563 22·957ha 56·73
6354 1·093ha 2·70
7651 3·149ha 7·78
3547 5·971ha 14·76
6336 3·198ha 7·90
5126 2·073ha 5·12
7726 3·676ha 9·08
6316 1·749ha 4·32
3412 4·971ha 12·28
7211 1·052ha 2·60
2506 ·919ha 2·27
2400 ·405ha ·26
4200 ·793ha 1·96
7700 ·967ha 2·39

20
1
2
8
9
11
12
35
5
4
14
34
3
15
16
17
33
26
28
29
30
22
31

1
2
3
4
5
6
6
7
8
9
11
12
14
15
16
17
20
22
26
28
29
30
31
33
34
35

LOUGHTON

LOUGHTON

Loughton started as two separate parishes either side of the Whaddon brook in the early medieval period, Great Loughton and Little Loughton. These can be easily identified today, Great Loughton being the village surrounding the church, and Little Loughton now but a few houses around the Green lying behind the Bradwell Road. In addition, there is the settlement that developed along Watling Street, now centred on the Talbot Inn and long known as 'Shenley End' or 'Shenley Inn'.

The population of LOCHINTONE, as it was called in 1086, was 62. In 1676 it had risen to 234 and by 1961 it had reached 402. Thus it had remained until the advent of Milton Keynes no more than a small rural village.

In the medieval period the land was owned mostly by the de Wolverton family and by the religious houses of Snelshall and Tickford. The Longuevilles acquired some monastic property in 1543. The manor sites are now represented only by earthworks, the Manor of Little Loughton by the moat, largely filled in, which encircled the present Manor on the green and the Manor of Great Loughton probably by the scheduled earthworks south of Leys Road in the fields of Manor Farm, although Old Farm has been claimed to be the site. These earthworks, which have not been investigated, comprise a moated platform and adjoining, a large square sunken area, probably a fishpond. Below this site the outflow from the moats and the adjoining field systems was canalised and run through a series of sluices with associated huts, probably some form of irrigation system. This area may well have been the fishery recorded between 1589 and 1604. Some years ago a rare Anglo-Saxon gold ring was found near-by.

There had been some small scale enclosures after 1485, but the original three-field system continued until the Parliamentary Enclosure award of 1769. It was largely a dairy farming area but the inhabitants were responsible for the repair of Watling Street through the parish, a responsibility they frequently failed to undertake. The first turnpike in England was established on Watling Street in 1706 between Hockcliffe and Two Mile Ash, and a new tollgate erected in 1740, although coaches had been running since 1658. Passenger coaches were running on regular schedules by 1754 and the first mail coach came through in 1785. Watling Street, always difficult through these clay lands, was re-engineerd by Thomas Telford after 1828.

Building materials available locally were restricted to some poor quality limestone, timber, and from the eighteenth century, brick made from clay dug at Coldharbour Farm, where Milton Keynes Bowl now stands. The earliest building still standing is, as usual, the church of Great Loughton, the church of Little Loughton apparently having disappeared early in the C19.

1 Church of All Saints **II***

The church has been the church for the combined parishes of Great and Little Loughton since 1408. It consists of nave, chancel and west tower, and fine south aisle and chapel which embraces the south porch and forms a chapel alongside the chancel. The earliest feature is the remarkable impost half-columns for the tower arch, probably C13, supporting a sharply pointed arch of early C14 date. The nave is virtually undateable but the single light windows at the west end probably replace lancets of C13 date. The chancel also has early medieval proportions but again the windows have been replaced in the later medieval period. To this modest structure was added, in the 1480's, using it is said, materials from the church of Little Loughton, the fine perpendicular aisle with its splendid moulded roof and crenellated parapet and a new west tower with its west door and window, later blocked by a despairing C19 buttress. The tower was thoroughly refurbished in 1984. Inside, the box pews were replaced in Victorian times by the present furnishings. The church has an interesting series of wall monuments: in the chancel two fine marble tablets presumably erected by John Crane of Loughton, one, of 1622 to his mother Felice Mortoft of County Durham, and the other, of 1624 to his wife Mary, daughter of Thomas Tresham of Newton, Northants, cousin of the religious eccentric, Sir Thomas Tresham, builder of the famous triangular lodge at Rushton, Northants. In the aisle is another fine monument, to the Hanslapp family, erected by the sole surviving son 31 years after the death of his father. The church also has a large Royal Arms of 1831 still bearing the escutcheon of Hanover which Victoria had to abandon six years later as, under Salic Laws, she could not inherit the German titles. The chancel has a good brass to the Rev. Hugh Park, rector, who died in 1516. There are six bells, two by Jordan dating from 1460 and two by Atton dated 1590 and 1631 respectively. The church was restored around 1826 and later in the C19 by E. S. Harris, between 1877 and 1883.

The graveyard contains no early stones, but a headstone now placed in the porch is to John Perrott, 1689. Some stones are worthy of note for their calligraphy. The stone wall round the graveyard is a listed structure.

COMMON LANE

Common Lane in 1969 was one of the remotest places in north Buckinghamshire, where cars were rarely seen and could hardly pass. It looped from Leys Road up on the cold high clay lands, to return to Bradwell Village, having served one or two isolated farms. However, its purpose might not have always been such, for at its furthermost elbow it met the parish of Great Linford precisely where the ancient Hundred meeting place, Secklow Mound was located. Now all is changed for Common Lane has now become the site for the City centre. The two farms in Loughton parish are no longer there, Rectory Farm, a C19 brick building against the lane, and Old Farm, which lay at the end of a rough track. This was again a brick building with traces of earlier fabric, which was demolished in 1976.

2 No. 12 Church Farm NL

Farmhouse, C16 or C17, rebuilt C19. Stone and brick, with modern tiled roof. Two storeys, the original building of two bays with a central through hall and stacks to the end gables, that against the churchyard being external and particularly large and had at one time diagonal brick shafts. The building has attached at its northern end a long range of farm buildings of stone with a corrugated iron roof. This range may well be earlier than the main house, and has survived its rebuilding in the C19. Internally the timber lintel over the main gable fireplace bears the initials RW and I.'W.

H2

THE GREEN

The green was the nucleus of Little Loughton Village and now has three important buildings and some cottages ranged around, with a brook running through the middle. A windmill once stood to the east of Manor Farmhouse.

3 No. 1 Cell Farmhouse II

Farmhouse of C16 origin, of colourwashed stone with a 1980's asbestos slate roof. It's most striking feature is a very large central stack with a moulded base and diagonal shafts of brick. It is of three bays, the panelled door opposite the side of the stack giving a lobby entry plan. Timber casement windows with wooden lintels. The stack to the left gable has been added, probably in the C19, and a single storey extension lies to the right. Internally the house has chamfered spine beams, and timber fire beams over the central fireplaces.

H3

4 Nos. 7 & 8, Manor Farm Cottages II

Despite its name, this building is a major house in its own right. It is of three phases, the earliest in the C16 comprising the southern end, a second the north end, and thirdly, the rear extension, itself of the C17. The first stage has a rear baffle entry and a large limestone stack incorporating a low oven, superimposed by a later oven, and between the room and the corridor a wattle and daub partition. In the north end, a window seat bears the graffito, 'William Perrot, 1691' and a wallpainting of a floral design on a timber framed partition. The roof over this part has curved windbraces. There are a number of doors and doorcases of the C16 and C17 and some C18 panelling. The south room has chamfered and stopped ceiling joists. The two leaning buttresses on the front are of recent origin. An interesting feature externally is a small stone fire window, lighting the inside of an inglenook, a not uncommon feature but rare in Milton Keynes. At one time part of the house was a shoemaker's shop.

H4

5 Manor Farmhouse II*

One of the major historic buildings of Milton Keynes. Local stone, with a striped tile roof. Early C16 and improved c.1580 by Valentine Pigot of Beachampton, Councillor at Law, and his wife Anne, whose initials appear on the porch. Pigot sold to John Crane who held the manor until 1655 when he sold it to Ralph Holt. A later owner, John Hanslapp. 1716–1735 rebuilt part of the house, probably the east end with its massive stone stack. A house has stood on the site since early medieval times for it was originally moated, the moat being still visible on the west side as a dip in the ground. The building consists of a central entrance to a cross passage and symmetrical rooms either side, that to the right being the equivalent of a low hall. To the left of the passage is a room, perhaps originally a service room to which has been added, in the early C19, a brick chimney stack, blocking an attic window, and replacing a partly external stone stack on the back wall. Beyond the hall there are two rooms, the second being a later C16 addition to the house, the roof timbers of which are massive but ill-fixed to the earlier structure. This part has a queen post truss with curved braces to the collar and the western end beyond a major wall has windbraces to a double purlin roof. To the rear is a lean-to dairy dated 1615, which still retains its Jacobean oak studded door. The hall has a good moulded ceiling and a very fine stone fireplace with blind spandrels and a date starting with 15 . . the last two digits having most unfortunately been obliterated by the fixing of a later fire crane. On the first floor, as well as another C16 fireplace, the central room has remarkably preserved grisaille wallpaintings of the time of the Pigots, fruity, with much scrollwork and at the top exhortations like FEARE GOD. These rooms originally ran the whole width of the house but have been cut back to insert a corridor. This part of the house may well have once served as a courtroom with an external stair. There is also a ledged original door and frame to the chamber over the porch. The house is reputed to have a ghost around the main staircase.

H5

H5a

6 Barns at Manor Farm II

A house of this standing must have had many outbuildings, and the diarist William Cole records that Mr. Holt had a handsome brewhouse. However now there are only two stone barns, both of which may well incorporate early masonry but which have been much remodelled in recent times. That in front of the house is said to be close to the site of the church of Little Loughton and to be built of some of its stonework. However this cannot now be confirmed. This barn has arrowslit vents in the south wall. The building to the rear, a milking parlour, has an offset stone plinth indicating that it was once a more important building.

SCHOOL LANE

7 No. 2 — II

House of c.1830. Painted brick and a slate roof. Two storeys. The building incorporated a gable of an earlier building at its left end to which has been added, in the C19, a baker's oven, the building being a baker's until recent memory. The house has five bays of 16-pane sashes and a door off centre. To the rear is a stone outbuilding incorporating some good quality stone, clearly taken from another building. It has been suggested that this may have been the church of Little Loughton.

8 No. 5 Church Close Cottage — II

Cottage. Late C18 or early C19. Local stone, refaced front and back in brick about 1840 and extended by one bay incorporating a single storey outbuilding. The rear elevation is that of a simple unsophisticated dwelling which has happily remained unspoilt by rewindowing. Gable stacks and a central staircase.

In the garden was another cottage which had a well in the kitchen with a pump.

9 No. 3 Beech Cottage — II

House, C18 or early C19. Stone with a brick facade and slate roof, extended to the left c.1860 in yellow and red diaper brickwork. The C18 doorcase has apparently been reset on the central porch. A stone cellar is present under the parlour left of the door and the fireplace on the gable against the road, now the kitchen, is of stone suggesting the C18 work is a rebuild of an earlier building.

A barn to the rear has traces of wattle and daub walling.

10 Elm House — II

House, c. 1820–1830. Brick with stone floor bands and a slate roof behind a parapet. Three storeys with a central through hall to a rear two-storey wing now containing the entrance and the service rooms. There are late Victorian extensions against this wing and the front has a Tuscan portico. Internally there is a cellar under the left room, with a window on the north side, and a plain early C19 stair with a moulded dado rail. The hall has an elaborate cornice.

11 No. 6 Rectory Farm — II

Farmhouse. Late C17 or early C18. Squared local limestone with a tiled roof. Two-storeys with cellar and attics. The windows are probably of the late C19 and have chamfered frames. Moulded timber eaves and three dormers.

12 Gazebo at Rectory Farm — NL

An octagonal structure of brick with a tiled roof below and facing the house, with Gothic door and window. A brick by the door has the inscription H.S.1839.

13 Barn at Rectory Farm — NL

Barn. C18, diaper brickwork with a corrugated iron roof replacing original thatch. Dormer with a pigeon cote. The interior has a hay loft and the building extends to the rear with former cattle hovels and terminates in a hay barn forming the farmyard enclosure.

H8

H9

H10

H11

14 Old School House **NL**

Church of England School, by William White, built by Alfred Hailey on glebe land in 1865 to accommodate 40 children, and extended in 1892 for a further 30. Red brick with tiled roof. Originally the school comprised a large double classroom with a toilet block at the bottom of the playground. To this was added a classroom at right angles and a new entrance and cloakroom. The building was converted to a dwelling in 1981 with a fine first floor drawing room. The school bell tower has been refurbished and the original bell, after some vissicitudes, returned to its original place.

H14

LEYS ROAD (North side)

15 No. 1 Shop and Post Office **NL**

Alehouse, formerly the Old Wheatsheaf, and now a shop and dwelling. C17 remodelled in the early C19. It was originally timber framed, with a large rear stack and internally a chamfered spine beam dating from the first build. Attached to its south end is a timber framed building of the C17, weatherboarded. The numbering of the trusses and slots for former windbraces suggest that it has been taken down from elsewhere and erected here.

H2/H15

16 Salisbury House **II**

House of the early C19. Pebbledashed with a slate roof. Four bays. The building was much remodelled c.1870–80. Modern central gabled porch and 20-pane sashes. The Kitchener family of Fenny Stratford moved to Loughton in the 1860's using this house as the family home, and acquiring property all along to School Lane.

17 Manor Cottages **II**

Pair of estate cottages, early to mid C19, extended to the rear to provide a third cottage towards the end of the century. Probably built for estate workers for Manor Farm. Limestone rubble with margin-glazed cast iron windows in lozenge pattern. Flush gabled windows to the first floor. The cottages are reputed to occupy the site of an earlier building.

H16

18 Manor Farmhouse, formerly Brook Farm **NL**

Farmhouse, now an equestrian centre. Mid C19, erected after 1867 when Lord Cadman of Shenley acquired the property. Although it occupies a site of much earlier buildings, it only acquired the name Manor Farm in 1835 when it came into the ownership of Henry Billington of Northampton. From 1788 it was in the ownership of the Vicar, the Rev. Stubbs and tenanted by a John Jarvis who continued until his son took over in 1802, the ownership having passed to a Mr Foster who, presumably with his kin, held it for the rest of the century.

19 Farm Buildings at Manor Farm **NL**

The main farm buildings are of interest as being the best example in Milton Keynes of the model farm principal of the mid Victorian period. The buildings extend out from the farmhouse and consist of two enclosed yards around which are ranged the various shelter sheds and loose boxes required by mid C19 farm management. The spine corridor connects the yards via a harness room and stables to the dairies and grain stores, and to an engine house, originally with a steam engine, for threshing and the many other uses mechanical power was being put to at the time. The wide centre block contained the bedding and fodder stores handy for the animal houses. The buildings were considered sufficiently innovatory to be published in the Illustrated London News at the time they were built.

H19

PITCHER LANE

H20

20 Beckett House NL

Former vicarage, built 1868 for Robert Charles Green, vicar of Loughton from 1864–1883, by Alfred Mailley & Co, a local builder. Colourwashed brick with a tiled roof. Recessed entrance with Green's monogram on the stone lintel. Small gables with cogged verges and six tall chimney stacks with oversailing heads.

In the grounds, the coachhouse and stables, also dated 1865 on the rain water hoppers. A stable boy's quarters are included on the upper floor.

GREAT HOLME

21

A group of late C19 farm buildings survived until 1983. These included a five-bay beast house and a three-bay implement shed.

WATLING STREET

Watling Street forms the south west border of the parish of Loughton. The settlement which grew up along the road primarily to serve travellers was thus split between Loughton and Shenley. This became known as SHENLEY END, corruptly SHENLEY INN, and remained so-called throughout much of recent history.

H22

22 Nos. 19 and 20 (West side) (Parish of Shenley) NL

Pair of semi-detached cottages built 1904 by Bucks County Council for policemen, Pebbledashed brick with tiled roof. Each cottage is of one bay with recessed lateral entrance and large timber casement windows. The front wall is extended as buttresses and the central chimney is battered showing an awareness of the vernacular movement in architecture being promoted at the time by C. F. A. Voysey amongst other architects. The shed on the right is where the steam roller for road repairs was garaged.

23 Charterhouse NL

House, three bays, with axial stack and stack to right gable. Considerably altered in recent times but a plat band and cogged eaves betrays the house to have C18 origins. It has a Westminster Fire Co. mark No. 20118, probably refixed from elsewhere.

24 The Old Plough NL

Hostelry, now house. C19 brick with two parallel slated roofs. One of a number of provisions for wayfarers along Watling Street.

To the south, a terrace of diaper red and yellow brick cottages dated 1898, indicating the late date to which this fashion of bricklaying lasted.

WATLING STREET (East side) (Parish of Loughton)

25 Milestone NL

Milestone, c.1830. Sandstone. Milestones with gabled tops and recesses for cast iron plates date from Telford's reworking of the gradients on Watling Street in the 1830's. Many of the plates have unfortunately disappeared in recent years due to the efforts of gypsies and collectors.

26 No. 15A NL

House, early C19. Pebbledashed brick with interlocking tile roof. Three bays with central porch and door. 16 and 20 pane sash windows.

H27

27 (The Bell Inn)

Demolished. A fine three storey three bay building of the early C19 with central doorway and flanking tap rooms. The sash windows had stone wedge lintels.

28 Nos. 25, 27, 29 and 31 NL

Terrace of cottages, c.1860–80, diaper red/yellow brick of local origin. Buildings much altered. A number of similar groups of cottages, all more or less altered, were erected along Watling Street at this time, including Nos. 11 and 13. The terrace 43–51 is c.1880.

H29

29 The Talbot P.H. II

Hostelry, now a public house and restaurant. C17 and C18, diaper red/blue brick with tile roof. Central carriage entrance to former rear courtyard. Rear elevation is a C19 rebuild with plate glass sash windows and extensions of 1970's. The Talbot was first mentioned in 1726 but a hostelry of this name existed in 1577. The innkeeper, the Newman's of 1749–1818 being perhaps the best known, maintained a smallholding and had a large barn and dovecote, the latter being demolished in the C19. Internally the inn has a large C18 fireplace formerly in a room known as the tap room. The roof is of late C17 or early C18 type and was converted later for servants sleeping quarters, and had a hand corn mill.

H30

30 Memorial Cottages (Nos. 35, 37, 39, and 41, Old style) NL

Almshouses built 1897 to commemorate Queen Victoria's Golden Jubilee. Red brick in garden wall bond with hard red brick dressings. Each cottage has one living room and rear service room, and each has a recessed sitting out place at the front. Brick vents to the roof space and moulded brick reveals to the timber windows. To the rear, hipped outbuilding containing a washhouse and closet. A Victorian postbox is set into the gable wall. Close by, to the south, was the Horseshoes Inn which later combined this service with that of a smithy.

31 The Fountain P.H. NL

Hostelry, C18 and C19. Colourwashed brick with a thatched roof. The original building is the two left bays with a central entrance, now with a thatched porch. This has been extended to the right by two bays in the late C19–early C20 and has been further extended at both ends.

H31

32 Milestone outside The Fountain P.H. NL

Milestone, C18, silicaceous sandstone with rounded top. There are now few traces of the inscription which once recorded the distance from London, and has been engraved with a benchmark of 297.4 ft above Newlyn Datum. This milestone pre-dates Telford's improvements and was probably erected by the Turnpike Trust in the mid C18.

BRADWELL ROAD

Apart from the Baptist Chapel, development along the road between Watling Street and Loughton village did not start until the last years of the C19.

33 Baptist Chapel NL

General Baptist Chapel, 1884, on the site of an earlier chapel of 1831. Red brick with yellow brick dressings. Iron glazed windows with radial heads within recessed panels having yellow brick corbels. Central round window within blind arch. Stork pattern shoe scrapers flank the arched entrance in a side annex, and to the rear is a large schoolroom, further extended towards the end of the century. The interior has an open timber roof of five bays.

In the graveyard, one headstone of 1855, to Richard Baker, earlier than the present building.

H33

34 Nos. 43 and 45, Meadowview II

Two cottages, now one house, early C18. Colourwashed stone with a thatched roof now covered with corrugated iron. One storey and attic bedrooms. The building has been extended by one bay to the south and in the late C19 housed the village post office. C19 timber windows and an original four-panelled door; all openings have keystones and segmental brick arches. The roof has simple tie-beams trusses. There were no rear windows until some 60 years ago.

H34

35 No. 53 NL

Two cottages, now one house, c.1830–40 utilizing the stone wall of an earlier building at the rear. Brick with slate roof, each cottage of two bays with a lateral door, one now blocked when converted to one house. A lean-to of 1963 is on the left.

In the front garden is a Cat's Head apple tree, a rare cottage garden species.

36 Loughton Lodge Farm NL

Farmhouse, now the National Centre for Badminton.

C19, of buff brick with slated roof. Two two-storey canted bay windows and a central door. Gable stacks.

Outbuildings include a large barn at right angles to the road, now sensitively converted for use of the sport.

H36

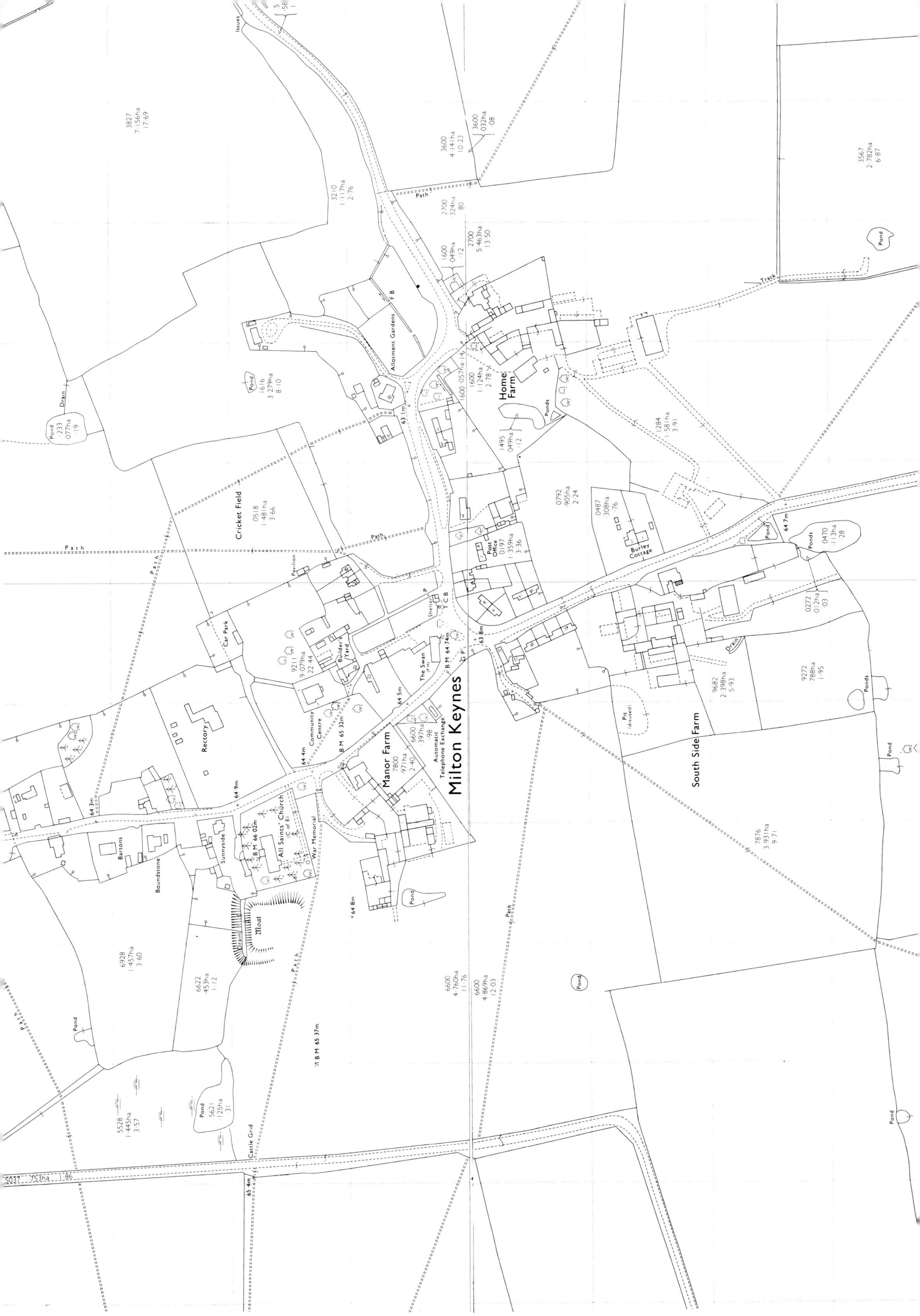
Milton Keynes
Manor Farm
South Side Farm
Home Farm
Cricket Field
Rectory
Allotment Gardens
Car Park
Pavilion
Community Centre
Builder's Yard
The Swan (P H)
Automatic Telephone Exchange
Post Office
Burley Cottage
All Saints' Church (C of E)
War Memorial
Sunnyside
Bartons
Boundstone
Moat
Cattle Grid
Track
Path
Pond
Ponds
Drain
Shelter
Issues
Pit (disused)

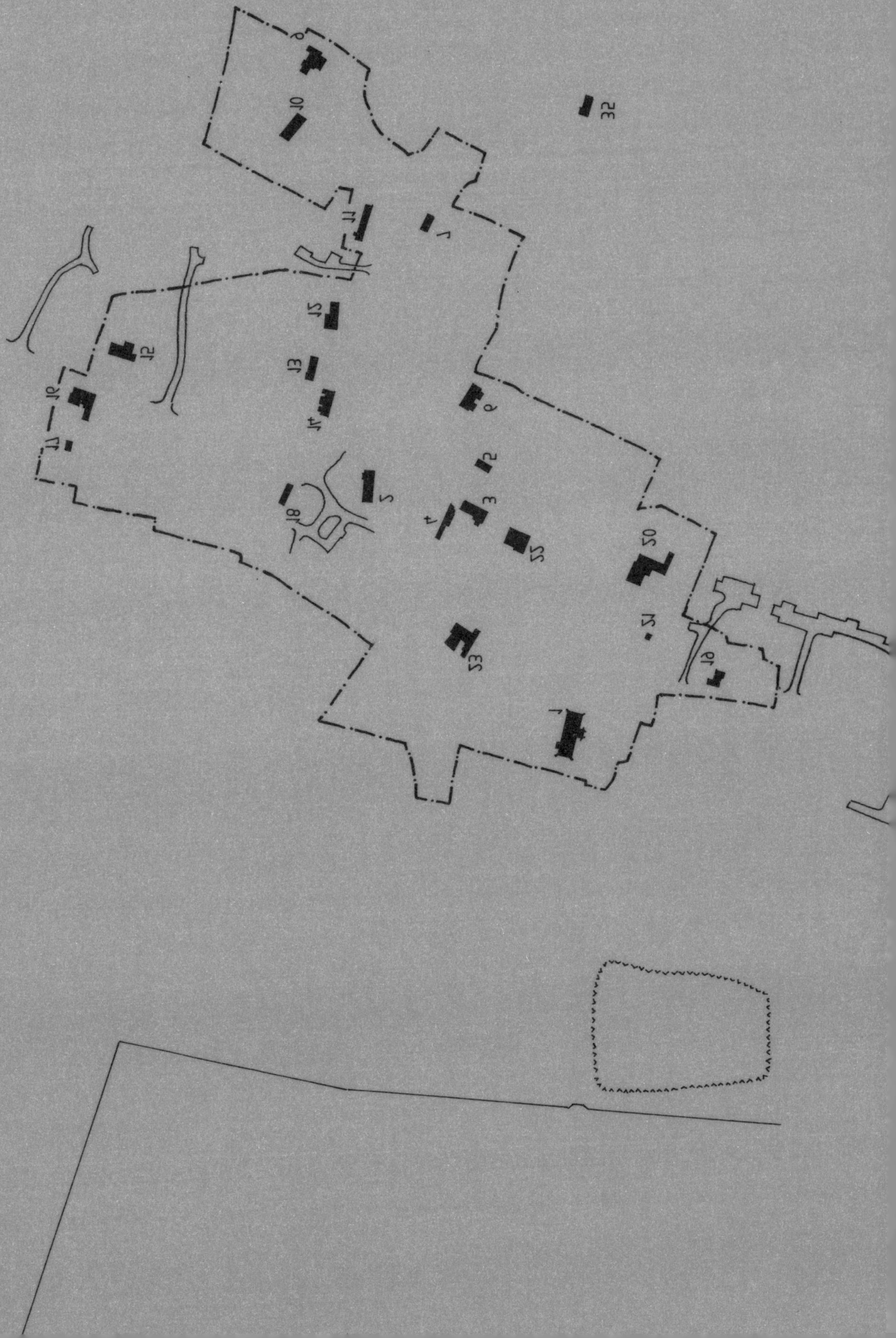

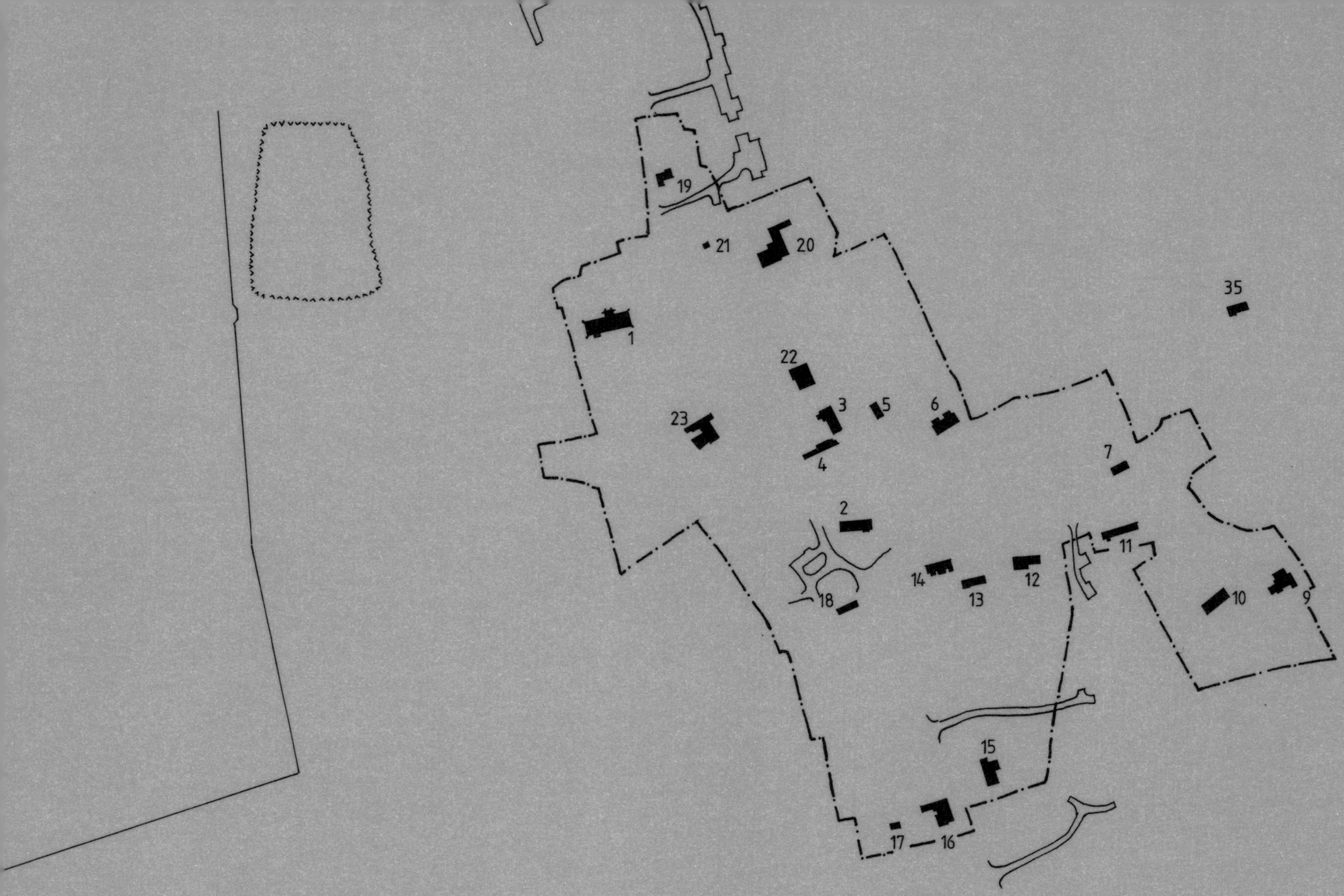

19
21
20
35
1
22
3
5
6
23
7
4
2
11
14
12
13
18
10
9
15
17
16

MILTON KEYNES

MILTON KEYNES

Milton Keynes village lies on a narrow spur of gravel between the valleys of the Ouzel and its tributary to the west. Here the former main route ran from Great Brickhill to Newport Pagnell, and here also is the junction of east-west routes of lesser importance from the Woolstones to Salford in Bedfordshire and beyond, this now reduced to footpaths in places. Prehistoric occupation is recorded within the parish, and Roman and later occupation in the vicinity of the church. In Domesday the village of Middleton, shortened later to Milton, which then belonged to Edith, Queen of Edward the Confessor, is described within Moulsoe Hundred, which was joined into the Newport Hundreds by the C13. Other than the church, little remains from the medieval period apart from a moated site east of the church, probably the site of the medieval manor which in the middle ages, owed the King the service of a mounted and armed knight for 40 days when required, and a curious site further to the west, called the 'Pondwykes' in 1418, likely to be the demesne fishponds. The mill, recorded in 1086, was probably that of Little Woolstone. The name Keynes derives from the family of Cahaines who held the manor from 1166 to the late C13 as well as property elsewhere in the country, Ashton Keynes, Wilts, Somerford Keynes, Gloucs, and Horsted Keynes in Sussex. The philosopher is probably a distant descendant. The population grew from 280 in 1801 to 334 in 1831, since when it steadily declined to 160 in 1971. The village has always depended on agriculture for its livelihood, and this has shaped its present appearance—buildings spaced widely over a less fertile area interspersed with paddocks and trees, until recently tall elms. The earlier buildings were of timber framing with wattle and clay panels, and thatch for the roofs.

1 Church of All Saints — I

The parish church, in origin a building of c.1200 which has in the C14, been largely rebuilt to become one of the more impressive parish churches of the area. It is of limestone, with tiled roofs. Nave and south porch, chancel, north chapel and a tower unusually on the north side.

Externally it is all of c.1330, indicating a period of prosperity or manorial favour in the village. Large three-light windows with handsome tracery and a fine south door. The chancel has a similar three-light east window, the outer order carrying a stilted arch. The tower is of three stages with a stair turret in the wall against the nave, and in the belfrey, five bells and a sanctus bell of the C17. Internally, the chancel arch is of the late C12–early C13 indicating not all was rebuilt, and the ornament of the tower opening is of similar date, perhaps re-used in this position. The chancel has a very fine sedile with double piscinae in range, ogee headed, with cusps on columns. The north chapel appears to be contemporary with the rest of the building and perhaps was included by those who sponsored the rebuilding as a family chapel. It became the village schoolroom in 1580, and was repaired after being in very poor condition in 1679. It has a good piscina decorated with ballflowers. Unusually, the tower also has a piscina and must have at one time had an altar. The church has few monuments, the most significant being the brass to Adam Babbington, rector, of 1427. There are a number of indents where there have been other brasses. On the sill of the north chapel are a number of Little Brickhill and Penn tiles of the C15, giving the name of the maker, Ricard. The Stuart arms are hung over the north doorway.

J1

BROUGHTON ROAD (North side)

2 The Swan Inn — II

A C16–C17 building ot timber framing and brick noggings replacing wattle and daub, and a thatched roof. Two storeys, two bays with central entrance. It has been extended in the early C20 to the right, also of two storeys. The framing is one panel high above ceiling level and it has two swept dormers. Internally the large inglenook beam has initials.

An inn called the Swan was first established here in 1550.

J2

3 No. 22 — NL

The oldest domestic building in Milton Keynes, perhaps the manor house of a branch of the Cahaines family. c.1300. Timber framed, having a two-bay central hall with its open roof raised on base crucks carrying arcade plates, and the central truss with a crown post and inverted braces. The whole roof is smoke blackened, including the thatch battens. This form of construction of great rarity and although of only modest proportions this building illustrates a line of evolution from the aisled hall. Its end bay was rebuilt in the C17 at which time it received a framed outbuilding, probably a dairy, and a stone stack inserted in the hall, allowing it to be floored over. It was further altered in the C19 when the two dormers were reconstructed and the gables infilled with patterned brick. One external stack has diaper brick patterning, but has been altered at least twice.

J3

4 No. 23 Swan Cottage — II

House of the late C17 or early C18. Brick on stone foundations, now rendered. Tiled roof. Two bays, two storeys, with external gable stacks and a long service wing. The oven to the east stack projects externally.

5 Barn to East of No. 22 — II

Barn, now a workshop. C18, timber framed and weatherboarded, and thatched roof half hipped at the ends. Three bays, with various added windows and doors, and a floor inserted in one part. To one side a brick lined saw pit survives.

J5

6 Nos. 27, 28, 29 and 30 — NL

A row of farmworkers cottages, c.1900–10, brick, each of one bay with lateral paired doors under a common pent roof and four-pane sashes. The last of the farm cottages.

7 No. 31 — NL

A two-bay cottage of diaper brickwork, two storeys with gable stacks. A third bay has recently been added.

J7

8 No. 35 Well House — II

A C17 farmhouse, with two timber framed bays and door to lobby entry, against the central stack. Thatched roof. An C18–C19 wing has been added to east end, and a C20 cross wing at the west. Internally the living room has a chamfered spine beam with notched stops and windbraces to the roof trusses. There is a cambered timber fire beam and a small oven in a secondary stack.

J8

BROUGHTON ROAD (South side)

9 Brook Farmhouse II

C18 farmhouse, largely remodelled in the early C19. Brick with a tiled roof. Two bays, extended by a further two bays.

10 Home Farmhouse II

A C17–C18 cottage, considerably expanded in the C19. The core building is of three bays with central hallway and door with flanking pilasters and hood. Extension to the left of two bays, C19, with segmental headed paned windows. Slate roof.

11 Nos. 1 and 2 NL

Originally a row of five farmworkers' cottages, now two. c.1860–80. Red brick with the merest patterning, and with low pitched slate roof all rather small scale. Timber windows and bead-panelled doors, all delightfully maintained.

12 No. 3 Abbot's Close II

C17, extended to the west in the C18. Roughcast brickwork with a thatched roof. Originally one storey and attic, with an extension of two storeys. Six panelled door at the left end of the lower build. Timber windows.

13 Nos. 4 and 5, The Old Post Office II

C14–C15, with C17 additions and later alterations. Timber framed with thatched roof. At the centre a cruck truss of chamfered blades and cambered collar carrying a king-post with curved braces to the post and principle rafters. The roof has heavy smoke staining from the former open fire. Stone chimney inserted probably in late C16 with brick flue through roof. Large chamfered spine beam in central ground floor room.

With No. 22, No. 4, Simpson and Bradwell Abbey barn, this is the fourth and most complete of the cruck trusses, and is a valuable glimpse of medieval building construction. Cruck construction, consisting of heavy curved timbers from ground to ridge, is the best documented of early regional styles. It is only rarely found in Britain east of Milton Keynes, another occurring at Husbourne Crawley. This one demonstrates a less common method of supporting the ridge.

14 Nos. 6 and 7 NL

A row of brick cottages dated 1890 and initials GHF. Two storeys each of two bays with a central panelled door, two storeys high with brick dentilled eaves and gable stacks. Doors recently replaced.

WALTON ROAD (East side)

15 Nos. 1 and 2, Burley Cottages II

Two cottages in a row, C16–C17. Originally timber framed with a thatched roof, the southern cottage partly rebuilt in C17–early C18 brickwork. The framed section has storey height framing, one storey and attic, with thatched roof swept over two dormers. The southern cottage is raised to two storeys and an attic, originally thatched, now tiled. The gable end has paired windows with a hood moulding over, and raised verges terminating in a brick stack, similar to the Manor House. A picturesque group.

J9

J11

J12

J13

J15

J16

WALTON ROAD (West side)

16 Southside Farmhouse II

Farmhouse of the C18, refronted in the early C19. Brick with tiled roof. Of four bays, with C19 rear extensions. Six panelled door in second bay with semicircular fanlight within a lattice timber porch with a rounded head and hexagonal patterned fascia.

17 Granary at Southside Farm NL

Granary, C17 or C18, timber framed and weatherboarded, and slated roof, raised on brick staddles. Door on south side, and the interior divided into bays for grain.

J17

18 No. 10 Nurse's Cottage II

A C17 timber two-bay framed cottage with storey height panels, one-storey and attic, and tension braces to upper panels. Thatched roof. The building has been extended eastwards in the C19 in brickwork, now whitewashed, and a lean-to thatched extension on the west. The main stack is on the east of the main block.

WILLEN ROAD (East side)

19 Ivy Cottage II

A C17 farmhouse, timber framed with whitewashed brick noggings, and thatched roof. One storey and attic, three bays, with a southward extension also timber framed and one storey.

J18

J19

20 Old Rectory II

An imposing parsonage built between 1693 and 1723 for the Rev. Dr. William Wootton on the site of a former rectory of stone and timber, the birthplace of the Jacobite Bishop of Rochester, and to where the litigatious protestant incumbant, Lewis Atterbury was appointed by the Lord Protector in 1654. The present building is of two storeys and attics, brick, with a tiled roof. The south front has five bays, with a further recessed bay on the east. The centre three bays are broken forward and pedimented, the heavy dentilled cornice continuing and returning at the ends. Stone moulded string at first floor level and gauged flat brick arches to the openings. Central timber doorcase with flat canopy on consoles, now with a glazed door. Twelve pane sashes to upper floor, those on the ground floor replaced, and two hipped dormers in the hipped roof. The building is double pile plan with central hallway and partly external stacks to the end gables. Single storey rear wing. The interior has contemporary panelling to the drawing room, but the main stair has been replaced in the C20. The clergy of the early–mid C18 were amongst the most wealthy of the community and frequently built themselves fine residences such as this one.

The walls to the road are separately listed. II

J20

21 Gazebo NL

A small gazebo in brick remains from what must have once been impressive gardens.

J21

22 Community Centre NL

Schoolroom, built 1859 for 60 children. Brick.

J22

WILLEN ROAD (West side)

23 Manor Farmhouse II

A major farmhouse of the village, C17 colourwashed brickwork with a tiled roof. Two storeys and attic, three bays with a north wing of two bays. The brickwork has characteristic plat bands and raised gables with kneelers, the windows divided by a central gable stack. Also two stacks in the centre of the house.

J23

24 Milton Hill NL

Farm buildings of brick with slated roofs, 1866, comprising a five-bay barn with perforated brick vents all round, and queen-post trusses, extended in line with a three-bay cow house, and the yard enclosed by a brick wall with shelter sheds on the two other sides. The initials TP and GP appear on the door jambs of the barn.

Shenley Church End
SHENLEY ROAD
MANSELL CLOSE
Manor Farm
Shenley Church End County Primary School
St Mary's Church (C of E)
War Meml
Hall
Rectory
Motte & Baileys
Reservoir
Water
Stag Lodge Farm
Stag Lodge
Home Farm
OAKHILL ROAD
Earthworks
Ford
Issues
Track
Path
Pond
Ponds
Tank
1761 12·172ha 30·08
1372 ·389ha ·96
0268 2·396ha 5·92
9285 4·020ha 9·93
1142 4·260ha 10·53
2531 3·915ha 9·67
1325 ·150ha ·37
9047 3·457ha 8·54
8729 1·297ha 3·21
7288 3·632ha 8·98
6373 4·499ha 11·12
5761 ·831ha 2·05
5149 10·178ha 25·15
7229 1·135ha 2·81
3973 7·864ha 19·43

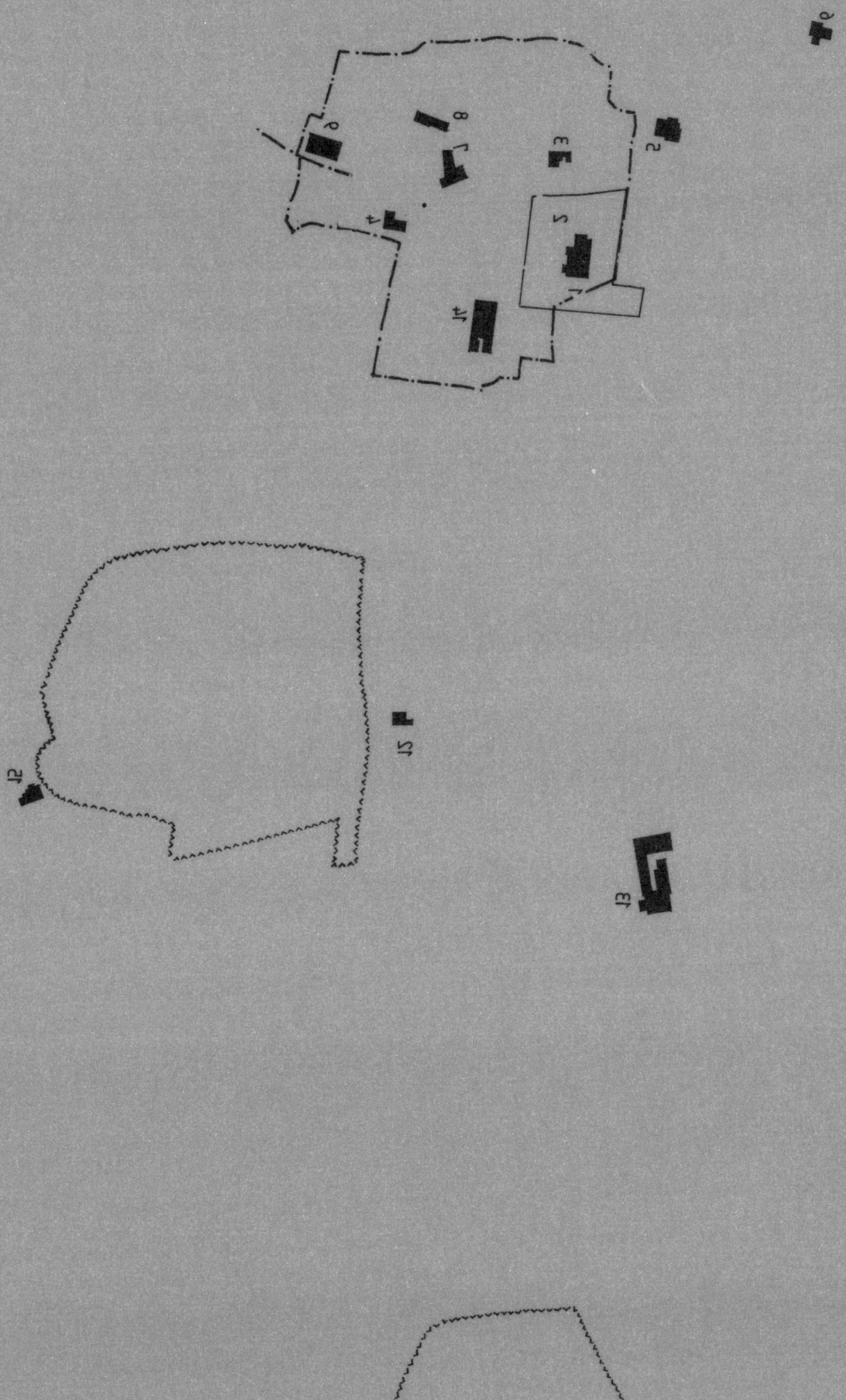

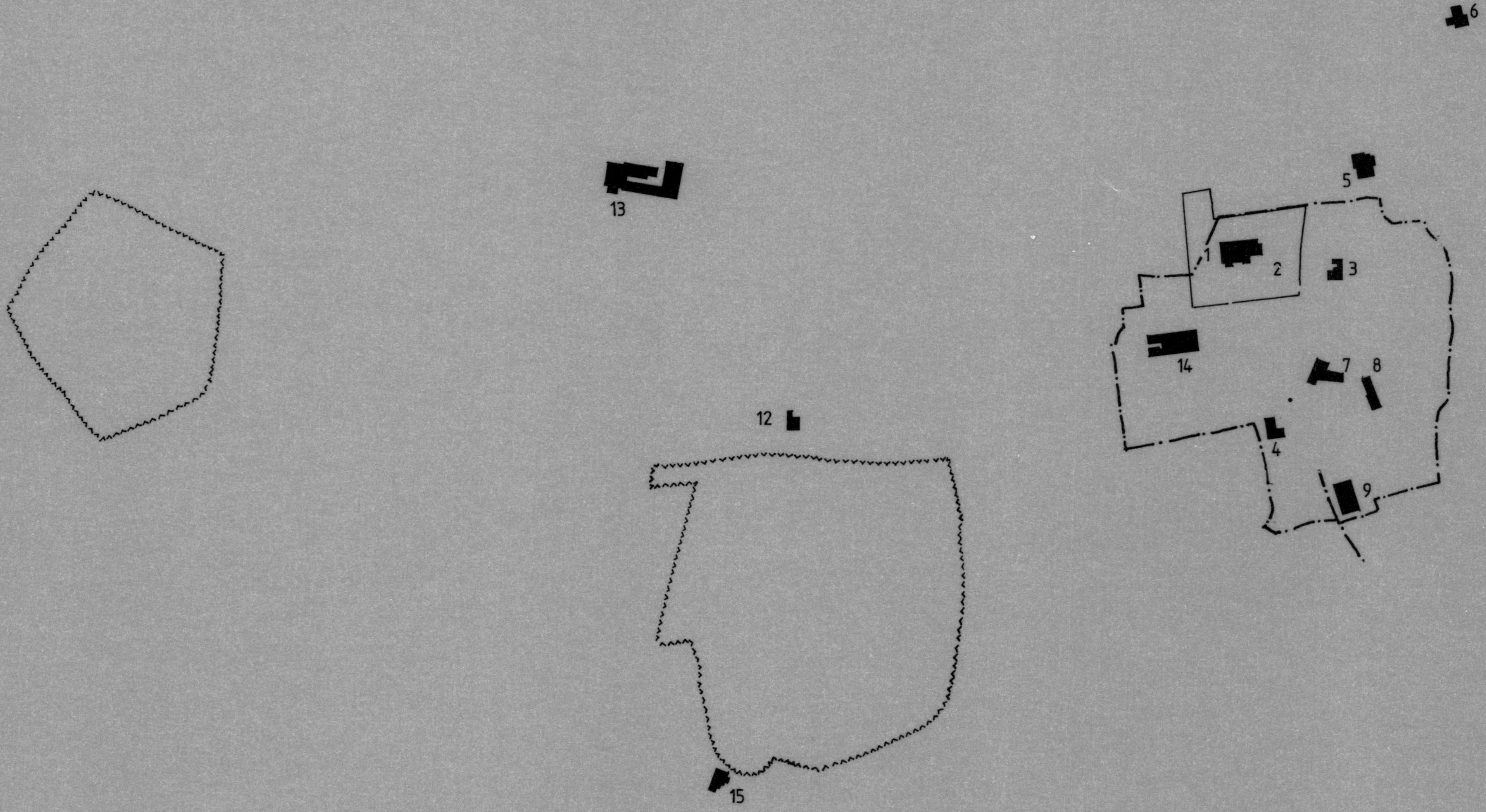

1
2
3
4
5
6
7
8
9
12
13
14
15

SHENLEYS

SHENLEY

Shenley first appears in the C11 Domesday survey under the name SENELAI. It is a parish in the Hundred of Mursley, later Newport, and is composed of two townships, Shenley Church End and Shenley Brook End, the latter already distinct at this early date by virtue of being within Cottesloe Hundred. The two were distinguished by various epithets such as Great and Little Shenley until the present usage became established in the later C18. The parish boundaries have been variable too, but these became established with Church End having 1659 acres and Brook End very slightly larger at 1662 acres.

Other than the church, the earliest visible remains are the earthworks of a motte and bailey castle or fortified manor in Oakhill Road, called The Toot. Some seven acres are enclosed within two ditched enclosures, with a small motte at one end, the northern enclosure having remained the manorial site for Church End until Matthew Knapp the Lord of the Manor demolished the house in 1774.

The manors descended through the Vache and Verdon families until the Knapp's of Little Linford acquired property in 1697. A park is mentioned as being in existence in the C16.

The parishes were partially enclosed in 1762–3 and finally in 1845.

SHENLEY CHURCH END

SHENLEY ROAD

1 Church of St. Mary I

Parish church for the whole of Shenley, with features of all periods from the C11 to the C16. An unusual plan, with central tower, a short nave with aisles and south porch, narrow transept chapels, and a chancel with a C19 vestry. The original building appears to have been cruciform, of which the transept chapels, with their small rubble stonework and elementary rebated windows are the earliest survivals. These must have been attached to an earlier and perhaps smaller tower, to which was added, in the later C12, the chancel with mid-wall string and windows with slightly pointed moulded heads and nook shafts, those on the south with shaft bands. The next major building phase took place in the early–mid C14 when the nave and aisles were rebuilt and a priest's door inserted to the south chancel wall. Major works again took place in the late C15–early C16 when the present tower was raised, probably as a result of a particular benefactor no longer recorded, together with the east and west windows, and probably the low-side window in the chancel.

K1

Interior:

There is much of interest in the church. The early Norman work is not in evidence, but the chancel is particularly fine, with three original side windows with doubled nook shafts and a dog-tooth string forming a hood mould to each window. In the centre of each side wall there is a multiple corbel, still in a fully Romanesque style, intended to carry vaulting, a rare occurrence in a parish church. A round-headed north door to an earlier chapel has a hood mould with beast terminals. Also, in the east wall of the south transept there is a capital built in which is equal to the best in English Romanesque work. The south arcade, with its well proportioned round columns and water-holding bases comes next, c.1200 establishing the nave at four bays. The north arcade represents an expansion of c.1350 at which time the nave walls were probably raised and a clerestory inserted. In the C14 the chancel was also embellished with a curious double piscina, and adjacent, a double sedilia with central arm rest, all under a segmental arch. The central tower was then rebuilt, c.1490 with its large triangular piers breaking into the east bay of the arcades. The north-east pier accommodates the rood stair and the spiral stair to the tower.

K1a

K1b

Interest does not end here, for the C19 also made its mark redolent of the period. The walls of the crossing and chancel have been stencilled, and encaustic tiles laid in panels on the floor. It has fine choir stalls and the eastern altar is still maintained properly dressed with a cupboard for the reserved sacrament, and tall candles. The whole has a validity of its own. The Victorian wall painting probably removed the traces of the paintings described by Willis in the early C18.

The font is a fairly plain octagon of the C15 and the pulpit has re-used long C17 oak panels in a recent tall oak octagon with a square tester.

The church has its share of monuments too. Perhaps the most significant is a wall monument in the chancel to Sir Edmund Ashfield, who died in 1577. It has a sarcophagus behind three marble columns supporting an open pediment with the Ashfield arms above: for its date a confident design in the use of the relatively new classical repertoire, more reminiscent of the first decade of the C17. A little later comes Thomas Stafford, died 1607 with his reclining effigy on a tomb-chest and his wife and family represented below, only the two daughters not holding skulls surviving him. It was Thomas's son that built the Almshouses with his legacy. A well-lettered tablet in the chancel commemorates the Rev. Matthew Knapp, who died in 1752. There are a few other wall tablets of later date. Two damaged brasses survive on the floor, one to Ann Kirteham, heir of Philip de la Vache, died 1427, and the other to Thomas Thirlby, rector, died 1432.

Other items of interest are the Royal Arms of 1772 over the south door, and an early iron-bound parish chest.

2 The Graveyard — NL

In the graveyard most of the older monuments are C19. South of the chancel the modest headstone of Mary Baker, 1744, is nicely engraved, and, also of the C18, two headstones, each to a William Kightley of 1761, hark back to the heavier modelling of C17 monuments. The conspicuous broken grey marble column is the memorial of Matthew Knapp, Deputy Lieutenant of Buckinghamshire, and related to the Knapp's of Little Linford. He died in 1863, having probably erected the Old Rectory. The C19 cast-iron screen and gates are work of an unnamed foundry. The village is famed for having a Glastonbury Thorn which is reputed to bloom at Christmastide.

SHENLEY ROAD (West side)

3 White Cottage — II

An early–mid C19 cottage against the churchyard, typical of the early Victorian period. Symmetrical three bays with central hallway and stacks to both end gables. It has been extended to the rear in recent times.

4 Guide Post — NL

At the junction of Oakhill Road with Shenley Road there is a C19 cast-iron guide or finger post, originally with three arms, now with only one, crowned by a ring reading BUCKS COUNTY. These signs, since the adoption of the Warboys international signing system, have now become scarce.

5 Shenley County First School — NL

School, built 1869, in a vernacular style with sensitively detailed brickwork and entrances with round arches and tile hoods. The cloakrooms and offices are towards the front with gabled schoolrooms lying at the rear. The rafters are exposed and shaped at the eaves, and the roof cantilevered over the gables.

K5

SHENLEY ROAD (East side)

6 No. 3 The Homestead II

A good example of a three-bay lobby entry house of a smallholder of the C17. Timber framed, the thatch now replaced with asbestos slates. The original entrance is now used as an access to a dairy added on the front at right angles in the C19. There is a large central stack of narrow bricks with a chamfered mantelbeam internally. The spine beams are chamfered with ogee stops only to the south room and the roof has clasped purlins. The framing has only one panel to each floor rising from a stone sill, and angle braces and jowled posts. A stone built lean-to store of indeterminate date is at the rear. The house was modified in the C19 by building a rear stair annexe replacing the original stair, and adding a stack to the north end gable providing the building with heating to the original parlour.

K6

7 No. 21 Manor Farmhouse II

Farmhouse, mid C18 extended in the C19. The C18 part comprises the taller right-hand block with raised gable walls, which was probably originally thatched, and a block to the centre rear. This suggests that the main building with the front entrance is originally C18, refaced or rebuilt in the mid C19 to which a second rear wing was added in rendered brickwork.

K7

8 Manor Farm Barn II

A timber framed barn lying to the rear of Manor Farmhouse containing three bays, extended to the right by a further two bays. The original building is C17, weatherboarded on a stone sill and a quarter-hipped thatched roof. Its roof has principal rafters joined by a saddle carrying the ridge plate. There have been many alterations, including having floors inserted for a granary. The addition is also framed but on brick sills, probably early C18. Both structures have internal braces to the posts and long windbraces, but the earlier only has external angle braces.

K8

9 Nos. 23 to 33, Stafford Almshouses II

Terrace of six almshouses, paired in two's built 1615 at the direction of the will of Thomas Stafford of Tattenhoe by his trustees, including his son, also Thomas Stafford, for four poor men and two poor women, each to have a house room, with a ladder to an attic, and a washplace at the rear, and garden. Internal partitions between pairs are of heavy timber framing, a form of construction characteristic of the period. At the centre a raised framed and rendered gable contains a dedication stone in a gadrooned panel, reading THIS ALMSHOUSE WAS CAUSED TO BE ERECTED BY THOMAS STAFFORD ESQ, DECEASED, AND WAS BUILT BY THOMAS STAFFORD HIS SON, ANNO DOMINI 1614. Through weathering it is now barely legible.

A result of the dissolution of the monasteries was that the destitute were no longer able to obtain charity and food from those in religious orders. This dire need was in time replaced by the duty falling on philanthropic landowners who were able to advertise their benevolence by providing these small single room dwellings with some financial support and care for the aged. In this case they were endowed with land in Great Linford. Those accepted for a tenancy were not the feckless, but those of good repute, 'unmarried and of good age and honest conversation' and were required to attend divine services at prescribed times. They received a gown annually, with a red cross on the left sleeve, and three pence per week for each man and two pence for each woman, equal pay being then unknown. Although poor when admitted, they frequently had not always been so and had often been people of honour and acclaim in their day, but had, through circumstances or age, fallen on hard times.

K9

OAKHILL ROAD (North Side)

Oakhill Road was originally a medieval and possibly earlier trackway leading from Shenley to Nash through Whaddon Chase, later reduced here to Oakhill Woods. Much of this land was apparently not brought into cultivation until after the medieval period, thus the buildings are without exception C17 or later.

10 Lawn Farm — Barn-II

Farmhouse, c.1870 on site of earlier farmhouse, of which little remains other than some stone walling incorporated into a former cow house, now linked to the dwelling. At the end of the yard there is a C17 timber framed and weatherboarded barn on stone sill walls, three bays, with lean-to former entrance to the centre bay. The structure has jowled posts and corner braces and the roof simple strutted trusses. The barn has been later converted to two levels, and an C18 stable attached to its northern end, having a pantiled roof. The name Lawn Farm derived from Furze Lawn in 1693, a rough grazing clearing in a wooded area.

K10

11 Grange Farm — NL

Farmhouse of 1887, of brick with a gable to the centre of three bays. Central stair hall. Three rooms deep. Both Woburn Abbey and Snelshall Priory had a farm (called a grange) in Shenley in the medieval period. Grange Farm is a clue to where it was to be found.

12 No. 10, Lodge to Shenley Park House — NL

Lodge, early C19 but much renovated in or around 1920. Significant for its timber verandah on three sides and bracketed eaves. The upper floor which is roughcasted, has brick surrounds to openings, bracket shaped on the sills.

K12

13 Shenley Park House — II

House of c.1805, formerly known as Shenley House, possibly built by the Knapp family, and later owned by the Selby Loundes, and later, occupied by Lord Cadman, the man who started the first ever school of oil technology in Birmingham. The site was previously occupied by a house, demolished c.1770. The present building is of brick, stone faced on its more important elevations, and with a wide overhanging hipped roof, all in a Regency style. There is a fine central stone portico, and on the south end, a handsome garden room of the 1920's with a fine patterned limestone floor, and a marble console table. Internally the house has a central hallway leading to a dog-leg stair at the rear. The reception rooms flanking the hallway have fine late C17 or early C18 panelling and bolection fireplaces. They must have been brought in, as was the excellent turned chestnut stair balustrade and the dentilled cornice to the hall.

K13

To the rear of the house are two wings, each extended in the C19 to include stables, carriage house and accommodation for the hunt. A curious feature is that the wings are linked at first floor level by a passage across the rear of the house, replicating the tall round-headed stair window.

14 The Old Rectory, Eagle's Wings II

Rectory, late C18 or early C19. A tall imposing building of three storeys on a stone basement, brick but the frontage rendered and painted. Three bays, the centre bay is a shallow three-storey arch, a Midland fashion, with a Doric portico in antis, and within, a wide segmental fanlight over paired doors, all raised over a perrault stair. The windows are tripartite 12-pane sashes with concealed boxes and the building has a moulded eaves cornice. Internally, there is a two-bay arcaded and groin-vaulted hallway leading to a rear stair hall. The mahogany stair is a replacement of 1972 and of fine workmanship. The one reception room has a contemporary marble fireplace, the other a C20 introduction. The building has various later extensions to the rear.

On the north side a range of stables defines the service yard. These have lunette windows and internally some loose boxes and iron mangers. They may be the kitchen and washing house described in a document of 1827. The garden wall along the road is C18, with diaper brick and half-round copings, rising in shaped form to the corner pier. When the garden was extended westwards in the C19 the shaping was repeated, and blue copings provided. II

K14

OAKHILL ROAD (South side)

15 Stag Lodge NL

Recorded as 'A capital newly built keeper's house' in 1875. Symmetrical of three bays, two storeys with central hallway six-pane sashes with stone wedge lintels and keystones, and gable stacks.

16 No. 1, The Dower House II

A more than usually substantial C17 farmhouse of a type probably once much more common in this area. Timber framed upper storey on brick and stone lower walls. Lobby entry plan with central stack, two bays to the right, and two forming the original parlour wing, at right angles to the left. The framing is two panels high, with jowled posts and corner braces. The interior has chamfered ceiling beams and a large fireplace with an oak mantelbeam. The stair has a few splat balusters on its upper flight.

K15

17 (Folly Farmhouse)

On Oak Hill and now demolished, a three-bay timber framed building with central brick stack rear wing and a thatched roof. It was later rebuilt with a brick frontage.

K16

OLD WATLING STREET

Watling Street, on its old course, forms the boundary between Shenley and Loughton parishes, presumably being a significant feature of the later Anglo Saxon landscape when the boundaries were being established. Thus the western side is within Shenley parish, and was long known as Shenley Inns.

The few historic buildings on the Shenley side of the Street are discussed under the parish of Loughton.

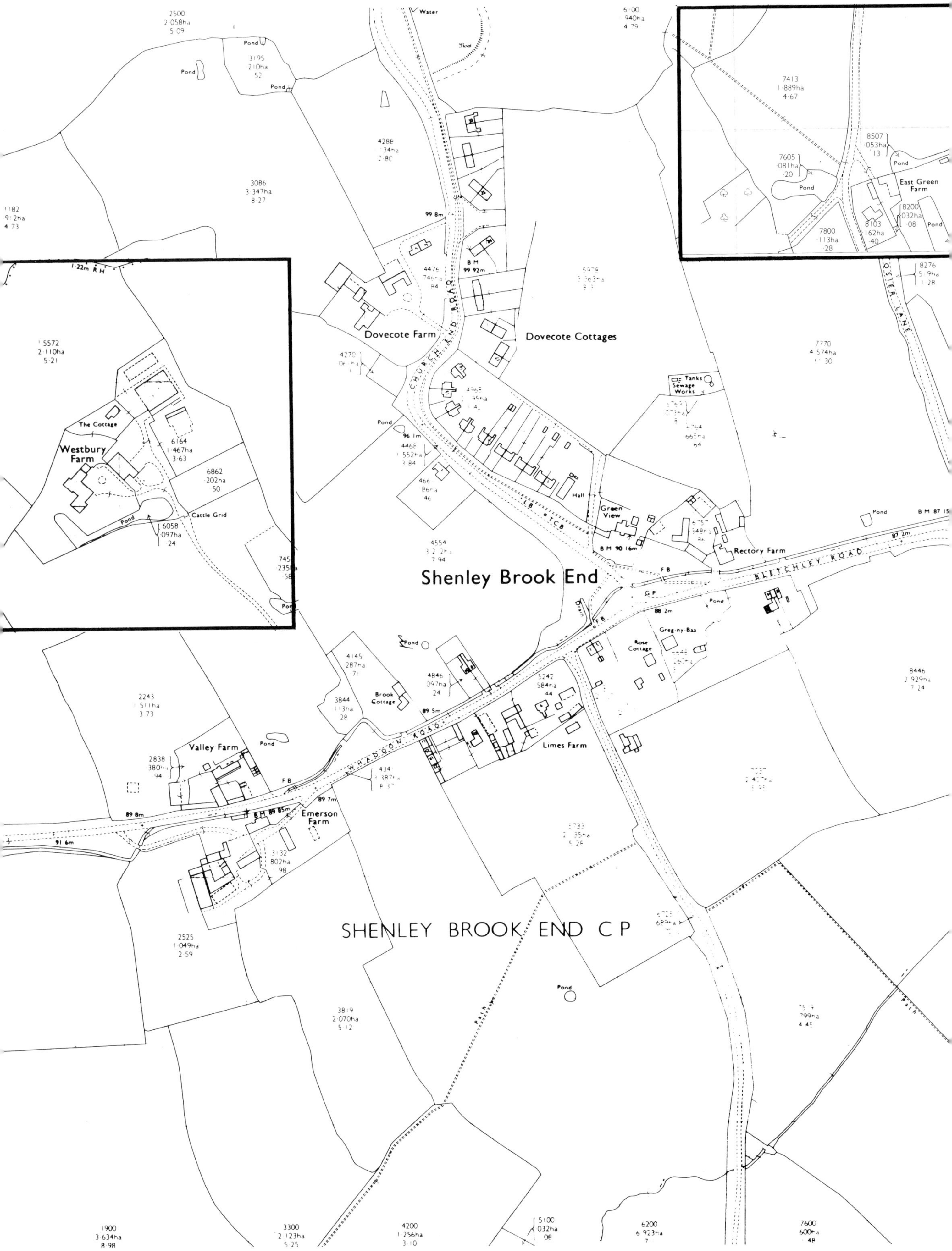
Shenley Brook End
SHENLEY BROOK END C P
Dovecote Farm
Dovecote Cottages
Westbury Farm
The Cottage
Cattle Grid
East Green Farm
Rectory Farm
Green View
Hall
Tanks
Sewage Works
Rose Cottage
Gregny-Baa
Brook Cottage
Valley Farm
Limes Farm
Emerson Farm
CHURCH END ROAD
BLETCHLEY ROAD
WHADDON ROAD
Pond
Water
F B
B M 90·16m
B M 87·15
87·2m
88·2m
89·5m
89·7m
89·8m
91·6m
96·1m
99·8m
B M 99·92m
2500
2·058ha
5·09
3195
·210ha
·52
3086
3·347ha
8·27
4288
7413
1·889ha
4·67
8507
·053ha
·13
7605
·081ha
·20
7800
·113ha
·28
8103
·162ha
·40
8200
·032ha
·08
8276
5572
2·110ha
5·21
6164
1·467ha
3·63
6862
·202ha
·50
6058
·097ha
·24
7770
4·574ha
4554
4145
·287ha
·71
3844
4846
·097ha
·24
5242
·584ha
·44
8446
2·929ha
7·24
2243
2838
3132
·802ha
2525
1·049ha
2·59
3819
2·070ha
5·12
1900
3·634ha
8·98
3300
2·123ha
5·25
4200
1·256ha
3·10
5100
·032ha
·08
6200
6·923ha
7600

28
18
24
19
20
21
26
22
23
27

28
18
24
19
20
21
26
22
23
27

SHENLEY BROOK END

Shenley Brook End is the second township of Shenley parish although it must have its origins in being a subsidiary settlement of Church End. It is itself of two settlements, Westbury and East Green and its history has also been involved with the small parish of Tattenhoe. There are a few earthworks representing earlier settlement, the more extensive being those around Westbury Farm itself, presumably a deserted village of that name which appears to straddle the two parishes. Also, on the road to Church End, a moated site lies on the top of the hill, and causes the road to re-align at that point. This is probably the site of the house of John De Grey which in 1803 appears as a splendid three-bay house, timber framed with three gables, the left bay a carriage entrance. Curiously it seems to have had a carved wood gallery extending along the whole front at first floor level, and similar to another sketched at the same time and said to come from a building called The Old House, now not identified. The loss of this important house typifies the later history of the parish, for in 1679 we see a goodly number of cottages clustered around the triangular village green, and as late as 1911 nine still stood, the wattle and daub replaced by brickwork. The present scattered appearance of the village is thus a monument to the public health legislation of this century and the enthusiasm of post-war development.

The settlement along the valley eastwards from Westbury Farm has recently been shown by excavation to be a village of C12–C13 date which was short lived and was largely deserted in the general decline of population in the C14.

CHURCH END ROAD (West side)

18 Dovecote Farm **NL**

House of the late C19, replacing an earlier farmhouse which stood against the driveway in front of the present building. Of brick, three bays and rear wing with a hipped slate roof. Central doorway with modern gabled porch leading to a through hallway. Six-pane sashes, those to the ground floor having stone wedge lintels. The building was later extended to the east to match.

During the building works in 1901 a substantial Roman building with a tesselated floor is reported to have been found partially under the floor of the house. This has not been verified since.

The property once belonged to the Guild of St. Margaret and St. Catherine, Fenny Stratford (q.v.) and, in 1680 was bought by the Knapps of Little Linford.

K18

SHENLEY ROAD (East side)

19 Green View **II**

House, formerly the Rose & Crown Inn. c.1850, extended later in the C19. Brick with a tiled roof. The original building was symmetrical about a central entrance in a forward brick porch with a moulded cornice. Original 12-pane sashes with wedge lintels have been mostly replaced with plate glass windows. Gable stacks.

K19

WHADDON ROAD

Brook End is the southern part of Shenley Parish gathered along the Shenley Brook. It is a settlement now without clear focus, the Green at the road junction being without the buildings on the west that existed in the C17.

WHADDON ROAD (North side)

20 Rectory Farm NL

Farmhouse, c.1840, on the site of an earlier farm. Diaper brick. Symmetrical elevation of three bays, with a bay window to the right of the central door with a fanlight. A contemporary rear wing.

In the yard to the rear there are two C18 barns, timber framed with weatherboarding, both with corrugated iron roofs.

21 Brook Cottage NL

An C17 cottage, very much altered in the C19 and C20.

22 Valley Farm II

Farmhouse. C17, extended in the C18 and again in the C19. The original building is of two bays with the entrance at the far left end opposite the main stack. It is timber framed, which is still visible at the rear, two panels high with corner braces. The stack appears to have been an insertion to the building, and was composed of unfired placer bricks. The roof is thatched. The early-mid C18 added a brick dairy, partly below ground and having a store above, to the right of the house, and the thatch extended. To this building the mid C19 added the rather prim left building of two bays about a central hall, with gable stacks and upper floor bedrooms. This is of diaper brick which was extended across the old timber house to meet the dairy. The house was converted to modern use in the 1970's.

23 Farm Buildings to Valley Farm II

Valley Farm has a number of interesting late C18 or early C19 farm buildings surviving. To the south there is a carthouse, probably of the later C18, of four bays with a hipped roof, open to the east. West of the carthouse there is a sheltershed of the late C18 or C19 of eight bays, the roadside wall of which links the carthouse to the C18 timber framed and weatherboarded barn with an asbestos roof. It has cart doors in the second bay from the north and later extensions. To the rear of the west end of the farmhouse lies a small square granary originally raised on staddles, now replaced with brick. It is timber framed and weatherboarded and is also probably of the same date. To the rear of the farmhouse, there is a timber framed granary on staddles, a type of building of which there are very few survivals in this area.

24 Westbury Farmhouse II

The major manor house of Shenley Brook End, now isolated within extensive earthworks of the former settlement, but still retaining a partial wet moat. It was the home of the Staffords who were related to the Dukes of Buckingham, from 1512, and Selby from 1732, later to become the Selby Lowndes in 1772.

The house is of various periods, the earliest a heavy timber framed section of the later C16, which possibly continued further south, to which was added a finely detailed C17 block at right angles and encompassing the north end of the earlier building, comprising two storeys, attic and cellar. This part bears a datestone reading E.S. 1670 (Edward Stafford) and has a moulded plat band and eaves. The north side has blocked brick arches, one probably an original entrance, and a gabled attic room. The south facing timber door on this block is an imported item of timber in an Iberian baroque style. The house has a single storey rear wing of the C18 to which has been added in the last 20 years a two-storey block parallel to the Stafford block. There are two four-flue brick stacks with diagonal shafts, partly restored.

K21

K22

K23

K24

Internally, there is a fine moulded stone fireplace in the Elizabethan block and some good overmantels on the first floor.

Opposite the house there is a C19 timber weatherboarded barn.

A windmill is recorded at Westbury in 1278, an early date for windmills in Britain.

25 Shenley Common South Farm — II

Now called Shenley Common Farm, the North farm having been demolished some years ago. C16 or C17. Timber framed, of three bays with a contemporary rear wing with a part underground dairy. The east gable has apparently been rebuilt in the C18 with a heavy plat band, and the building was refurbished c.1890 when it was re-roofed and three dormers added to the front. A C19 scullery extension with boiler and flue is added to the west gable. Gable stacks.

The farm is remarkable for preserving the character and buildings of the pre-war period, with cowsheds around a stockyard, barn and pigsties, and a well kept kitchen garden, all delightfully evocative of mixed farming before the age of cost accountancy and agri-business.

K25

WHADDON ROAD (South side)

26 Limes Farm Barn — II

Barn, C17 or early C18. Timber framed with half-hipped tiled roof. Three bays with central cart doors. The roof has slender wind braces.

27 Emerson Farm — II

Farmhouse, early-mid C18. Brick, some vitrified and red brick surrounds to openings. Five bays. Lobby entry plan with central stack and stair. Central doorway and C19 timber casement windows. Plat band and dentilled eaves. Roof is half hipped. Various lean-to structures at the rear and pig sties backing on to the road. Over the door there is a Sun Fire Insurance mark No. 104115, dated 1748.

There are a number of Emerson tombs in the churchyard.

To the west of the farmhouse there is a granary, originally on four by four staddles and probably of the early C19, and a three-bay weatherboarded framed barn with central cart doors. II

K26

28 Howe Park Farmhouse — II

Farmhouse just within Shenley parish although the approach road is in Tattenhoe. Farmhouse of c.1840, but on the site of an earlier building marked on the 1801 Selby Estate map. It is of three bays with wings to the rear. This side has become the main entrance with a central door and 12-pane sash windows with segmental heads. The building has been rendered and has a slate roof.

K27

OSIER LANE

29 East Green Farmhouse — II

Farmhouse of the late C17–early C18. Timber framed with rendered brick infilling. It consists of two independent blocks at right angles, now joined by C20 lean-to structures. The main block is that on the west, of two unequal bays with a central door and C19 bay windows. At the north end there is a large fireplace supporting a chamfered spine beam. A stack has been added to the other end. To the rear the second, narrower, block has one stack. The framing is slender, the second block having long tension braces. The roof has clasped purlins.

To the left of the entrance there was until a fire of January 17, 1981, a timber framed barn and stables which bore an unrecorded date. The walls were three panels high, the lower panel being equal in height to the upper two.

K29

Simpson
Simpson Lodge Farm
Aircraft Navigation Beacon
Ponds
Tank
Holmfield
Grand Union Canal
Towing Path
GROVE WAY
M P 37
M P
G P
70·8m
B M 72·65m
74·1m
69·3m
70·5m
B 488
Path
Track
Pond
Simpson Meth Church
White Cottage
Wayside
SIMPSON ROAD
ABBEY RD
Halls
The Forge
Shelter
Five Acres
St Thomas's Church
(C of E)
War Meml
Ponds
El Sub Sta
Warren Bank
Simpson House
63·7m
65·7m
E Sub Sta
P O
The Plough (P H)
T C B
L B
F B
The Walnuts
Manor Farm
B M 64·08m
64·0m
B M 79·75m
Hill Farm
Hedgerow
Brook View
Hillview
Royston
The Apiary
Pond
The Mount
70·7m
B M 71·09m
72·8m
Simpson Br
Moats
Fish Ponds
8970
·316ha
·78
8271
·827ha
2·04
0067
·551ha
1·36
0067
3·861ha
9·54
5759
·592ha
1·46
8558
3·841ha
9·49
9750
·340ha
·84
2155
2·929ha
7·24
0456
·364ha
·90
0950
·851ha
2·10
4753
4·428ha
10·94
0547
·061ha
·15
0646
·295ha
·73
2540
2·658ha
6·57
3641
·401ha
·99
0038
1·155ha
2·85
1238
·754ha
1·86
0633
·697ha
1·72
0038
·073ha
·18
4736
3·796ha
9·38
4620
1·685ha
4·16
0019
1·994ha
4·93
0019
1·094ha
2·70
1820
9·115ha
22·52
4212
·786ha
1·94
5307
·146ha
·36
9307
·259ha
·64
9406
·057ha
·14
0001
1·013ha
2·50
0001
·511ha
1·26
0001
·081ha
·20
8200
3·364ha
8·31
2200
·425ha
1·05
2200
·494ha
1·22
3700
2·419ha
5·98
3700
17·061ha
42·16
5300
·360ha
·89
5800
·032ha
·08
5300
2·700ha
6·67
5800
·040ha
·10
1390
4·316ha
10·67
0084
·121ha
·30
0073
3·345ha
8·27

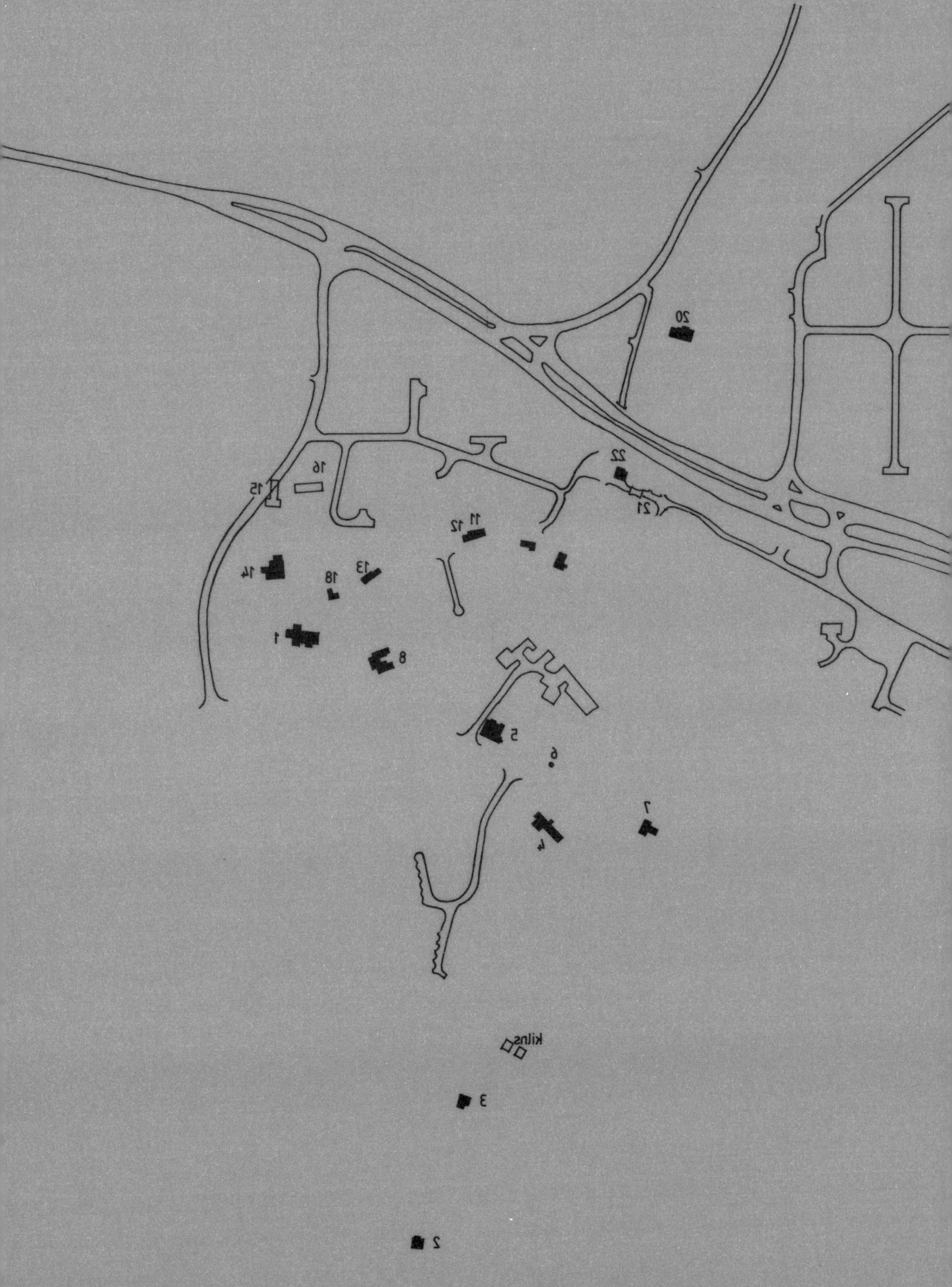

1
2
3
4
5
6
7
8
11
12
13
14
15
16
18
20
21
22
kilns

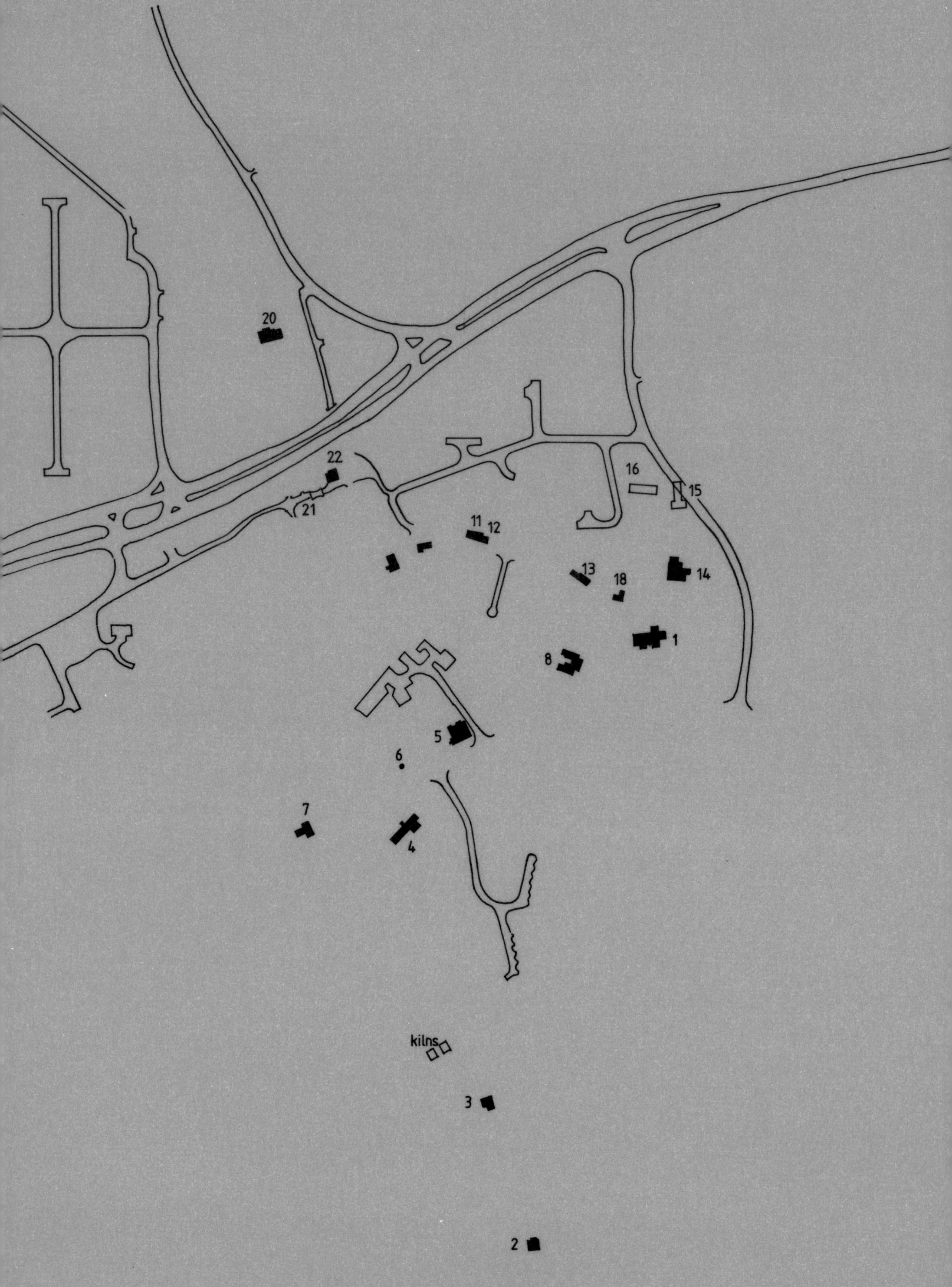

20
22
21
16
15
11
12
13
18
14
1
8
5
6
7
4
kilns
3
2

SIMPSON

SIMPSON

Simpson, Siwinestone in the C11, is the first valley village along the Ouzel north of Watling Street at Fenny Stratford. This route from Leighton Buzzard to Newport Pagnell is of at least Saxon age, and provided the main communication link between the settlements at about one mile intervals on the western side of the valley. Simpson is a parish of 1365 acres, but this included a chapelry later to become Fenny Stratford. It was enclosed by Acts of Parliament of 1763 and 1771. The manor house stood at the south-west end of the village, a seat of the De Grey and later, the Hanmer families. This was demolished in the early C19, leaving only a moat and associated ponds close to the river, to be seen today. This is a scheduled monument and has not been investigated archaeologically. In 1800 the Grand Junction canal was cut through the parish and later the Bedford Railway came. The parish was united with Woughton in 1956. The buildings of the village were, it appears, once all timber framed with thatched roofs. Many have since disappeared, five since the RCHM survey of 1911.

1 Church of St. Thomas and St. Nicholas B

Anglican parish church. C14 and C15. Limestone with odd Brickhill stone and a tiled nave roof, and slate to the chancel. Nave without aisles, transepts with a crossing tower, and chancel. A north-east vestry was demolished in C19. C13 south porch. The building is largely of the early C14 with varied Decorated style windows much repaired in 1873 and later in 1892 by J. M. Scott at the cost of £1,810, but one square-headed C15 chancel window remains, blocked in the C18. In 1710 the chancel and transepts are recorded as being ruinous. It has been suggested that a close succession of builds started with the crossing and continued with the nave, chancel and transepts. The tower is C15.

Internally, the nave has one of the finest late medieval roofs in this part of North Buckinghamshire, but was underdrawn with plaster up to the late C19. It has moulded ties, and two collar beams with long arch braces, and two tiers of hollow moulded windbraces to two purlins. It is of four bays, the end trusses against the walls are of hammer-beam form. The chancel has a painted and varnished C19 roof. There is a stoup by the south nave door with sexfoiled ogee head. The crossing arches are narrow, and of late C13 date, contrasting with the wide span of the nave. There is a large wall niche in the north transept and squint doors join both to the nave. The east nave wall has a Hanoverian Royal arms with the letters G R 2, and a flying stair of c.1904 from the upper rood-loft door to the tower ringing chamber. There are a number of interesting monuments, in the chancel, a proud obelisk wall tomb with a bas-relief roundel of weeping Justice by J. Bacon R.A., 1789, for Sir Walden Hanmer, M.P. a barrister, died 1783, and a good architectural wall monument by Bayliss, 1738 for Job Hanmer (who lived at Broughton), and his wife. Further tablets are for Edward Hanmer, 1821, with arms over, and for Arabella Hanmer, died 1828, by H. Hopper. In the nave two tablets, one to Charles Warren, builder of Simpson House, died 1872, and the other his wife, died 1841. There is also an unfixed round-headed headstone of 1638.

L1

SIMPSON ROAD (West side)

2 No. 105 NL

Cottage. c.1850. Dark red/yellow diaper brickwork with blue brick quoins. An unspoiled example of a late Victorian cottage using local materials and probably built for workmen engaged on the canal. Similar examples of the use of local brick can be found at No. 416 and No. 105, Main Street, the latter now covered over.

L2

3 No. 107 Hillcrest NL

House of late C19, with tripartite windows also unspoilt. In the garden a shed has recently been erected on old staddle stones. Close by is the site of the brickworks and a canal wharf lay in what is now the garden.

SIMPSON ROAD (East side) II

4 No. 422 and The Old Bakehouse

House of the C15–C16, remodelled and extended in the C19. Brick, with roughcast on the front and tiled roof. The central block of three bays contains the remains of an open medieval hall house, with a later back-to-back fireplace with oven and salt cupboard. The purlins and one windbrace survive in the roof, and an end collar truss. The east end of the building is probably slightly later, still timber framed, and with a C19 rear wing.

L4

SIMPSON ROAD (North side)

5 Simpson House II

House, formerly known as Simpson Villa. c.1830, built by Charles Warren. The ground floor has line rustication and an imposing central entrance of two three-panelled doors with Roman Doric half-columns in antis and an elaborate fanlight. Windows to both floors are unusual in having margin glazing at the top and bottom of the sashes only. Wide modillion eaves. The lean-to has scalloped verge board. The building was extensively refurbished about 1972.

L5

6 Gazebo to Simpson House NL

The grounds of Simpson House were famous in their day for their grottoes, rockwork, fountains and fishponds. All that survives is the gazebo or summer house, early C19. Half-octagon in plan, the walls covered with vitrified kiln waste probably from the local brick kilns, into which is inserted conch shells. Three sides have doors with architraves and a timber entablature. A seat is placed against the rear wall, and the interior has a plaster ceiling and cornice.

L6

7 Manor Farmhouse II

Farmhouse, c.1840–60. Yellow brick with tiled roof. Central six-panelled door in doorcase with a fanlight and canopy. 12-pane sash windows. Plat band and moulded timber eaves. The gable end has been treated as a dentilled pediment with redbrick lozenge decoration and the gable stacks are panelled. There is a pebbledashed earlier rear wing, with a good door and flat timber canopy.

8 Nos. 187 and 189 II

A pair of cottages, c.1840–50, of diapered brick and slate roofs, each of one bay with 16-pane sashes and doors with fanlight and canopy. No. 189 has been altered.

L7

SIMPSON VILLAGE (South side)

9 No. 203 II

Cottage of the C17. Timber framed with brick infilling and thatched roof. The original structure is of two unequal bays of framing raised on a stone sill, with much re-used timber and long tension braces. The right bay appears to have been the main living room with a service room served by a door now blocked on the left. Internally the large inglenook fireplace has been modified in recent times. It had a clasped purlin roof.

L9

10 No. 205 The Poplars II

Farmhouse. C18. English bond brickwork with tiled roof. Original six-panelled door, the top panels being glazed. One original leaded casement window, the other being replaced in the early C20. A brick over the entrance is inscribed SEAR NEWMAN 1792, whose tomb is to be seen in the churchyard. The house has an original rear wing on the right and a C19 wing on the left.

L10

SIMPSON VILLAGE (North side)

11 No. 458 II

Semi-detatched cottage, C18, English bond brickwork and thatched roof. On the elevation there is a brick inscribed R[D 1797. To the west, a timber framed and thatched barn, clad in pitched corrugated iron, and a shelter shed extends to the north forming a yard.

12 No. 456 II

Semi-detached cottage attached to right of No. 458. C16, refaced in the C19. Timber framed with brick infilling and thatched roof. The frame exposed on the end elevation has heavy curved braces and inside the house has a cruck truss against the party wall. There are only two other full cruck trusses known now in the Milton Keynes city area, one is in the priory barn at Bradwell Abbey, there dated to c.1320. It is probable that this form of construction was once much more extensive over the area in the late medieval period.

L11–12

13 No. 442 II

A thatched cottage of the C18 with casement windows and gable stacks. Wing on the left is a former two-storey cottage.

14 The Rectory

House, 1872. Perhaps by Richard Sheppard. Red brick, with yellow and red banded brick lintels and a blue and yellow brick plat band, otherwise quite plain. There are cross windows, and the main entrance has a boarded door and a wider five-light fanlight with a label mould. There is some stained glass in the upper parts of the windows. It replaced a parsonage which comprised a hall, parlour, kitchen with buttery and pantry and small stores.

L14

15 (Rectory Farm)

To the rear of the Rectory, a small farmhouse of the mid C17, timber framed with brick. It has a rear wing containing a sitting room, kitchen and scullery, remodelled in the C18. The framing had two panels to each of two storeys.

16 (Rectory Farm Barn)

Excavated after demolition in 1972, a five-bay timber framed and weatherboarded building built before 1674 when it was described in a terrier, with a central threshing floor and opposed cart doors, and a lean-to structure at the east end. It had jowled posts and angle braces to the tie beams. Two panels high and centre bressumer, it had originally been infilled with staves and wattling, but whether this was originally daubed is not known; it may well have been left open like some barns still standing in Herefordshire. Two C17 traders tokens were found on the floor, one made for a trader in Fenny Stratford. A range of cow hovels stood on the other side of the yard to the south.

17 (Manor House)

A major Manor of the De Grey's of Wilton who acquired the property by royal patent in c.1569. The C17 and C18 seat of the Walden and Hanmer families, demolished about 1810 by Charles Pinfold of Walton; the site is now only identified by earthworks including a moat and fishponds close to the river on the south side of the main road.

18 No. 436 The Forge

A pair of simple C19 cottages, whitewashed brick and slate rooofs with a central stack. The left cottage has a rear extension.

L18

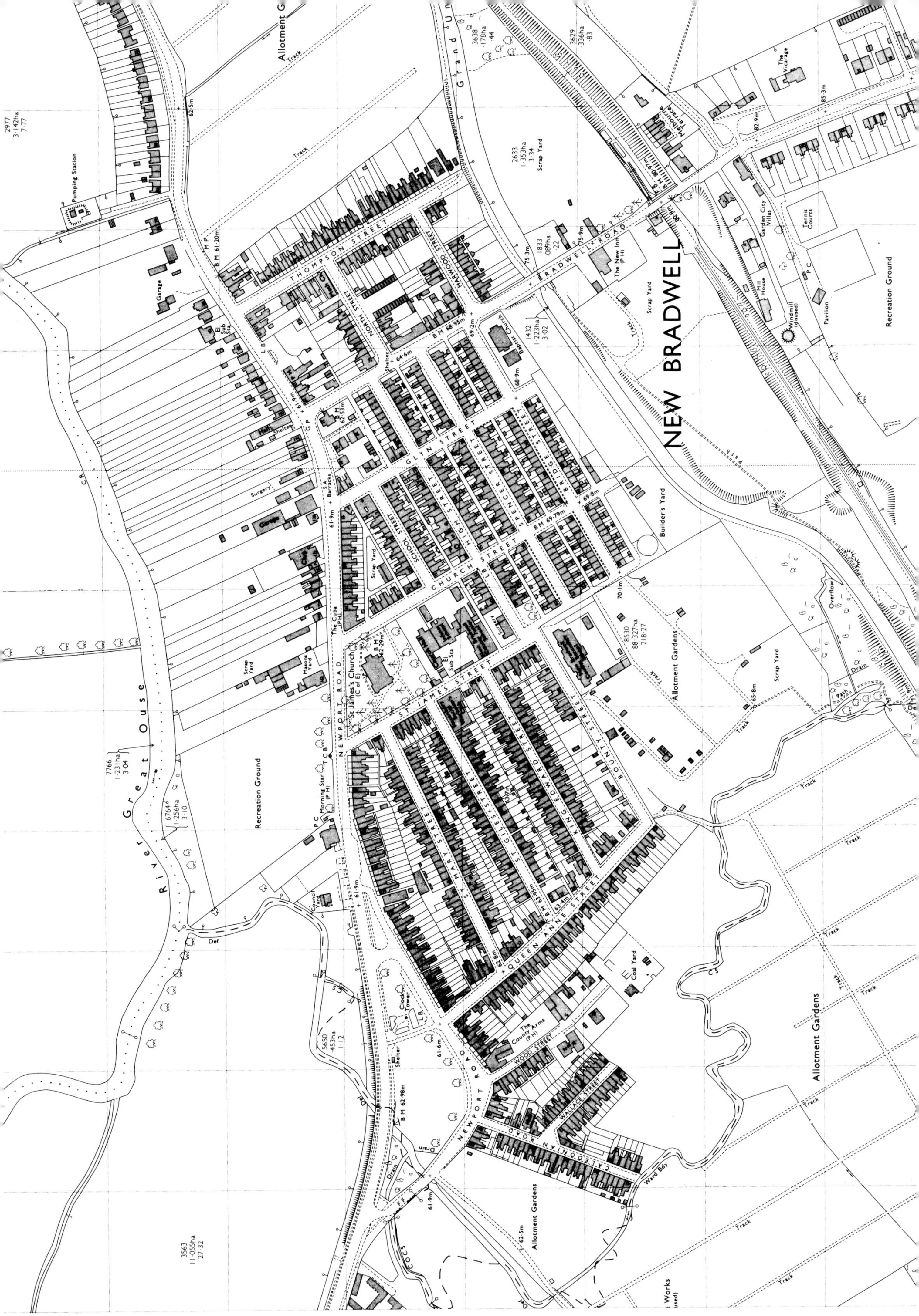
NEW BRADWELL
River Great Ouse
Recreation Ground
Allotment Gardens
Newport Road
Bradwell Road
Thompson Street
Harwood Street
North Street
Glyn Street
School Street
High Street
Spencer Street
Bridge Street
Church Street
St James Street
St James's Church (C of E)
St Mary Street
St Giles Street
King Edward Street
Bounty Street
Queen Anne Street
Wood Street
Wallace Street
Caledonian Road
Morning Star (P H)
The Cuba (P H)
The New Inn (P H)
County Arms (P H)
Clock Tower
Pumping Station
Garage
Surgery
Scrap Yard
Builder's Yard
Coal Yard
Masons Yard
Council Yard
Windmill (disused)
Mill House
Garden City Villas
Tennis Courts
Pavilion
The Vicarage
Melbourne Terrace
Baptist Church
Barracks
Overflow
Track
Grand Union Canal

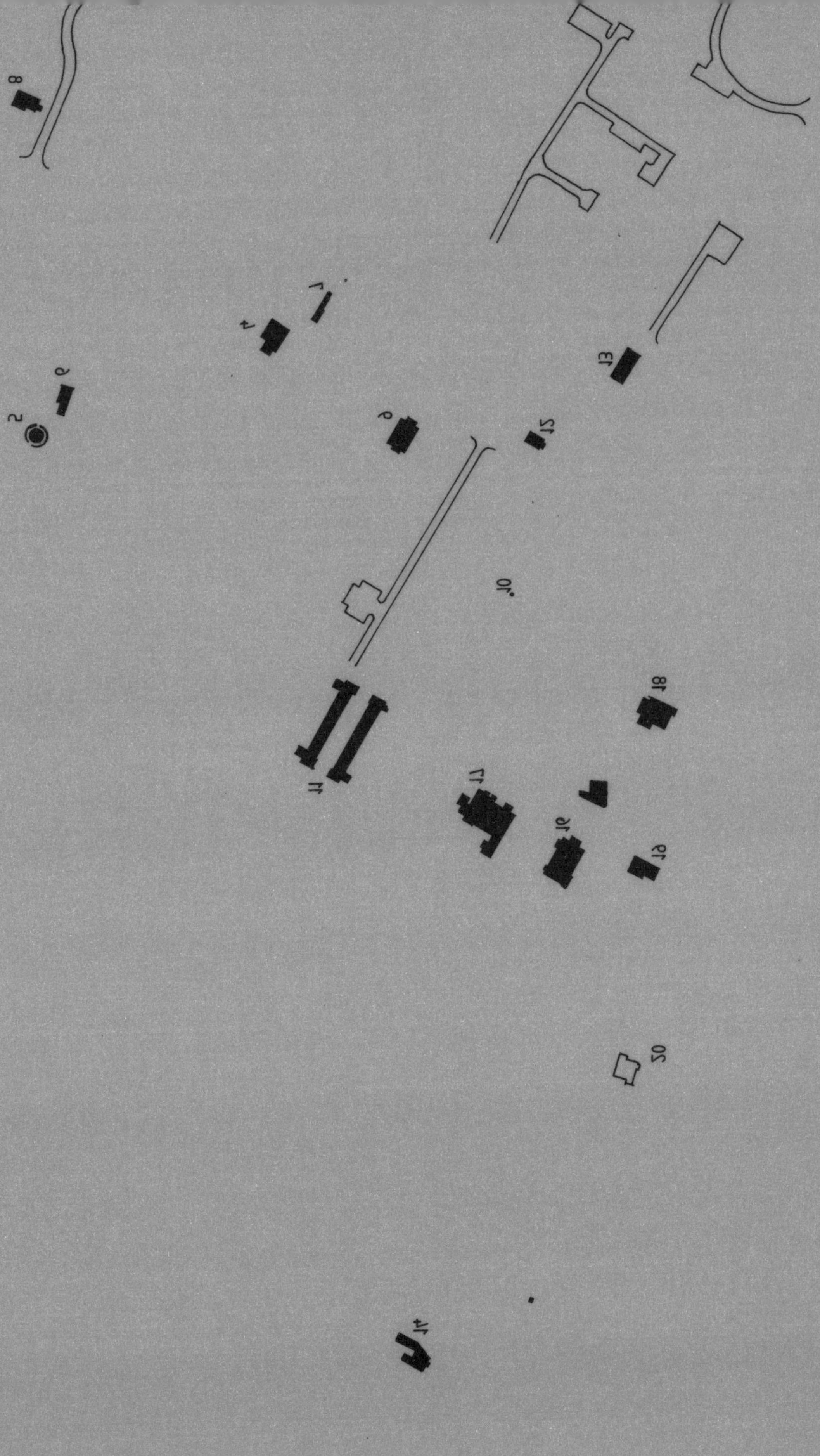

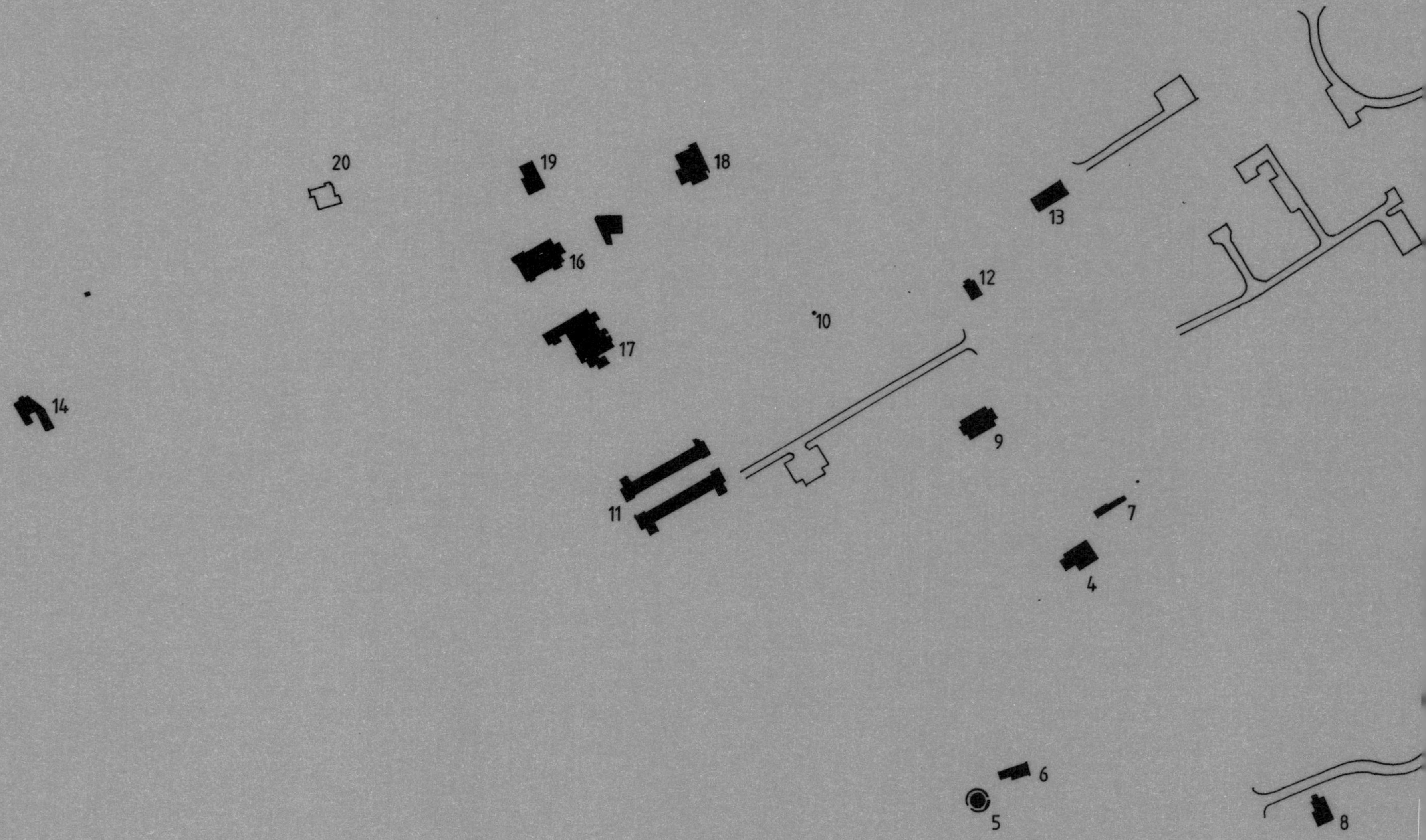

20
19
18
13
16
12
10
17
14
9
11
7
4
6
5
8

STANTONBURY and NEW BRADWELL

STANTONBURY AND NEW BRADWELL

STANTONBURY

Stantonbury is one of the medieval parishes partly included in Milton Keynes. The village of Stantonbury, situated low down by the Great Ouse became a deserted village, having been depopulated by Sir Nicholas Vaux, friend of Henry VIII, and who made arrangements for that last great occasion of medieval chivalry, the meeting of crowned heads on the Field of the Cloth of Gold. This old village, which acquired its name from the Berry or Barie family of the C13, was just outside the designated area of Milton Keynes, but is included here as it has lent its name to part of the new city. This area is known as Stanton Low as opposed to Stanton High, where there was a farm called Greaves Farm. Near Stanton Low was a large Roman courtyard villa with mosaics and scenic wall decorations and bath suites, a sumptous affair and possibly the most senior villa in the district. The C17 manor house which lay to the south-west of the church and demolished in the C18 is a rather romantic site. In 1736 there were only four farms and a few cottages in the parish; some of the people may have been engaged in the local industry of stone extraction—remains of the stone pits are still visible to the east of the church, close to the humps and bumps of the deserted village. There may have been some brickmaking in the parish or close-by in Bradwell immediately after the Civil War, possibly there specifically for the building of the Manor House. The destruction of the village remains took place in 1955–56, watched by J. K. Tull and others, who recovered the plan of a two room house. Of the little church something remains, for it stood in good condition until around 1945 but then hastily decayed until it was made redundant, following which the roof fell or was removed. It is an object lesson in how quickly a substantial building will disappear.

1 Church of St. Peter II

Held at one time by the priories of Goring and of Bradwell, this interesting little church has early C12 or even earlier origins, consisting of a short square nave and a C13 chancel and north aisle, the latter apparently demolished in the C16 when the porch was added. It had a timber clad western bell turret with a tiled roof. Its chief glory was the C12 chancel arch, which was moved to St. James', New Bradwell in the 1950's and fixed on the west wall. The west nave wall, which still stands, was a rebuild of the C15, but incorporates part of an earlier structure, a mysterious arch at low level. An underground tunnel extending in a northerly direction was discovered early in this century, and opened again in 1938. The church, which had many a fine monument, is now just a ruin. A painting of the building by John Piper is now in Aylesbury Museum.

M1

2 (Stantonbury Manor House)

This house of Sir John Wittewronge built 1662–68 lay to the south west of the church, the levelled platform still being visible. It was of brick with stone windows and had a parlour 34ft 8in by 19ft 8in. Detailed accounts of its building, and of those employed on the works, have survived and make fascinating reading. Extending eastwards, south of the church, are earthworks of the former gardens.

3 (Stantonbury Farmhouse)

A handsome farmhouse in local limestone with a tiled roof stood to the east of the church until the late 1950's when it was overtaken by gravel extraction. It was probably C17 in origin with a lobby entry plan, and developed into a three-bay two storey house in the later C18. It had timber casement windows with wood lintels and a central and one gable brick stack.

M3

NEW BRADWELL

New Bradwell was formed about 1840 from the northern end of the old parish of Bradwell and was awarded this independence as a result of the rapidly increasing population of railway workers. Until then it had been little more than a farmhouse or two along the old Newport to Stony Stratford turnpike, from where a lane branched off to Bradwell itself. The advent of the canal in 1795–1800 brought some development on this lane associated with a wharf. Stone quarrying supplying lime kilns supported a small local industry until 1843, the pits being on the east side of the road on what has since become known as the 'island', and to locals as 'Aunt Mary's', between the canal and the later railway. In 1843, having no more available land in Wolverton itself, the Railway Company commenced a scheme of housing for its employees in Bradwell, with a direct rail connection into the works, and a small station in the cutting at New Bradwell. The new development included a school, and church and is an interesting example of C19 planned urbanisation.

Away from the Railway Cottages, the first development took place on 'Corner Pin' and 'The Gravelfield' behind, later Thompson Street. Most of Newport Road and the network of streets to its south were built up in the 15 years from 1890–1905, Caledonian Road and Wallace Street being first. These houses are of a standard industrial type, with front and back rooms and a side passage with a stair. Almost every permutation of design can be found commeasurate with sound construction and economy; including the odd glazed tile in the centre of the King Edward Street houses, cogged eaves, and the occasional curiosity such as 'Barbara's' in St. Mary's Street, with its admixture of sawn stone and fruity panels. The old turnpike was later straightened in the early C20 leaving a cut-off area, since landscaped like a green and given, in 1962, the violently plain memorial clock.

BRADWELL ROAD (West side)

4 The Wharf Inn (formerly the New Inn) II

Built 1804, close to the wharf, for the refreshment of those on the canal. Local stone with a tiled roof. Three bays, double plan, and much altered and added to since. It had a cellar capable of holding 100 hogsheads and a large range of outbuildings including coke and salt houses.

M4

5 Windmill II

The only standing windmill with sails between the Chilterns and the Warwickshire/Leicestershire uplands. It was built between 1803 and 1817 by Samuel Holman, who had purchased a corner of a field called the Yawles, the attraction of this spot being, in addition to its high elevation, the proximity of the newly constructed canal wharf. It is a limestone tower, unusual outside Somerset, with a raised walk for tending the sails. The cap was originally a close fitting boarded one with external chain wheel. This, and the internal machinery was replaced or restored by the last traditional working millwright, R. Thompson & Son of Alford, Lincs. and it is now in working order. There are two pairs of stones, one pair of French Burrs and a pair of Greys (Millstone Grit), underdriven from the vertical shaft, each pair linked to separate governors. The cap contains the brake wheel and windshaft, a huge iron casting weighing some two tons. The cap is turned by hand from a chain wheel at the back, an old fashioned device even for the time it was built, the drive passing to the front of the cap through a linkage of universal joints as simple as the original invention of Robert Hooke. A sack hoist is friction driven from a rubber beneath the wallower. The sails are new, with spring shutters or shades, replacing a pair of spring sails and a pair of common sails spread with cloth. The mill had a chequered history and probably at one time had an auxilliary steam drive for when the wind failed. It ceased working about 1870–80. A guide book is available.

M5

Old stone quarries that probably supplied the walling stone for the mill lie at the bottom of the access path. They also supplied a lime kiln at the south end. Gravel was also extracted in the C19 near the canal overflow, called the 'eight arches'.

6 Mill Cottage II

House, early–mid C19 and much altered. No doubt where the miller lived. Stone with a tiled roof. It originally had a central stair hall and rooms either side but has since been opened up.

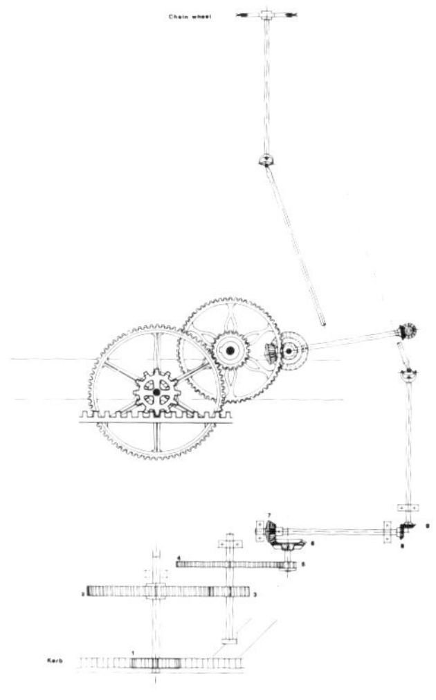

M5b

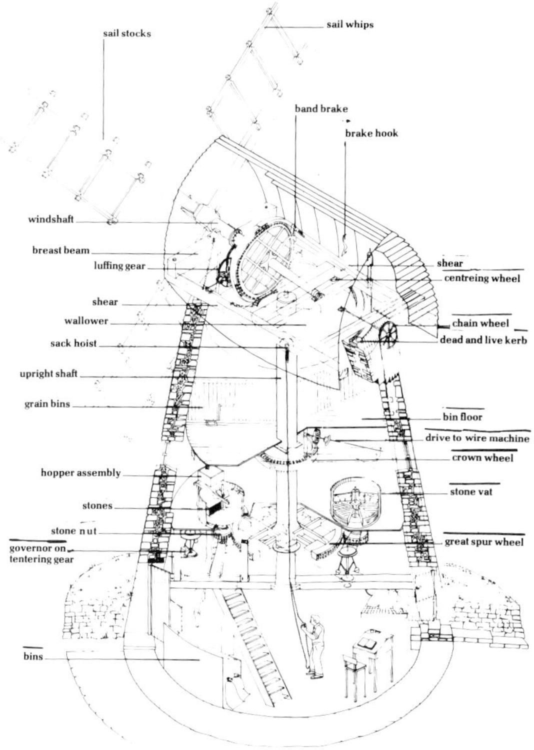

M5a

BRADWELL ROAD (East side)

7 Wharf Cottage NL

A C19 cottage built for the attendant on the wharf.

8 Old Vicarage II

Vicarage for New Bradwell St. James, by G. E. Street, 1858–60 and an important example of Street's modest domestic style suitable for Vicarages. Red brick with a mansard slate roof. The west front has a three-light stair window, and the cross wing on the south has a two-storey bay on the east. The sash windows of the main part are paired under a relieving arch and have angular heads. Attic windows appear in the peak of the gables.

M8

BRADWELL ROAD (West side)

9 The New Life Church

Baptist chapel, now an evangelical church, c.1935 in an Art Deco style with cubist glazing bars in the large windows characteristically filled with pastel coloured textured glass. It was first built with a flat roof but replaced with the pitched roof a few years later.

As with the Progressive Workmen's Club, an interesting example of a passing style of architecture poorly represented in this area.

M9

HIGH STREET (North side)

10

On the corner of Glyn Street one of the few examples remaining of the old McDowall & Steven & Co. Ltd. cast iron pillar box, c.1910–20.

HIGH STREET (South side)

11 Railway Cottages II

The development of railway housing in New Bradwell took place in two stages, following the Company's purchase of the land in 1852 to relieve the shortage in Wolverton itself. Firstly, 118 houses were built in High Street (Bradwell Road) and Spencer Street (Middle Street) in 1853, to be followed by a further 69 in the remaining part of Spencer Street and Bridge Street. The total of 188 dwellings were in yellow stock brick with red brick dressings and gauged lintels, each row of 12 to 18 terminating at either end in three-storey houses for higher grade workers, engine drivers and the like. They were probably designed by McConnell and built by J. Parnell, builder of Rugby who was to build Rugby School and Keble College, Oxford, for William Butterfield.

Three houses at the west end of High Street were demolished by a bomb in October 1940, and 164 houses were demolished c.1973. Two terraces of the first build at the west end of Spencer Street were eventually saved, to be converted and modernised in c.1976. These are a salutory example of what can be done to provide good dwellings through careful renovation and conversion.

M11

NORTH STREET

12 Baptist Chapel NL

Chapel of c.1860, now a shop. A simple building with a gabled elevation and porch, and with round headed lights. Nicely turned brick roundel appears in the gable. Pierced ridges. The schoolroom to the south with cast iron windows was probably built first. It was replaced c.1935.

THOMPSON STREET

13 Methodist Chapel NL

Primitive methodist chapel, 1865 of four bays with a modern porch, and to the rear a three-bay Sunday school in a similar style. Margin glazed windows. The building has a record of seven foundations stones.

NEWPORT ROAD (South side)

14 County Arms NL

Public house of c.1854. Three storeys with a projecting porch and painted stone details. It originally had some fine crestings. This is the part known as 'Corner Pin', presumably from the sharpness of the bend.

15 Cuba P.H. NL

Public house of c.1860, stucco, with plaster architraves to openings, round-headed on the ground floor, and segmental on the first floor.

16 Church of St. James B

Anglican church, 1858–60, by George E. Street, for the London and North Western Railway Company, the builder being J. Mills of Stratford-upon-Avon. Cosgrove Stone with Ancaster dressings. Nave with a south aisle, and chancel. Tower in the north-west corner, early Decorated style, with lancet windows. As it cost £4,430 by the time of its consecration, the upper stage of the tower and spire were omitted, and like most things postponed, was never completed. The chancel arch from St. Peter Stantonbury has been fixed against the west wall of the nave, and remains in spite of the incongruity, the outstanding example of decorated Norman architecture in Milton Keynes. It was here in 1909 that the Rev. J. N. A. Guest discoverd that the building had never been licensed for certain sacraments, including marriage, and warned his law-abiding congregation that they were living in sin and their children were illegitimate, creating such great consternation that the Home Secretary of the day had hurriedly to put matters right.

A toll house formerly stood on the bend of the road east of the church.

M16

17 Community Hall and Workshops II

Schools. 1858, by G. E. Street, now craft workshops and a community hall. The original building is of rock faced limestone with fish tailed slate roofs. A picturesque composition, consisting of a number of schoolrooms connected by a corridor, all quite generous for its time. Large chimneys, now reduced in height, and a delightful sharply pointed bellcote. Internally the schools are utilitarian, with high rooms and open trusses. The building remained a school until recent times and received extensive red brick additions on the south side early this century.

M17

NEWPORT ROAD (North side)

Due to the wetlands of the river, no development took place on this side apart from on a narrow strip close to the road itself.

18 Progressive Workmen's Club NL

A two-storey clubhouse of c.1910, with a large gable to the street, and a caretaker's house at the side. Interesting in that it is practically the only building in Milton Keynes showing an awareness of the Art Nouveau style in architecture which became fashionable for a brief period in the early years of the C20 century.

M18

19 No. 162 Leys Villa NL

House, 1904, of brick with stone details, with an ambitious and ill-proportioned door and carved panels below the windows. Attached on its east side, the monumental mason's showroom, with an overlarge pediment filled with unhappy sea monsters. The initials on the house are of the Gurney family. All splendidly individualistic.

M19

20 (Morning Star P.H.)

A brick public house of 1860, two storeys, three bays, including a large assembly room at the rear. Seriously damaged by fire and demolished c.1984 and replaced with four houses.

STONY STRATFORD
Watling Street
HIGH STREET
LONDON ROAD
CALVERTON ROAD
Calverton End
CLARENCE ROAD
WOLVERTON ROAD
VICARAGE ROAD
VICARAGE WALK
QUEEN STREET
KING STREET
KING GEORGE CRESCENT
SAINT MARY'S AVENUE
RUSSELL STREET
NEW STREET
YORK ROAD
PROSPECT ROAD
MILL LANE
HORN LANE
OXFORD STREET
SILVER STREET
CHURCH STREET
MARKET SQUARE
Horsefair Green
CORONATION ROAD
KINGSTON AVENUE
FRANKSTON AVENUE
WOODSIDE
Galley Hill
Cemetery
Allotment Gardens
Jubilee Terrace
Temperance Terrace
Franciscan Preparatory School
Stony Stratford County Primary School
Stony Stratford Methodist Church
The Baptist Church
Calverton House
Burnham House
Stratford House
York House Youth Club
Telephone Exchange
Bus Station
Warehouse
Clinic
Garage
Car Park
Caravan Park
Tennis Court
Tennis Courts
Bowling Green
Swimming Pool
Sports Ground Cottage
Pavilion
Leather Works
Foot Bridge
Weir
Path
Water
8735
73·908ha
182·65
9268
1·543ha
3·81
4342
·413ha
1·02
3745
1·880ha
4·64
3353
1·045ha
2·58
3338
·194ha
·48
3520
5·630ha
13·91
4523
·421ha
1·04
5421
·299ha
·74
5517
·340ha
·84
5707
·170ha
·42
6006
·397ha
·98
4806
·380ha
·94

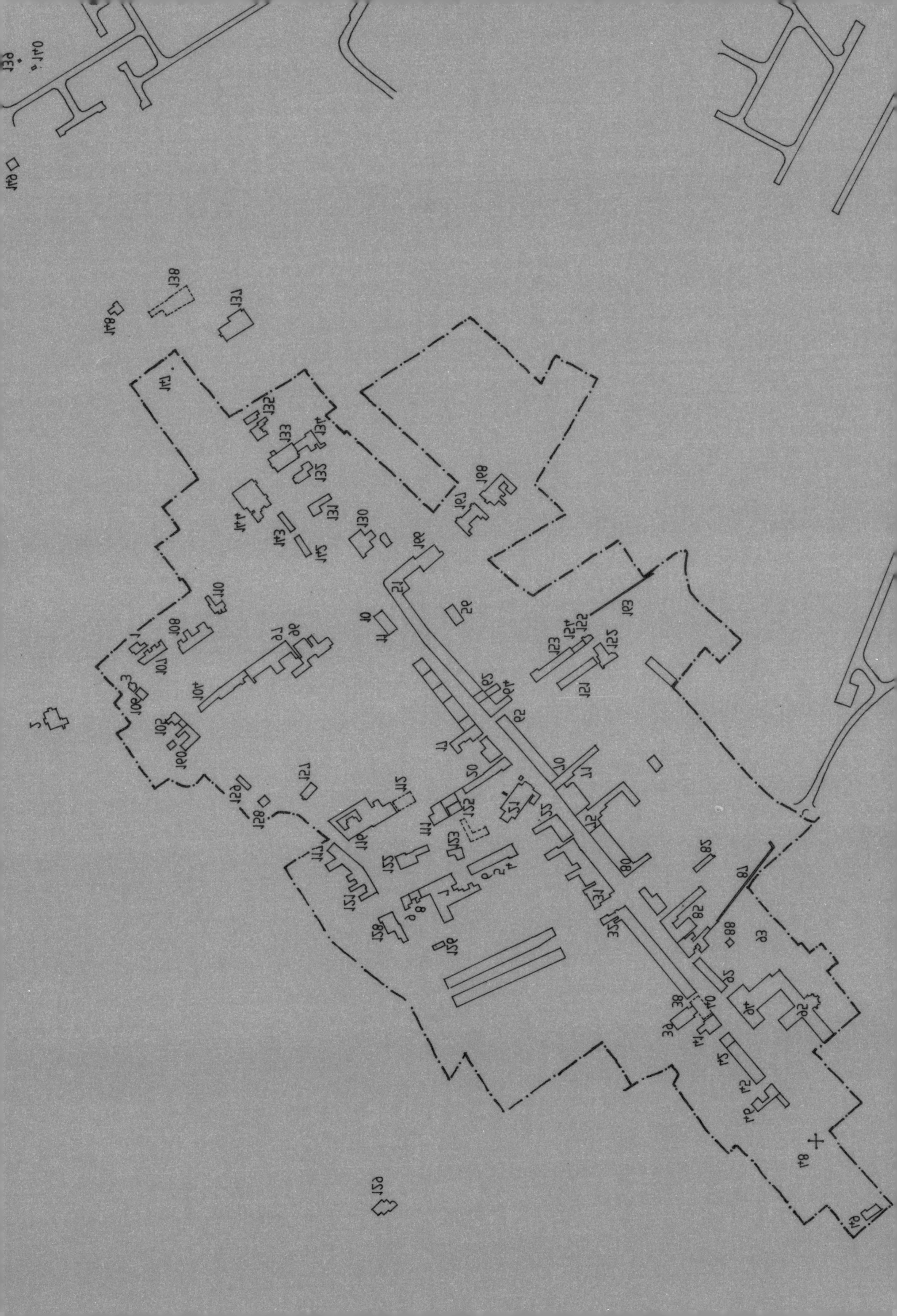

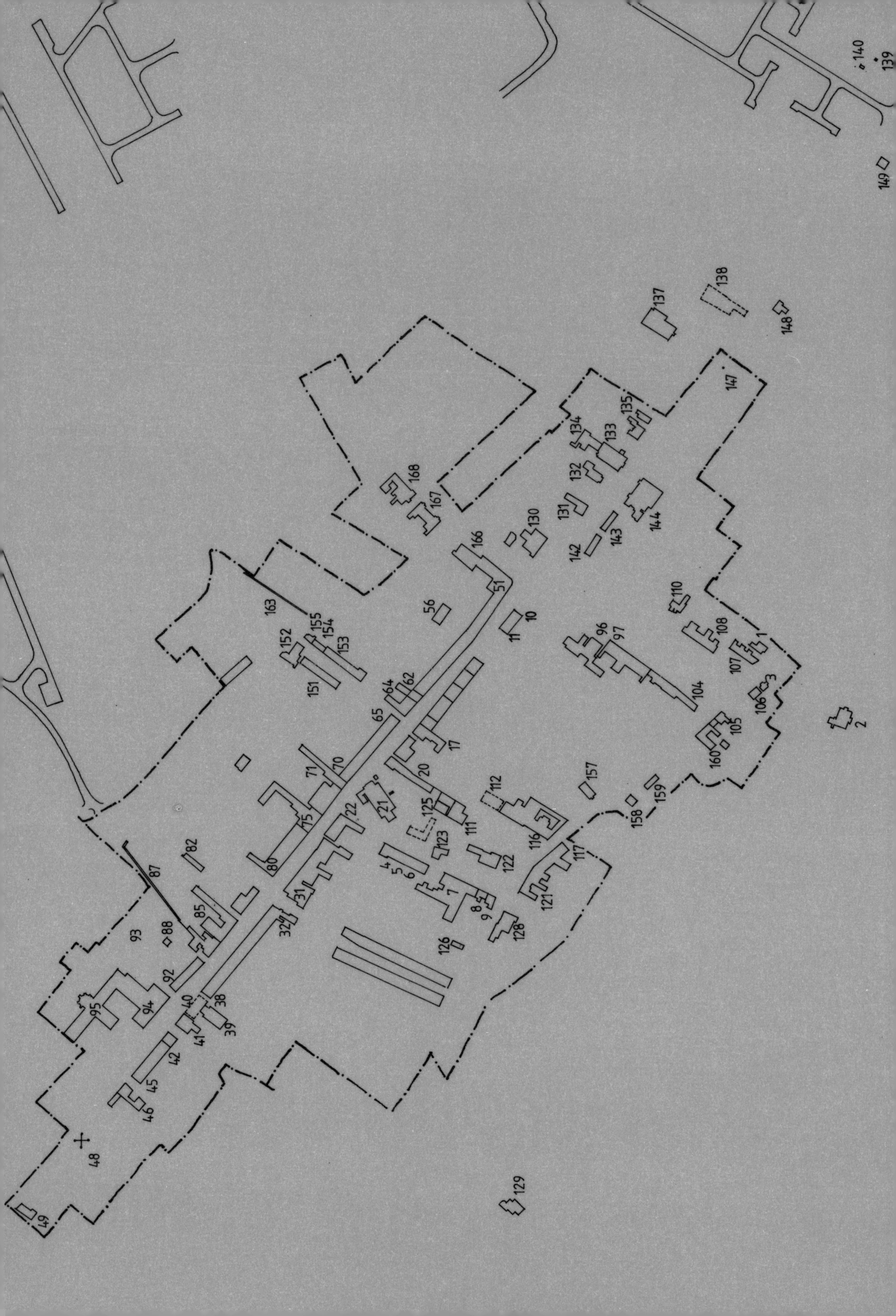
140
139
149
138
137
148
147
135
134
133
132
168
167
131
130
144
143
142
166
51
163
56
10
11
110
155
154
153
152
151
96
97
108
107
104
64
62
65
106
3
105
2
160
17
157
159
20
71
70
112
21
22
125
158
75
123
111
116
117
82
80
4
5
6
122
87
1
121
31
8
9
128
85
32
88
93
126
92
40
38
95
94
39
41
42
45
46
48
129
49

STONY STRATFORD

STONY STRATFORD

Stony Stratford has by far the greatest concentration of historic buildings in Milton Keynes. Its origins are obscure. Across the River Ouse in Northamptonshire there is Old Stratford, and here evidence for Roman occupation has frequently been found in the sand quarries. This is higher land, and as it is equidistant between two known Roman posting stations: it is most probable that some arrangement for changing horse would be available, particularly that this is the first large river to cross on Watling Street, north of the Thames. Significantly, the well-known hoard of temple trappings with dedications to Jupiter and Vulcan were found nearby. Such temples were frequently to be found at river crossings and boundaries of native territories. Being on rather higher well-drained land, this location would have been attractive for settlement. Stony Stratford first appears in the records with the foundation of a market in 1194. A market at this position where travellers were likely to be held up crossing the Ouse marshes is most probable. Significantly, the High Street widens on the spit of gravel extending towards the river suggesting an early street market, but this no doubt would be inconvenient, and we see evidence of a planned town layout in the Market Square area, discussed below. When this took place cannot yet be said, but there is no doubt we have a flourishing if small community present in the roadside ends of the old parishes of Calverton and Wolverton in the medieval period. There are records of many kings of England passing through in the medieval period, and repeated on the famous occasion of the abduction of the boy king Edward V from under the noses of the Woodville's of Grafton Regis nearby.

With the mid C17 came coaches running on staged routes at economical prices. This brought very many more people through the town, which was a convenient half to one day's journey from London, thus a place to stop and eat and stay the night. This led to a boom in catering establishments and all that went with them, and the heavy use the old Watling Street was getting eventually led to the first turnpike in England being made between Hockcliffe and Stony Stratford, and commented upon with interest by Daniel Defoe c.1725.

The C17 has left much more documentary evidence, and some buildings have survived from that time hidden under later alterations. Twelve local traders issued their own token currency in the period 1657–68, more than anywhere else in Buckinghamshire except Wycombe, indicating the importance of commerce to the town. Stony Stratford suffered a series of devastating fires in 1703, 1725, 1736 and 1742, and many minor ones. In these fires the timber framed and thatched buildings were particularly vulnerable; in 1742, 146 houses and a church were destroyed, and blazing thatch fell as far away as Old Stratford. The town that survives today is basically a town built of the local poor quality limestone, faced up from the C18 onwards in locally made brick. Celia Fiennes notes in 1697 that it is a modest stone built town where everyone appears to sit outside their houses making lace. This they continued to do in Silver Street and elsewhere up to the First World War, it being an important cottage industry. The stone quarries were all around, particularly on the Beachampton Road, and near the village of Cosgrove where they can still be seen. Bricks were made to the south of the town where clay was available, up to the mid C19, by the builders themselves, George Wilkinson, Thomas Freeman and Alfred Hailey being registered as brickmakers as well as builders. From the mid C19 the town expanded considerably to house workers from the Railway Works at Wolverton, and many new roads and back development remains from the later decades of that century.

STONY STRATFORD

Calverton Road

Development took place along Calverton Road only after c.1860. The east side was developed as far as Augustus Road by 1906, and extended in the early 1930's. The west side did not commence until the latter date.

1. No. 1 **NL**

House, c.1860, for William Hillyer, built by Cowley. Brick with small limestone rubble facades. Hood moulds to the sash windows. A bay window was added on the south side for Mr. W. J. Crisp, by E. Swinfen Harris in 1896.

N1

2 Calverton House **NL**

Vicarage, now flats. 1852, for the Rev. Christie. Yellow brick with moulded string, now partly rendered. Exaggerated overhanging gables to porch and roofs.

3 Lodge for Calverton House **NL**

Lodge in a mid-Victorian cottage-orne style. Stone, gabled, with timber windows. There were originally two.

CHURCH STREET

Church Street probably formed the northern side of the early medieval Market Square planned layout. By the C17 there had been building on the south side within the Square, but this never became very substantial and has largely disappeared. The fire of 1736 destroyed 53 houses, most of which seem to have been in Church Street, thus the present buildings are a rebuild, or new buildings built in the mid C18 or later. Some have been replaced in recent times.

N2

4 No. 14 **II**

House, mid C18. Brick with a tiled roof. Three bays. Central six-panelled door in a pedimented doorcase. C19 large paned sash windows replacing the C18 windows in the same openings. Stone wedge lintels with raised keys to the ground floor. Dentilled eaves and gable stacks. One dormer.

5 No. 16 **NL**

C18 house totally refurbished in the C19. Painted brick and modern tiled roof. The fascia over the door extends over where a shop window was located on the left.

Nos. 18, 20 and 22 have little historic value as buildings but contribute greatly to the group. No. 18, is early C19, and is listed, No. 20, late C19, and No. 22, of the c.1960's.

N4–6

6 No. 24 **II**

C18 house, painted brick with a tiled roof. Three bays including a former carriage entrance on the right. Six-panelled door and C19 sash windows. One dormer.

7 No. 36 (Sharp & Woollard) II

An interesting wide frontage, probably originally two symmetrical houses built in the early C19. Stone, rendered to ground floor and brick facade above.

A four-bay entrance formed with pilasters and cornice, both end bays slightly setting forward, only one now with a door. The pediment over has narrow tryglyphs. Sixteen-pane sashes with rendered wedge lintels and slightly raised keys. Paired modillion eaves. To the rear a currier's factory, built c.1880, two storeys. seven bays with weatherboarded openings along the top for ventilation. Prior to this it appears that it was a manufactory for lace accessories. Sharp & Woollard are the oldest manufacturing firm in the town, the Woollard family supplying a host of prominent citizens in the C19.

N7–8–9

8 No. 38 II

House, C18. Brick and timber framing, perhaps part surviving from before the fire. Two storeys and attic, two bays. Central early C19 door of six panels within a canopy and reeded doorcase. Sixteen-pane sashes but a canted bay on the left. Two dormers and an C18 brick stack, heightened when the adjacent property was built. It has a C19 rear wing.

9 No. 40 II

An C18 brick house, two storeys, two bays. Central part-glazed door in an open pediment. The C18 windows were altered in the early C19 and are now 16-pane sashes with segmental headed openings. In the centre is a wooden sundial with three knobs, dated April 17, 1739, the maker's initials being H.A. It has an inscription W(illiam) M(ead) TEMPUS ET IGNIS OMNIA PERDUNT, a sad commentary on the fires. An overlarge bay window has been added in the late C19. C19 rear wing.

HIGH STREET

N10

10 No. 5 II

Shop with dwelling over, 1881–3, by E. Swinfen Harris. An imposing structure in brick with timber framed third floor, the framing infilled with brickwork, alternate panels rendered and having impressed sunflowers, a motif favoured by the Aesthetic Movement. The gable ironwork favoured by this architect bore the initials WRW and has recently been taken down from the main gable and should be put back. These were probably the initials of W. Watson, a master carpenter.

11 No. 7 II

Two shops with a dwelling, now offices, over. c.1840–60. Red brick with gauged red brick arches to 16-pane sashes.

N12

12 No. 23 II

A C17 building, timber framed with stone gables, rendered and with quoins to the front. The only example of exposed timber framing in Stony Stratford. The building is of two bays with chamfered spine beam and fire place at each end on the ground floor. To the rear is a bakery.

13 No. 25 II

A stone building with an C18 brick facade using blue bricks in header bond between red window dressings. Six bays of sash windows with a Tuscan doorcase in the fourth bay. The interior was refurbished in the early C19 with a stair well and stair, probably contemporary with the parallel rear block. Adjoining to the left is an extension of C19 over a carriageway to the rear. This was the first garage and petrol station in Stony Stratford. This extension is not listed.

N13

14 Nos. 27, 29 and 31 II

The Furniture Centre is a late C19 stone building with gables, built on to an C18 brick building (No. 27) with sash windows and a dormer. On the front is a Sun Insurance plate. Listing refers to No. 27 only.

15 No. 33 NL

Shop with flat over, having carriage access to the side. The facade is of the late C19. Frederick Ancell, builder and local benefactor, lived here.

16 No. 39 and 41 II

The ironmongers shop incorporates three buildings, the most northerly being of two bays, C17 or earlier, timber framed with a rendered facade. The upper floor has been raised and the partitions still have some wattle and daub infilling.

This building and the Old George have together a picturesque collection of stacks in hand made clay tile roofs.

The main building is a mid C19 rebuild to the front of two earlier properties of which little survives.

17 The Old George II

A C17 three-bay building probably originally of stone rendered to the front. The elevation has interesting C18 two-storey sashed bays with triglyph frieze and cornice. It has a stone rear wing which has been subsequently raised to two storeys. Internally there is a large fireplace now blocked. The low floor level indicates antiquity and this is probably the George, a hostelry mentioned in 1609.

18 No. 43 II

A late C17–early C18 three-bay shop with side carriage entrance. Rendering over stone. C18 sash windows and attic dormer to the rear. Interesting plan, with a rear range of buildings.

19 No. 45 II

This C19 building has a Britannia Fire Insurance mark.

20 The White Horse P.H. II

This hostelry first recorded as belonging to a guild in the early C16 originally continued to the churchyard. It had the right of common pasture in Calverton. The present building is largely C18, of stone, rendered to the front and has a central carriageway tall enough to accommodate stage coaches. The carriageway is closed by good C18 fielded and panelled doors. Tripartite 12-pane sash windows. The rear a long range formerly with stables and ostlers accommodation.

N16

N17

N20

21 Church of St. Mary and St. Giles **B**

Anglican parish church, originally a chapelry of Calverton. Of the medieval church only the tower survived the fire of 1743, a C15 structure of four stages with a west door. The medieval church had a chapel built before 1500, later to become the chapel of St. Catherine in which the Rookys monuments were located. The nave already had galleries in 1640. Most of this building was then destroyed in the Great Fire of 1742 and after some years of fund raising, was rebuilt by David Hiorne, the chancel being completed by 1757 and the remainder by 1776–7. The fine Gothic polygonal apse with its curious tracery may be of later date. This was replaced in 1928 for road widening by the present short square apse by C. Hare. The C18 structure has a nave of five bays with tall clustered wooden columns bringing the aisles to equal height like a German hall church. It has a wooden vault throughout and galleries on similar smaller columns, the galleries having once reached the east end. Hiorne's larger church of Tetbury, Gloucestershire has many points of similarity. He also extended the merlons of the tower parapet to give the church its characteristic profile. The windows were later replaced in heavy stonework by G. E. Street in 1876. The font is C19 and the pulpit preserves marks of the latest fire, in 1964, after which the church was redecorated by P. Foster. Below the gallery is a series of small windows with glass probably by Powell, commemorating the parents of local architect, E. Swinfen Harris, who added the Chapel of the Blessed Sacrement and the vestry in 1892.

In the churchyard the handsome lychgate is of 1931 and a large chest tomb of 1849, to Alfred Hailey, the builder.

NL

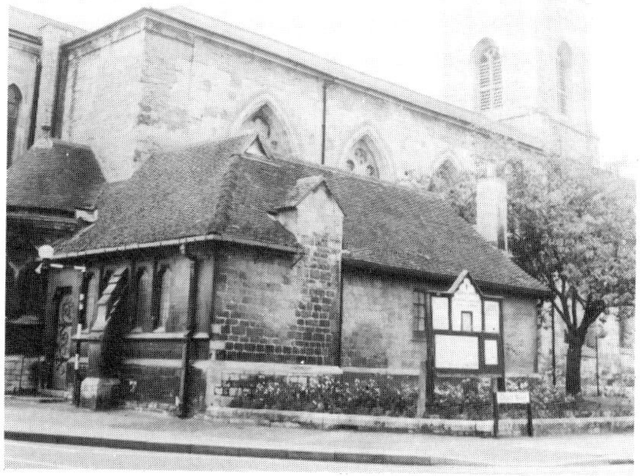

N21

N21a

22 No. 59 (Frazers) **II**

House. C18, rebuilt 1820–40. Brick, rendered to the High Street. Panelled soffite to the eaves. A wide reeded doorcase with canopy gives access from Church Street.

23 No. 61 (W. F. Taylor, Jeweller) **II**

House of C17 or C18 with an C18 gabled facade. Two storeys and attic. A good C19 shop front with pilastered side doors. Round headed sash window to the attic. The curved gable to the street with central feature is a Dutch form not found elsewhere in the area.

N23

24 No. 63 **II**

A shop premises similar to No. 65, probably built a little earlier.

25 No. 65 **II**

Building of c.1880, one bay wide. Bay window on first floor.

26 No. 67, Lloyds Bank **II**

Bank and offices. 1887, on the site of Oliver & York's Bank of 1843. Red brick with terracotta details. Moulded arched door and stone heads to windows in shallow bays. The bank was founded in 1820 in an C17–C18 house of two storeys and attics, and had a columned portico over the pavement.

N27

27 No. 69 **II**

House, Stone, C19 facade over C17 structure with high pitched gabled rear wing. Central six-panel door with tall canopied doorcase. Four-pane sashes but with tripartite sashes to the ground floor, that to the left with a rusticated fascia and cornice.

28 No. 71 (J. S. Cowley) **II**

Shop and dwelling. C18 with a C19 facade, two bays, with C19 arcaded shopfront and margin glazed central doors.

N28

29 No. 73 (Cox and Robinson and Hazeldine) II

Two shops with flat over. Early C19. A stuccoed facade with 16-pane sashes and good shopfronts at ground level.

30 No. 75 (Cox and Robinson) II*

House and chemist's shop. Early C19 facade. Two bays. A strikingly good shopfront with pilasters the lobby to the shop and house entrance. Six-panel carved door. The house has a delightful bay window with concealed sliding shutters. Keystones and wedge lintels to the upper windows. The interior is an unusually fine specimen of a C18–C19 apothecary's shop complete with much contemporary glassware and fittings.

N30

31 No. 77, Conservative Club II

House. Late C18. Formerly York House school. Rendered four-bay facade of two storeys with attic. Six-panel door with fluted case and carved bracketed canopy. Keystones to the C19 plate glass windows, plat band and dentilled eaves. The building has an extensive rear dwelling, c.1890, possibly an unrecorded work of E. S. Harris. A recent rear extension covers the bay window at the rear.

32 No. 79 II

House, now solicitor's offices. Brick with a rendered facade of 1830–50 with drawn ashlar, palmette moulded fascias and modillion eaves.

N32

33 Nos. 81 and 83 II

Formerly the Talbot Inn, now two shops. Originally a timber framed building of the C15–C16. Four bays with a former open fire bay at the north end, and originally extending beyond where No. 79 now stands. It has a two-bay rear wing, probably of slightly earlier date, the framing between the end stone wall replaced in brick in the C18. The stone of the gable has initials TW and EH, and a date 1696. The front roof has wattle and daub partitions and double purlins. The front was rebuilt in brick in the early C19, and later the open side passage was built over and the fine round-headed door added. Excluding churches, this is the oldest building in the town.

34 Fox and Hounds P.H. II

A two bay house, probably of the C18 but much remodelled in the C20. A Fox and Hounds is recorded in 1690 which may have been on the same site.

35 Nos. 89 and 91 II

A pair of timber framed houses of the C17 or early C18, refronted in the later C19 with Gothic style windows. Two attic dormers appear behind the parapet.

N35

36 Nos. 93 and 93A II

A rendered facade of the early C19 over an C18 structure. No. 93 has a good Victorian shopfront.

37 No. 97 and 95, The Cross Keys II

Now offices and bank, this building retains the earliest externally visible feature in the town, the late medieval moulded frame to the carriage opening. It now has 16-pane sashes to the upper floor and a shop window with intersecting glazing bars at ground level. The interior has much exposed timber framing, some of it of the C16, and chamfered spine beams. Some rafters in the front roof are carved Elizabethan work re-used in this position. The building became the Cross Keys Inn (the badge of St. Peter).

N37

38 No. 103 II

House. Late C17–C18 with an early C19 symmetrical facade. 20-pane sashes on the ground floor. Door with six reeded panels and flat canopy. The building housed one of the last dame schools in the town, and was extensively renovated in 1982–3.

The garden wall on its north west side is also listed. II

39 Church of St. Mary Magdalen NL

Roman Catholic church and presbytery to the rear, 1957–8 by Deakin & Laing. Pleasing interior.

40 (St. Oswald's House)

The church is on the site of St. Oswald's House, an imposing C18 house of seven bays, three storeys, the window with moulded architraves and classical entrance. Its demolition was a great loss to the town and included a famous mulberry tree. It was occupied by Surgeon-General W. H. Bull, the eminent local doctor.

N40

41 No. 107, Rothenburg House II

House, 1892, by Edward Swinfen Harris as his own dwelling, incorporating the gable of the C18 cottages on the site. Harris was a local architect with a practice in London, and favoured the domestic revival style evolved by contemporaries, E. W. Godwin, Philip Webb and others, many of whom he knew. The house was built in his mature years after his travels in Europe where he had sketched and absorbed details from Germany (Rothenburg) and elsewhere. The interior has a balcony over an open hall, and numerous inscriptions, the one over the door NISI DOMINUS being the opening words of Psalm 127 'Except the Lord build the house, they labour in vain that buildith it'. The black streaks under the windows are tar resulting from the 1900 local elections when Harris stood as the Liberal candidate, and Tory feelings ran high.

N41

HIGH STREET (South west side)

42 No. 119 II

This building of the C18 has a brick dated 1775 or 1776 and internally some timber framing, presumably surviving from an earlier building on the site.

43 No. 117 II

An C18 house of two storeys and attic, the facade much altered.

44 Nos. 119 and 121 II

Built as one building, C17 with a facade of the late C18 or early C19. Stuccoed with end quoins and rendered keyed lintels. No. 119 attemps to be symmetrical but has a later bay window. The facade conceals a C17 structure internally, with attics and dormer window.

It was at one time a bakery, and has a fine timber roofed outbuilding recently converted to a dining hall.

N44

45 Nos. 125 and 127 II

A modest two-bay house of the late C18 with an original door, canted bay and dentilled eaves, and one dormer in the roof.

46 No. 131, The Rising Sun II

A stone building with a brick front. Early C18. Two storeys and attic, five bays with a panelled door and modest canopy, and a venetian window over. The building has a plat band and cogged eaves, and at ground level, a later bay window. Unusually the roof is of gambrel form to allow more headroom in the attics, now with two gabled

N46

dormers. The two ground floor sash windows have heavy glazing bars, the upper windows being later. The house retains a stable range and a stone carriage house at the end of the yard. It later became the Rising Sun public house and was favoured by the local Irish community until closure in c.1974.

47 No. 135, Coventry House II

A brick pair of cottages built in the late C18, now one house. Each was of two bays. The raised gable verge suggests it may have been thatched.

48 No. 157, Site of the Eleanor Cross

In front of No. 157 stood, so it is claimed, the famous Eleanor Cross. These crosses of which there were 13, were erected in 1296, wherever the bier of the Queen Eleanor of Castille rested on its journey from Harby in Lincolnshire to London. Four still survive, at Lincoln (fragmentary), at Geddington and Hardingstone in Northants, and at Waltham Cross, Essex. They are of two types, the accounts having entries such as that of £63.13.4d paid to John of Battle, but without an entry to pay for effigies, suggesting that the Stony Stratford cross was of the simpler type, perhaps like Geddington. The location has been disputed, but Browne Willis records that he was informed that foundations were visible near the Horseshoes Inn in the early C18. The precise location of this inn cannot be confirmed. The Cross was probably destroyed as an idolatrous monument during the Civil War. A plaque commemorating the Eleanor Cross can be seen over the archway.

49 No. 185, formerly the Barley Mow Inn NL

Probably built as a hostelry in the C18, now mostly early C19, having the public rooms against Watling Street and the three-bay house facing oncoming travellers. The local stone was originally rendered with plaster surrounds to windows and end pilasters. It still has a good six-panel door. Deeds of the site extend back to the mid C18. It may be the site of the White Horse Inn granted by Queen Elizabeth I to Christopher Carne in 1584. The field to the rear is the Town Close, from long ago the town's public open space, with a bathing station on the Ouse at the bottom.

N49

Between the former Angel and the Rising Sun the buildings are all later C19 infilling partly replaced in the present century, Nos. 169 and 171 being the earlier with its 16-pane sash windows.

Temperance Terrace, a late C19 yard development of 1892 has, at the end, two cottages added shortly after. These have red and blue brick details with impressed sunflower patterns fashionable some 10 years earlier.

50 Ouse Bridge NL

A handsome bridge of 1834–5. Millstone grit. Three shallow arches on two piers with rounded cutwaters, the stonework rusticated and having a dentilled cornice below the parapet. The bridge is last in a long line of attempts to make a safe crossing of the Ouse, the first major river crossing north of London. The Romans probably bridged it hereabouts, but evidence for this has yet to be found. The wide valley was a notorious quagmire and when the water was high, several delays might be experienced, thus the early need for accommodation nearby. The medieval bridge appears to have had a chapel of St. James near the north end. The C18 bridge was of three arches with two side culverts; this collapsed on a notorious night in early 1835, under the heavy load of vehicles carrying plate glass making machinery, after which the present bridge with its long causeway was built, including, near the centre, a toll gate and keeper's cottage. This was abandoned in 1857.

N50

HIGH STREET (North east side)

51 Public Hall II

British School, now public hall and dance studio. 1844. Yellow brick probably from Fenny Stratford, extended in red brick to round the corner. Girls and boys entrances at opposite ends with multi-paned fanlights and arched narrow first floor windows. In the early C20 it had a canopy around the corner as a shelter for the tramway passengers.

N55

52 No. 2 II

Shop with dwelling over. c.1840–60. Brick with first floor bay windows and paired modillion eaves. Late C19 glazed tiles to side entrance. Pleasant shop front with blind box.

53 Nos. 4, 6 and 8 II

A brick building of the early–mid C19, now with modern shopfronts. Listed for their value as part of a group.

N56

54 No. 10 and 12 II

C18, refronted 1872. Windows with elliptical arches on first floor. Outbuildings at the rear of brick with some timber framing. Formerly The Gate Inn.

55 Nos. 14 and 16 NL

Two shops separated by wide entry to The Retreat. 1892, for F. W. Woollard. Stone with brick dressings. Long modillion canopy and first floor gabled bays. Varied ceramic finials and arcaded ridge to roof. The building has nearly symmetrical rear wings in English bond, and sash windows throughout.

56 The Retreat II

Four almshouses, 1892. Brick and stone with three cogged gables and ventilated openings. Casement windows, the panes diminishing to the top. Gable stack with very tall pot and the centre gable has a ceramic finial.

In the wall to the right, two stone fireplace lintels of C16 and a small ogee headed light, all recovered from the former guildhouse of St. Mary which stood on this site. II

N57

57 No. 18 II

Shop, now house. C18. Two-storey, two bays with tripartite sashes and central door.

58 Nos. 22 and 24 II

Two shops. C18 or early C19. Stucco on stone. Three bays with panelled door and fanlight in a fluted Ionic doorcase. Four-pane sashes. No. 22 is probably an extension of one bay to No. 24, the latter incorporating earlier work.

N59

59 Nos. 26 and 28, Rose and Crown P.H. II

House, formerly the Rose and Crown Inn. C16 or earlier. Stucco on stone. Two-storey, four bays. No. 28 has a four-panel door and shop window linked under a common canopy. Various small paned windows. Interior has, on first floor a later C16 stone fireplace with moulded jambs and head. This building is said to be where, in 1483, Richard, Duke of Gloucester, later Richard III, apprehended the boy king, Edward V, and his brother the Duke of York and carried them hence to the Tower of London and their eventual demise. During alterations in the early C20 an Elizabethan grisaille wallpainting was discovered on the upper floor.

60 No. 30 **NL**

Here stood the National School, built 1819 and extended in 1858. The present building is late C19, rather surprisingly.

61 No. 36 **II**

House, now shop. C18. Brick. Two-storey and attic with first floor 12-pane sashes and a hipped dormer. Two-bay rear extension of the C19. Stone stack. This was once the Vicarage House and was where E. Swinfen Harris the local architect was born in 1841.

N61

62 The Swan P.H. **NL**

The present public house was built in 1915 on the site of the former Swan Inn. The Swan yard to the rear was once the notorious Ram Alley, redeveloped with a terrace of six brick cottages in 1864. The yard still retains some stone walls.

63 Nos. 38 and 38A **II**

Shop and dwelling, now offices. C18, refronted early C19 diaper brick. Three storeys. Late C19 shop front with tall cast iron columns. The four-pane sash windows have keystones, the top centre window blocked. To the rear, a large C18 two-storey range.

64 No. 40 **II**

A small shop of the C19 tucked in against the side of New Street.

65 Nos. 42, 44 and 46 **II**

Two shops, late C17 or C18 brick, two storey and attic. Refronted C18. C18 sashes in later boxes. One hipped dormer on No. 42, a small dormer was unfortunately removed from 44–46, which was probably built as one house.

66 No. 48 **II***

House. C17, the front block rebuilt in the late C17 or early C18. Stone with stone quoins and plat band. Two-storeys, cellar and attic, four window bays. The entrance up steps, is a four-panelled door in panelled doorcase and has a very fine shell canopy. Eighteen-pane sash windows with moulded surrounds. Heavy dentilled eaves and two gabled dormers. The interior has excellent panelled rooms and a fine dog-leg stair rising from the stair hall, and having inlaid wood quarter landings. To the rear is the C17 timber-framed wing with central spine beam and leaded windows, and stone outbuildings. To the front area, cast iron railings, rising to the entrance.

N66

67 No. 50 **II**

Restaurant and dwelling. Late C18–early C19. Stucco on brick, three-storeys. Good shop front with a doorcase having a stepped keystone bearing the number, and flanking pilasters. 12- and 16-pane sashes and moulded modillion eaves. In an outbuilding there is a deep well, now covered over. Wells were in common use throughout the town until after 1900, when the water supply and sewerage disposal system was improved after a series of outbreaks of typhoid. London Road relied on wells up to the 1930s.

68 No. 52 II

Shop and dwelling. Late C18–early C19. Three-storeys, four- and nine-pane sashes and a moulded modillion eaves.

69 No. 58 II

Shop, early C19 refronting of an earlier building. Two storeys, with a canted bay on the first floor, and particularly fine cast iron railings.

70 No. 62 II

Shop. Mid C19. Three-storeys. It has a good shopfront with elongated pilasters and large fanlights. Cast iron railings of two types are set over the fascia. Canted central bay on the first floor. To its right, No. 60 demolished in the late 1960s, was one of the oldest buildings in the town.

71 No. 64, Bull Hotel II*

An important hostelry of the early C19. Brick, of five bays with a cobbled carriageway through the second bay, and a symmetrical elevation to the right. Central panelled doors in doorcase with three-quarter Tuscan columns and a wide spreading cornice. Sash windows with keyed wedge lintels and moulded timber eaves. Sash windows, tripartite at the ends of the first floor. On the front of the building is the magnificent wrought iron bracket carrying the inn sign, probably made in the early C19 using all the frills of traditional blacksmithing. The building replaces an C18 structure, the present entrance being in the carriage entrance.

The building has a tall two-storey rear wing, partly of stone, formerly the carriage house and stables. It has a Norwich Union fire mark. II

Clare Stables, also to the rear, is a stone structure rebuilt in the C19. It has a lunette window over a large opening to the yard.

The large building to the rear was the bus garage for the Eastern National Bus Company.

N71

72 No. 66 II

Shop and dwelling. Mid C19. Three-bays, three storeys with keyed stone wedge lintels and billet moulded eaves. In the centre a six-panelled door in a heavy doorcase.

73 No. 68 II

Shop and offices. Mid C19. Rendered stone with a C19 shopfront, extended as a pilastered front over panelled doors. Plate sash windows to the first floor, with moulded surrounds and cornices. Long two-storey range to the rear of diaper brick, extended a further two bays in stone. Garden wall of stone faced in rat-trap bond, an economic way of laying bricks unusual in this area.

74 Nos. 70 and 70A

An early C19 two-storey pebbledashed building with five pilasters to the shopfront and two panelled doors.

75 Nos. 72 and 74, Cock Hotel II*

Hostelry, Mid C18. Stone, fronted in brick, three-storeys, nine bays, with an entrance in the fifth bay under a magnificent wood doorcase of the highest quality: Corinthian columns supporting an entablature with a garlanded frieze and carved pulvinus. It has been claimed, with little authority, that it came from the interior of the demolished block of Claydon House. Above is a Diocletian window and all windows to the three centre bays have Gibbs stone surrounds and stepped keystones.

N75

HIGH STREET (North east side—continued)

Others have the stepped keys only. Moulded eaves. The two left bays are now a shop and have a six-panelled door of the early C19. The right end bay projects over a through carriageway to the rear and has a cast iron balcony. Etched glass to the dining room and entrance doors. On the front, another fine wrought iron hanging bracket and inn-sign. The Cock Hotel is now the most imposing coaching inn of the town, from where as many as 20 stage coaches departed daily up and down Watling Street. It was left to the town in 1520 by Thomas Pigot of Beachampton as a charity for the repair of the bridge and causeway over the Ouse. C18 landlords here and at the Bull vied with one another with their tall stories, hence the origin of the well-known metaphor. Here in June 1792 the meeting was held with James Barnes, the builder of the Kennet & Avon Canal, to initiate the building of the Grand Junction Canal that was to affect the Milton Keynes area in the next two decades.

To the rear is a range of building of various dates, part with a patterned roof. This ends in a two-storey carriage house with a recessed central entrance and rounded head, key and abaci, and a cobbled floor. This building now bears the golden lettering that once adorned the front. II

In the car park to the rear, formerly the Inn yard, is another carriage house with four shallow saucer recesses on the north gable. II

Along the east of the carriage way is a stone wall, probably C18, some 2m high, also listed. II

76 No. 76 II

Shop and offices. c.1820. Stucco. A three-storey building with a good symmetrical shopfront with end doors and canted windows. The upper floors have fluted pilasters and modillion eaves. Small square bays to the first floor and 16-pane sashes throughout. It has a two-storey extension to the rear. Listing includes the south side outbuildings, now part of Timor Court.

N76–80

77 No. 78 II

Shop and dwelling. Early C19. Stone with brick refronting. Three-storeys, 16-pane sashes with keyed wedge lintels and dentilled eaves. To the rear, one two-storey wing with a small round headed sash window with lobed glazing bars. A stone outbuilding formerly with this property is now part of Timor Court, raised in brick to two storeys. It has 35-pane windows.

78 No. 80, National Westminster Bank II

Bank and offices. Diaper brickwork, stuccoed to ground floor. Early C19 12-pane sashes with keyed wedge lintels. End doors with two fielded panels and radial fanlights, that on the left within a fine Ionic doorcase. It has recently been improved with round-headed windows on the ground floor and the doorcase moved from the right hand door in 1975–6. Dentilled eaves. A rear wing has a traceried fanlight in the gable.

79 No. 82 II

Shop. C18. Brick. Three storeys, two bays. Shopfront defined by Ionic half-columns. Sixteen-pane sashes with wedge lintels and dentilled eaves. Long range of C18 brick outbuildings with a rounded window, an oculus, in the gable. Probably built at the same time as No. 80.

80 No. 84 **II**

Shop and offices. Mid C19. Brick. Good shopfront with unusual Composite pilasters and small twisted columns to central recessed door. Stone window lintels and multi-coloured brick relieving arches.

81 Nos. 86 and 86A **II**

Shop and offices. Stucco and brick. Early C19. Sash windows and modillion eaves. Corner windows to No. 86A at rear and attached C19 range with former coach house and stables. A side passage leads to The Manse.

82 The Manse **II**

House up a narrow alley through No. 86. Mid C18. Brick. Two storeys and attic, five bays. Central panelled door with canopy. Twelve-pane sash windows with flush boxes to first floor. Plat band and moulded eaves. Gambril roof with dormers and gable stacks. Single-storey outbuilding to the east. An interesting and relatively unaltered example of a Georgian house built following the Great Fire of Stony Stratford.

N82

83 No. 88 **II**

A mid C18 post-fire building, now rendered on the front and built up as a parapet. Shop front modern. At the side, a passageway probably of great antiquity, leads to Timor Court at the rear.

84 No. 90 **II**

Shop and surgery, C18 or earlier with C19 façade. Two bays. Moulded box cornice with acanthus consoles. Thick walls suggest this may incorporate walls of a pre-fire building.

85 Nos. 92 and 94 **II***

Hostelry, now restaurant and hotel. Mid C18. Stone with a brick façade and stone quoins. Three storeys and attics, nine bays. Central carriage entrance with depressed keyed arch and braced doors. Flanking brick pilasters connect plat bands and moulded brick eaves. Panelled door in doorcase in third bay, and C19 shop windows added to No. 92. 9- and 12-pane sashes with gauged brick lintels. Three dormers and gable stacks. The interior of No. 94 has a fine C18 dog-leg stair, the balusters recently refixed upside down, and a curious half-cellar of stone, possibly a survival from a pre-1742 structure. To the rear is an elegant assembly room, a facility much favoured in the C18, which has an early C18 chimneypiece with a panelled overmantel. A date stone in the north wall reads W.E.1687. The building was once the Swan, alternatively the Three Swans or the Swan with Two Necks, first mentioned as a possession of Bradwell Priory in 1526.

N85

86 No. 96, Tower House **II**

Offices and dwelling. C17 with C18 front block, remodelled and heightened in the mid-late C19. Three storeys. The façade has stone lintels and quoins to the plate glass windows, and a canted first floor bay. The cobbled yard to the side opens to a fine range of C18 stone stables and coachhouse with a brick façade and hipped roof. Inside there is a good C18 circular stair in a stairwell with a coved ceiling and Gothic window, and a fine floral WC pan.

The walls and panelled piers at the front are separately listed. **II**

87 Walls to No. 96

The walls and panelled gate piers at the front are separately listed as being important to the setting of the stable block. II

The garden walls on the graveyard side of No. 96 are of limestone, with tiled copings. They are an important part of the setting of the churchyard and the footpath through from the High Street.

88 Tower of St. Mary Magdalen II*

Tower of parish church of east Stony Stratford. C15. Stone, of three stages with tall bell openings, impressive gargoyles and gables in the parapet to the former pitched roof. The west window is curiously assymmetrical and there are blocked openings to the pitch-roofed north aisle and to the nave and the tower, at the west end of the aisle. A square panel on the west front has no known purpose. The interior has no floors and only the remains of the circular tower stair. The church was a casualty of the great fire of 1742, fire stained stone being still visible especially at roof level. The tower was saved from demolition by the intervention of the local notary, Browne Willis, founder of the Society of Antiquaries of London. Some pre-fire headstones survive in the graveyard, which was extended over the building area after the disaster and was in use until about 1865. Although much weathered, some stones have lettering of a very high standard.

N88

89 Nos. 98 and 100 II

Pair of late C18 houses, now shops, stone, rendered to the front. No. 100 has 12-pane sashes and cogged eaves. No. 98 has a doorcase of the early C19.

90 No. 102 II

House of early C19 with contemporary door, doorcase and rear 16-pane sash window.

91 No. 104 II

House of C18 or early C19 with a rendered facade and plat band.

92 No. 106 II

House, now surgery and offices. C18. Stone, rendered to the façade. Three bays with mid-C19 door, doorcase and later canted ground floor bay windows. It was once an inn called the Drum and Monkey, later the Coach and Horses.

N90–92

93 The Old Vicarage II

House, C17 or C18 with an early C20 brick front and original rear wing. Stone, possibly always one bay with large inglenook stack and services in the rear wing. The building occupies the land formerly belonging to The Malletts. Said to be the dwelling of the priest for St. Mary's Church.

94 Nos. 104 to 116 II

Six houses in an impressive three-storey and attic row, with ashlar stone fronts now much repaired. Mostly C19 but No. 104 C18, and very much altered. No. 116 built or radically altered 1863 when the properties became the staff houses for St. Paul's School. Chamfered casement windows and curious arched doors. The row occupies the site of the Horseshoe Inn, the leading C18 hostelry of the town in the C18, and another inn, the Red Lion, mentioned in 1529 stood somewhere near the same spot. The right end building used to have a stone sundial dated 1773.

N94

95 Stratford's Restaurant and Dwellings II

St. Paul's public school, later Fegan's Homes for homeless children, cigar manufactury, convent of Franciscan friars, and now a restaurant and houses. Built 1863–5 by Goldie and Childe, for the Rev. W. T. Sankey. A most imposing building of local stone with brick dressings, comprising a chapel with apsidal end, entrance gatehouse and assembly rooms in an ambitious German Gothic style. The gatehouse has a Wagnerian quality and there is a rear stair turret, all of which adds much to the skyline. Internally the chapel has fittings of marble and stained pine of high quality. The assembly room, now subdivided, has ceiling paintings. The school closed in 1896. J. W. C. Fegan, who then acquired the property in 1900, was a London evangelist whose exertions were also extended to the townspeople. It too finally closed in 1962, many remembering their somewhat harsh education with a degree of affection.

The fine moulded arched entrance, with the later stone wall along the High Street, are separately listed. II

George Goldie (1828–87) was a Roman Catholic, and who, in partnership with Childe, were favoured by the Catholic Church for its buildings. They built Upsall Castle, Yorkshire. It is unexplained why they should be employed here, particularly as earlier, Sankey had H. Woodyer prepare a scheme.

N95

N95a

Beyond this development the High Street comprises mostly C19 industrial housing, ending in the Gas Works, now a caravan sales area.

HORSEFAIR GREEN (North side)

96 Baptist Chapel II

Baptist Chapel, 1823, built to replace an earlier chapel on the same site built for the thriving congregation that was first founded in 1657. Inside the porch, a C17 two-light timber framed window with an C18 leaded iron casement is said to be from the original building. The present building has wide pedimented gable set back from the road, of red brick with paler headers. Originally with central round headed pair of doors, and two side windows, and three corresponding windows at the upper level, the ground floor was altered c.1974 with the addition of the porch. The gable has a curious segmental arch and within, a tablet recording the building. On the right an extension of 1935, founded by the notable local Baptist, C. J. Woollard, leading to a four-bay schoolroom at the rear.

Inside there is a C17 pulpit and a gallery over the entrance, and a panelled timber ceiling. There are also some interesting monuments.

The forecourt has iron railings and a lantern on an overthrow. There are also nine headstones set to the side, all of the first half of the C19, and including William Aveline, father of the developer of Wolverton, and members of the Wallis and Willmer families.

N96

97 No. 7 **II**

An extension of No. 8 and contemporary with No. 9. One bay, three storeys, early–mid C19 house with side passage. A small blocked arch in the gable originally lit the attic. The paired modillion eaves run across No. 8 and 9.

98 No. 8 **II**

A fine three-bay three-storey house of stuccoed brick, being an early C19 remodelling of a mid-C18 house on the site. Central stone gabled porch with a pair of doors with etched glass. 16-pane sashes, but two nicely detailed small square bays with dentilled entablatures on the ground floor.

99 No. 9 **II**

Contemporary with No. 7. Two bays with an elegant door and doorcase in panelled reveals, and finely gauged carriage arch on the left, now filled with a window. All 16-pane sashes with raised keys. It has a coloured Royal Insurance fire plate.

100 Nos. 14 and 15 **II**

Originally one thatched stone built house, probably early C18, No. 14 being a C19 subdivision of the buildings. Two small raking dormers to the attic, and all other windows replaced. No. 15 has an inglenook fireplace internally.

101 No. 16 **II**

A continuation of Nos. 14–15 in brick on a stone sill, also early C18. Two bays, with paned windows and timber lintels. It also has an inglenook fireplace internally.

102 No. 17 **II**

Early–mid C18 cottage, two storeys and attic but lower than its neighbours and originally thatched. It has symmetrical elevation set off-centre due to the large stack on the right. Fire mark of the Phoenix Insurance Co.

103 Nos. 18 and 19 **NL**

A pair of early C19 cottages with original doors and canopies, No. 18 still with its 16-pane sashes and original glass.

104 Nos. 20 and 21, with 43 Silver Street **NL**

An early–mid C19 block of two-storey cottages, No. 21 with its original sashes, and those of No. 20 replaced later in the C19 with thinner glazing bars. The splayed corner originally had a door to a fourth cottage.

105 No. 22 **II**

Formerly the Royal Oak P.H. facing down Horsefair Green. An early C18 brick building now roughcasted and painted, with central plat band and a door off-centre to allow a through passage behind the central stack. C19 windows, being canted bays on the ground floor. The thatch has been replaced by slate.

106 Nos. 25 and 26 **NL**

Early–mid C19. Two cottages with grouped doorcases. No. 26 takes the biscuit for insensitive rewindowing.

107 Terrace: 27 to 32 inclusive **NL**

An interesting terrace of six cottages of 1858–9, set back at an angle, the two centre ones sharing a large gable and an entry to the rear. Brick, with nicely turned and gauged heads to openings, and doorcases. No. 28 has unfortunately been altered and painted.

108 No. 34 **II**

A three-bay house of the mid C18, three bays with a long rear wing. Brick, with an open pedimented door case and strange painted fanlight. C19 casement windows.

109 No. 35 and 35A, Dene Cottage **II**

An interesting building but not striking externally. C18, and partly timber framed, altered in the C19 and windows renewed in the C20. Painted brick facade of three bays, with a central pedimented reeded doorcase, clearly a local effort. No. 35 is the cross wing.

Chamfered spine beams in the main block.

110 No. 38 Calverton Lodge **II**

An early Victorian yellow brick villa standing in its own grounds behind a contemporary wall and gates. 'L' plan with a large gabled porch set at an angle in the re-entrant angle. Tudor Gothic pointed windows with chamfered surrounds and glazing bars. Small gables over the upper windows. To the rear two extensions of 1850–70.

The front wall and gates are separately listed. **II**

N105 & N162

MARKET SQUARE

The Market Square is perhaps the most fascinating geographical item about Stony Stratford, for it speaks clearly of a deliberately planned development of the town. Of this the records are silent, for it is not a completely new settlement such as would have attracted comment or licence. Nonetheless, it is an ambitious scheme that converted the end of the medieval tenement plots into a large square, and is of a scale that could only be undertaken by a large landowner. That it took place on the west side of Watling Street perhaps indicates that it was the proprietors of the Manor of Calverton that were responsible, and as this scale of urban planning found particular favour in the C13 and early C14, it is possible that the landowner responsible was the Earl of Oxford. However, there was a grant of a market in 1194 by Richard I, the second earliest market in Buckinghamshire, suggesting that it was already a place of significance. Its origin must for the present remain speculation: what is clear that at some stage in the early history of the settlement the town required more market space than was afforded by Watling Street itself, and that the space needed was found to the rear of the High Street properties. This urban space is still bounded by Church Street, White Horse Yard, and the back lane on the south-west. Whether the church of St. Giles was already in position cannot be told as its subsequent history has obliterated any early evidence, but it would not be unusual if the square was planned as an adjunct to a pre-existing churchyard which up to then had serviced partially in this role.

As frequently happens, ephemeral market booths became more substantial, remained overnight, from feast day to feast day, and eventually were replaced in permanent materials, thus the centre of the square acquired buildings, now represented by Nos. 21 and 33 and the Victorian Police Station and Court Room.

111 No. 1 — II

Now the most conspicuous building in the Square, preserving the line of the north-east face of the planned area. A house of c.1812, three storeys, double pile in plan form with two parallel roofs. A C19 shop window has been inserted into the north west corner but otherwise it retains its nine- and 12-pane sash windows. The entrance is in a single storey extension to the rear, with a vermiculated lintel and key.

N111

112 No. 3 and 4

This is Stony Stratford's most disastrous loss in architectural terms. A very fine house of a wealthy C18 merchant, three-storeys, five bays, brick with stone raised quoins and, on the ground floor, C19 shop windows. Its siting here reminds one that such a central position overlooking the market was one to be aimed for by the leading citizens, an attitude still prevelant abroad but which has been lost in Britain. The interior had some fine panelling. The Health Centre is a very inadequate replacement for the dignity and urban scale reflected in this building.

113 No. 7 — II

An C18 house, also of double pile plan, now offices. It is of two bays, rendered brickwork, with a central six-panelled door (a modern replacement) with an excellent curvilinear fanlight in an open pedimented doorcase. The windows are C19 replacements to the same pattern as the originals.

N113

114 No. 8, Market Place — II

Formerly the Queen's Head public house, later the Wolverton Urban District Offices and now offices for an estate agent. Three wide bays, being a C19 refacing of an earlier house. Wide door and doorcase and triple windows each in an eared pediment and cornice. It was also known at one time as the White Hart.

115 No. 9, The Crown P.H. II

Public house C17 and C18. Two storeys and attic. Rendered brick with a tiled roof. Central six-panelled door with a bracketed open pediment and fanlight. Twelve-pane sash windows grouped in threes and four. Two hipped leaded dormers with bottle ends in the apexes. Moulded eaves. An C18 brick stack appears on the rear slope of the roof. There is a C19 assembly room and other contemporary rear extensions.

N115

116 No. 10, Higgs, Butcher II

House of the early C18, stone, with a brick front, now rendered. Adapted to become a shop of the early C19. Two storeys, three bays. Central paired doors within a recessed entrance. Sash windows, but a shallow bay with rounded corners to the shop, with a butcher's grille vent over. Moulded eaves.

The interior of the shop is boarded, with meat rails and a safe. It is a rare survival of a C19 shop.

To the rear, an interesting range of outbuildings ranged in diminishing sizes, one with a pair of carriage doors with spiked cresting. One of the most picturesque groups of the town. II

N116

117 No. 11, The Old King's Head II

A house of the C16–C17, at one time an alehouse. Rendered brick with a tiled roof. Three bays, with axial stack between the second and third bays. Entrance to central bay through a six-panelled door in a timber doorcase with a bracketed canopy. Casement windows and moulded eaves and two hipped dormer windows.

Internally the stone stack has a fine C16 moulded fire lintel.

118 Nos. 12 and 13 II*

An interesting house of the C17 refaced in ashlar limestone in the C18. No. 13 now a shop with side entry. Four bays. Entrance has a four-panelled door in a stone eared architrave and a baroque acanthus keystone and flowing leaves, much in the style of Henry Bell, probable architect of the Sessions House, Northampton, of 1678. Windows have 12-pane sashes, the lintels flush with ogee heads and raised keys connecting to the plat band. Timber dentilled eaves. Above the door a datestone reading I & M A 1790 and arms of the Arnold family, parted per pale, clearly a later addition to the building.

The property was a pin makers factory in the C19, the work being carried on in outbuildings to the rear.

N118

119 No. 14 and 15

Now one house, No. 14, but originally a pair of early C19 shops. Three storeys, of brickwork, rendered on the ground floor and provided with one splendid paned bow window each and a common dentilled fascia covering the two doors between them. Blind panels cover the party wall on the two upper floors. The end stacks are rebuilt.

120 No. 16, Cowley's Bakers II

House of the late C18, three bays, with a six-panelled door and bracketed open canopy. Wide 16-pane sashes with wedge lintels and stepped keys. Modillion eaves. The window to the left has been altered in later times. The baker's ovens are in the rear wing.

121 No. 17 II

House. Later C19. Rendered and slated. Two bays with a central arched entrance now converted to a window. Tripartite windows with raised wedge lintels. Side entrances, that to the right in an extension are set back behind a curiously recessed corner and provided with a fanlight and bracketed pediment.

N119

122 No. 19, Magistrate's Courts and Probation Office NL

Built 1865, with large hard red bricks and slate roof. Windows and doors have heavy flush stone arched lintels. The former identification panel has been rendered. A large rose window fills the south west gable. It was originally two separate blocks either side of an earlier brick structure on stone footings. A new wing was built in the 1970's. A confident building not unaware of advanced architectural fashions of its day, it has nevertheless always received a bad press due to its plainness and hard materials as much as to its first use as the Police Station.

N122

123 No. 21, Sun and Moon House II

Rendered brick house of one build with No. 33 and at one time four cottages. A lease on the site dates from the reign of Charles II (1660–72) showing that this part of the Market Square was already in occupation by that date.

124 No. 33 II

One build with No. 21 and consisting of the fourth, easterly bay, of that house and its back wing. Mostly early C19, with 16-pane sashes in rebated boxes. The back wing is roofed independently.

125 No. 26 II

Numbered out of sequence, this is a pleasant C18 house, originally symmetrical with a central panelled door in a pedimented doorcase. 12-pane sashes, the lower ones tripartite with raised keys. Dentilled eaves to the slight gambrel roof, an unusual feature in this area outside Stony Stratford, only appearing elsewhere at Fenny Stratford. The building was extended by one bay eastwards in the C19 and pebbledashed. One central hipped dormer.

N125

MILL LANE

Mill Lane is, with Silver Street, a fossilization of the medieval back lane to the High Street plots which ran from the Horsefair on Calverton Road, returning to the High Street against the Barley Mow. With the development of the Market Square its clarity was changed, and in later times has been retained as a road only as far as the access drive to Stratford Mill. Beyond here it is still a public footpath and retained some useful function in that it's name is recorded as Harlot's Path.

Development along the Mill Lane beyond the ranges of outbuildings to the High Street properties did not take place until the later C19, when a number of terraces were erected. Nos. 12–16 are characteristic and have not lost too many of their original details. They are of brick, slated with blue crested tiles (only two retaining these), sash windows and two-panelled doors in dignified doorcases with bracketed canopies. No. 16 has cast iron railings to the front garden wall.

126 Laura Cottage II

A curiously placed cottage developed on the rear of a High Street plot in the late C19. Three bays, nicely maintained, one sided with original sash windows and door central to the two eastern bays on the north side and blank on the south.

127 No. 1, Ouse Bank Cottage II

Cottage of the late C18 or early C19. Three bays with a central panelled door in a timber doorcase, and to the left, a small window to a larder, perhaps once an entrance to a second cottage. The roof line has been altered between two end parapets.

128 Stratford House II

A house of the early C18, altered and refaced at the front and side c.1840–60. Three bays, with a wide central door and rendered doorcase, and large six-pane sashes. This elevation is rendered and lined, with rusticated quoins at one end. Three hipped dormers. The right stack is C18, on a stone base. Gothic eaves detail. There is also an arched porch to the garden with a cast iron balustrade. The front wall against the road is balustraded.

N128

129 Stratford Mill NL

A water mill has stood on this site at least since Domesday. It is probably the mill bought by John Penn in 1581 and held by that family, a branch of the Penns of Chalfont, Bucks and the United States, until 1618. The present building has been rebuilt again and again and now only retains the last six phases of rebuilding. The earliest section is undateable, being a stone structure over the mill leet. A three bay structure was added to this in the late C18 or early C19 in a dark red brick. The original building was then almost totally rebuilt in brick in 1883 by James Rogers and raised to three storeys, with a wing to the south. This was also enlarged in 1875 by E. Swinfen Harris, taking the form of a high three-storey extension of the living quarters with the upper floor slate hung and gabled, the gable having his characteristic ironwork finial. Once again, in 1890 Harris was called upon to extend by building, in his more developed style, a smaller parallel block on the north side of his earlier work, and with an oriel window over the gable entrance. Subsequent additions have generally been of inferior work, some being post 1939–45 war. The 1883 building, which had round end tie plates by Roberts of Deanshanger, was destroyed by fire in November 1985.

The mill leet still has water to the canal below the race although there is no longer a wheel. Across the yard facing mill field there is the apex brickwork of an overflow tunnel.

N129

LONDON ROAD (North east side)

130 The Plough Inn II

Church Schools, commenced 1867, and built 1873, by Edward Swinfen Harris, and one of his more colourful schools. Rock-faced limestone with brick dressings. Tiled roof. It consists of two double classrooms at right angles to each other, (originally with a glazed timber partition dividing each) and a third room, probably for infants, at the rear, the remaining angle filled with the ablution block. The south-west elevation has paired shouldered windows divided by a turned slate column, and date and the parish insignia, the lys, on the stack. The porch is also original. There is a bell-tower, and the gable facing up London Road has fanciful brick details. It was converted to a public house in 1937.

N130

131 No. 13 II

A late C18 building of two storeys refaced in the early C19 with abundant stone detail, a string, ground floor window dressings to the bays and a small scale portico. Also stone moulded eaves. The rear extension of c.1850 has been heightened.

N131

132 Church Hall II

Parish hall, 1892, by Edward Swinfen Harris. A picturesque building for the Rev. G. P. Trevelyan, perpetual curate of Wolverton St. Mary. It is of four bays, buttressed externally, of rock-faced limestone with ample brick dressings. It has a lean-to timber-framed entrance porch with patterned brick noggings and a gable door with an elegant hinge in which Harris excelled. Round window in the gable, and at the rear, a kitchen annex with shouldered windows. On the side it has a pompous dedication in Latin by GVLIELMVS P TREVELYAN, the priest. The interior has open trusses and curious turned baluster supports. It is all charmingly detailed and small in scale, but somehow lacks the conviction and assurance of Scott's adjacent church.

N132

133 Community Centre C

Formerly the parish church of Wolverton St. Mary, 1863, by Sir George Gilbert Scott, formed from parts of the parishes of Wolverton and of Calverton. Coursed limestone, with flush dressings, used in a rather severe Gothic style. Paired lancet windows and a round gable window. North aisle added 1867, with double chamfered arcade on octagonal columns. The building was converted to a community hall c.1975 by D.Sim, and a lean-to porch added, and toilets replacing a gabled south porch.

N133

134 Vicarage II

A vicarage of 1864, extended twice later in the C19. 'T'-shaped with a parish room attached at the bottom of the 'T' and connected to the church. Limestone, with tall stone mullioned windows, the upper floor having raised flush dormers with gables. Bay window facing garden added 1892. Tiled roof. An open roofed parish room links the house with the church.

135 No. 19, Otley House NL

A pretty Gothic villa of c.1880, probably for Edward Hayes, the owner of the adjacent engineering works. Coursed squared limestone with flush dressings, and a dark coloured tiled roof. Two storeys, with windows with pointed heads, but a stone mullioned window to the drawing room and a canted crenellated bay to the cross wing at the south end. The pointed arched door is within an open moulded Gothic porch. Carved bargeboards and a small oriel window on the south side.

N135

136 Stables to Otley House NL

Stone and yellow brick. Pigeon lofts over the gable and the pitching door over the stables. Crested tiles.

137 York House II

House of c.1840–50. Now a Youth and Community Centre. Red brick with large yellow brick pilasters and a hipped slate roof. Three storeys, three times two bays. Wide fibreglass portico and glazed doors from rehabilitation of c.1970. 16-pane sash windows with gauged brick lintels. Moulded stone cornice at first floor and eaves level. It has two contemporary rear wings, one a stable block, all in yellow brick. Timber extension containing the stair.

N137

138 Hayes Boatyard, Watling Works

The large building on the north side of the garage was originally part of the boatyard of Edward Hayes. He started in the Wolverton works and later became an agricultural engineer, later specialising in marine engineering developing into full scale boat building. Tugs up to 70ft in length were towed through the town by steam traction engine and launched sideways into the wharf at Old Stratford. The yard started in 1840 and the business finally closed in 1925, having built boats for Britain, France, Russia, Egypt and others.

139 London Road Cemetery NL

The lychgate, designed by E. Swinfen Harris. Timber framed on a stone base, supported on two posts with moulded brackets to a brattished tie, the hipped roof propped by turned corner balusters. Perforated gates with spikes. Although on a small scale it is an original and imaginative solution to the same problem that was handled more pondorously and expensively at St. Giles churchyard in 1931.

140 Store NL

The cemetery store, also by Harris, is again a happy design with a pointed arched door with another of his original hinges.

N140

141 Cross NL

A churchyard cross with three steps and carved drum, the shaft terminating in a crucifixion scene. C19 but almost convincingly medieval.

LONDON ROAD (South west side)

142 Black Hall NL

Now an inconspicuous building of stone, but probably of C18 or earlier origins. Two bays, extended by single storey structures either side.

143 Nos. 10, 12 and 14 No. 14, II

A row of three-storey brick cottages, No. 14, with cogged eaves the earliest, dated 1837, No. 12 later, and No. 10 later still.

144 Calverton Limes II

A very large house, now the C.I.U. Mid C19, completely covered by a front block by Edward Swinfen Harris of 1870 for S & B Daniell, surgeon, and full of querky detail. Bands of limestone rubble, all laid differently, herringbone, upright, and random, all with brick quoins. Tiled roof. A slightly recessed central part, with a cross wing on the south, and a parallel wing on the north. Central entrance under a decorative gable with a carved roundel, and an arch with nook-shafts. The cross wing has a canted two-storey bay window and pierced bargeboards. Other windows with shouldered heads and sandstone columns, not unlike the Plough opposite. In 1890 Harris added a lean-to extension with another door at the north end, connected to a caretaker's house at the rear. The two builds illustrate the evolution of his work over 20 years. It was converted to a working men's club in 1947.

N144

145 No. 24 NL

Early C19. Five bays, conspicuous for its interesting two-storey bay window with diamond lattice glazing.

146 Nos. 26, 28 and 30–32 NL

A row of C19 terrace cottages built in that order out from the town.

147 Milestone by No. 46 NL

c.1830, a sandstone tapered pillar dating from the reworking of the Stony Stratford to Hockcliffe turnpike. The cast iron plate is lost.

148 No. 62 II

Early C19, a well-balanced façade of three bays with a central reeded doorcase and door, and a thin canopy on consoles. Wedge window lintels with raised keys, the windows destroyed by re-windowing.

149 No. 108, Galley Hill House II

A pair of one-bay three-storey cottages, now one house. Stone, with a brick facade, early–mid C19. 16-pane sash windows.

150 No. 110 NL

A vigorous Victorian house of 1885, once occupied by and built by a local. Symmetrical, of blue bricks with ample stone details, including an elaborate entrance and canted two-storey bay windows either side, rusticated and with much carved work. Pierced parapets over the porch and bays, the latter terminating in urns in front of the steep gables. General de Gaulle once made use of the facilities here.

STONY STRATFORD

NEW STREET

New Street was a development of 1863 of a jetty off High Street leading to a footpath towards Wolverton.

151 Nos. 3 to 17 inclusive II

Terrace of 7 cottages, 1862. Brick with plat band and leaded windows, each opening with a pointed brick arch. Each attic bedroom is provided with a large gabled dormer.

N151 & 152

152 Masonic Hall and Temple II

Infants school and parish hall, 1863–4, by Henry Woodyer for the Rev. W. T. Sankey. The parish floor was on the first floor with access via a stair tower in the corner. Now a masonic temple with common room below. Brick with dressings and tracery to the windows. Continuous blocked dormer both sides.

153 Nos. 2 to 16 inclusive II

Terrace of eight houses, built 1863 for the Rev. W. T. Sankey. Rock faced stone and brick. A picturesque group with leaded windows and hipped dormers, the end cottages gabled and with initials and date. Brick dentils. The terrace continues to the east with a pair of slightly earlier cottages with sash windows, the doors grouped under a common head.

At the High Street end a second gable is that of the stables with an adjoining yard.

154 Nos. 18, 20 and 22 II

A pleasant group of buildings listed for group value.

155 No. 24 II

House. c.1863. Rock faced stone and brick, with canted gable to Russell Street and a single storey rear extension. Leaded windows with brick pointed lancets. An interesting design making a satisfactory end to the group.

PROSPECT ROAD

156 Prospect Road was a development of a 'yard' in the 1890's with cottages for railway workers.

SILVER STREET

Silver Street is the medieval back lane, a continuation of Mill Lane to Market square, renamed in 1887 in honour of Victoria's silver jubilee. There are three buildings of interest before the explosion of development in the late Victorian period.

157 Methodist Chapel II

Chapel, 1845, simple brick box of four bays, gable to the street. This has a heavy Doric entablature of a portico, and either side, round headed windows, the architraves stopping at a string. The windows have been altered and the portico columns replaced c.1950. The interior is very plain.

To the right, two schoolrooms, now a meeting hall, built c.1900 of bright red panelled brickwork, and two gables.

N157

Oxford Street has, at Nos. 1–2, a stone pair of cottages of the early C19, and leads to Horn Lane, now an almost forgotten backwater of stone walls and sheds. Here stood the Pest House in comparative isolation from the town.

158 No. 14 NL

Fire Engine house, now an office, built 1864 as a result of another major fire in 1848. Pointed arch, now glazed, within a gabled elevation having stone dressings and finials. It housed the voluntarily manned engine.

159 No. 22, Belmont House II

An elegant frontage of c.1830. Brick, originally three bays, the flanking bays slightly set forward of the centre and ends. Central simplified pedimented portico, the door now fixed. 12-pane sashes, the lower with small bracketed heads. The building was extended to the right by two bays, entirely in character, to contain, in the end bay, a carriage entrance in an elliptical arch.

160 No. 32, Burnham House formerly The Chestnuts II*

A fine C18 house of three bays, gable end to the road. Brick with stone footings and ashlar quoins, extended by a further two bays in the early C19, when the house was re-windowed with its present 12-pane sashes and stone keystones. Plat band. The centre window is blocked, and it has a bay window on the ground floor. The extension has a continuous cornice over a handsome door and canted bay. The gable against the street is raised, with stone kneelers and copings. To the rear an extension with strap pointing contains the entrance.

Internally there is fine panelling in the drawing room.

N160

161 Summer House II

In the garden, a mid-C19 schoolroom also designed for musical performances. It has windows with 'Y' tracery and a crenellated porch.

162 No. 34 II

A mid C18 house of two storeys, two bays, with raking dormer to an attic. Tyrolean rendering, probably over stone. Very steep roof of slate replacing thatch, and one raking dormer.

VICARAGE ROAD

Vicarage Road was formerly Back Lane, the lane between the back plots and the open fields. Even now the buildings on the town side are service outbuildings for the High street properties, some stone, some brick forming an interesting group housing workshops and small businesses.

Opposite is noticeably later development. Cottages 8, 12 and 14 have ashlar limestone ground floor with Hollington stone quoins, and brick above. The traditional stone walls with tile copings as around the garden of No. 68 and 94 are significant features.

163 Walls to Vicarage Walk II

The stone wall on the north-west side of Vicarage Walk formerly contained the garden and coachhouse of the Vicarage built by the Rev. W. T. Sankey in the early 1860's, the Vicarage standing where St. Giles Mews now stand.

The walls on the south-east side are the backs of the interesting but unlisted group of three pairs of cottages Nos. 28–33, The Gardens, red brick with yellow brick end pilasters.

RUSSELL STREET

Russell Street, named after the developer, is a continuation of the back lane to rather shorter plots than Vicarage Road. It was developed with brick terraced cottages c.1890–1900. The County First School was built c.1910.

WOLVERTON ROAD (North side)

Wolverton Road is a continuation of the old valley road from Beachampton to Newport Pagnell, and formed the southern boundary to Stony Stratford. It was turnpiked in 1844 after it was redirected through New Wolverton and a tollbar and cottage erected at Debb's Barn.

164 Forester's Arms II

Public House. c.1830–40, once the Brewer's Arms. Stone and diaper brick with purple headers. 12 and 16-pane sashes with keyed wedge lintels. Modillion cornice. The ground floor was faced in the late Victorian period with glazed bricks and stained glass to the windows.

165 Nos. 5 and 7 II

Two shops and dwellings. 1840, built by Wilson. Windows altered.

166 Congregational Church II

Independent chapel, 1823. Red brick. Two-storey symmetrical facade with brick dentilled pediment and round headed windows and central door. Schoolroom attached to the right with similar windows.

The forecourt has cast iron railings and gates with dog rails. II

N166

167 Nos. 15 and 17 17

Two semi-detached houses. c.1870. Red brick with blue strings and end gables. First floor windows have multi-coloured brick and stone heads and half-hipped dormers. This was the first building to be erected on Wolverton Road proper. To the east lay the town's recreation ground.

168 No. 19 II

House, 1883 by Edward Swinfen Harris for Dr. Paddy Maguire, one of Harris's best works. Brick, nicely detailed, with timber framing in the gables as was popular within the domestic revival movement of the time. Picturesque carriage entrance with bottle ends inset to the lintel, and stair tower. The yard was too narrow to turn a carriage and had to be adjusted later. The client's initial appears on the windvane, and on the large stone fireplace in the entrance hall.

The low front brick wall and gate piers are separately listed. II

N168

169 Wolverton, Stony Stratford and District Light Railway

To the rear of Nos. 23–41 was the depot of the famous tramway, built 1886–7 between the Railway Works and the Barley Mow, and extended first to Old Stratford later in 1887, then to Deanshanger. It was of 4ft gauge and the builder was Charles Wilkinson. It operated initially two locomotives made by Krauss of Munich, and later replaced by Green, and Brush and other locomotives. After closing in 1889 it was re-started in 1891, and in 1910 the High Street and Deanshanger sections were abandoned and it turned round in front of the Forester's Arms. It was closed during the general strike in 1926.

N169

WOLVERTON ROAD (South side)

170 No. 2

Once the schoolmaster's house for the Church Schools, built 1872–3 by E. Swinfen Harris. Rock faced limestone with a half hipped tiled roof and ironwork finial. The shopfront is a late alteration.

The remainder of Wolverton Road on both sides was developed around 1865–70 around the King Street junction, and later, between 1885 and 1900 across the town's playing fields. There are some buildings of interest, the Duke of Edinburgh P.H. is of stone, with fine cast iron railings to the common canopy and etched glass to the bay windows. No. 57 has curious dog-tooth decoration around the windows, No. 73 has a hollow carved cornice. No. 99 is of 1866 and no doubt the work of the Rev. W. T. Sankey as New Street.

There is some moulded brick detail on 98–102, and on 22–26 South side. No. 36 has ceramic tiling in the porch.

171 YORK ROAD

York Road was the result of development of c.1896–7, responding to the needs of the railway works. It was pushed through between Nos. 77 and 79 High Street, following the long curved line of the property boundaries. A large house was erected at the rear of No. 77. It is a low two-storey building with two gables and entrance under low eaves between them. The gables have moulded bargeboards. The name was originally called Homelands, and later became known as York Road after York House school at the High Street end.

Beyond the garden ends, the street was fully built up with terrace cottages in a robust late Victorian style, variety being achieved by grouping together those with hipped gables between pairs set forward with straight gables. The doors are raised over steps and flank entries to the rear. The street has fortunately retained its plate glass window sashes but only a few of the fine moulded doors.

N171

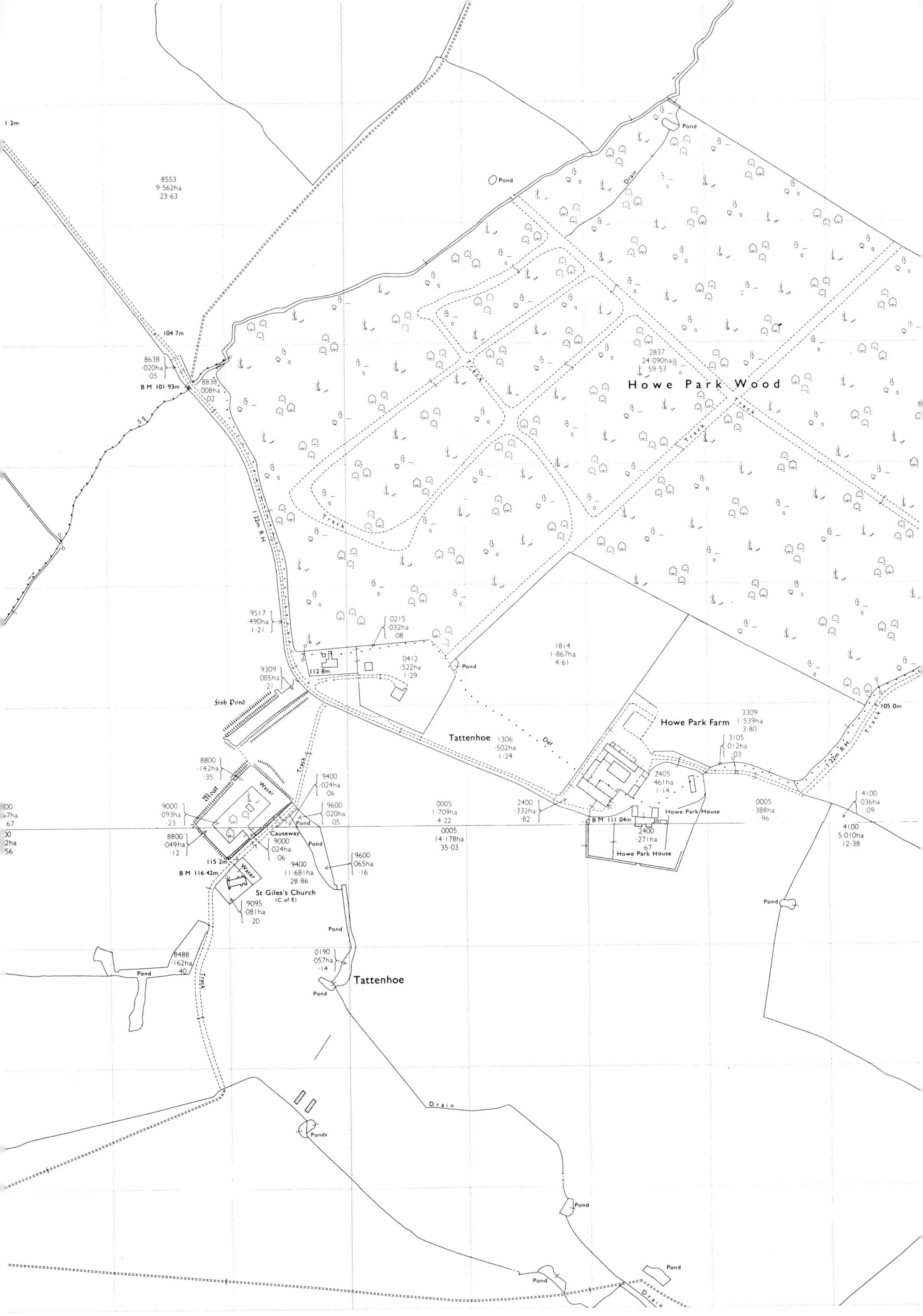

8553
9·562ha
23·63
Pond
Pond
Howe Park Wood
2837
24·090ha
59·53
Track
Track
Track
Track
104·7m
8638
·020ha
·05
8838
·008ha
·02
BM 101·93m
SS
1·22m R H
9517
·490ha
1·21
0215
·032ha
·08
0412
·522ha
1·29
112·8m
Pond
1814
1·867ha
4·61
9309
·085ha
·21
Fish Pond
Tattenhoe
1306
·502ha
1·24
Def
Howe Park Farm
3309
1·539ha
3·80
3105
·012ha
·03
105·0m
1·22m R H
8800
·142ha
·35
Moat
Water
9400
·024ha
·06
9600
·020ha
·05
0005
1·709ha
4·22
2405
·461ha
1·14
2400
·332ha
·82
Howe Park House
0005
·388ha
·96
4100
·036ha
·09
9000
·093ha
·23
Pond
Causeway
0005
14·178ha
35·03
BM 111·04m
2400
·271ha
·67
Howe Park House
4100
5·010ha
12·38
8800
·049ha
·12
9000
·024ha
·06
Pond
9400
11·681ha
28·86
115·2m
BM 116·42m
Water
9600
·065ha
·16
St Giles's Church
(C of E)
9095
·081ha
·20
Pond
Pond
8488
·162ha
·40
Pond
0190
·057ha
·14
Tattenhoe
Pond
Drain
Ponds
Pond
Pond
Pond
Drain

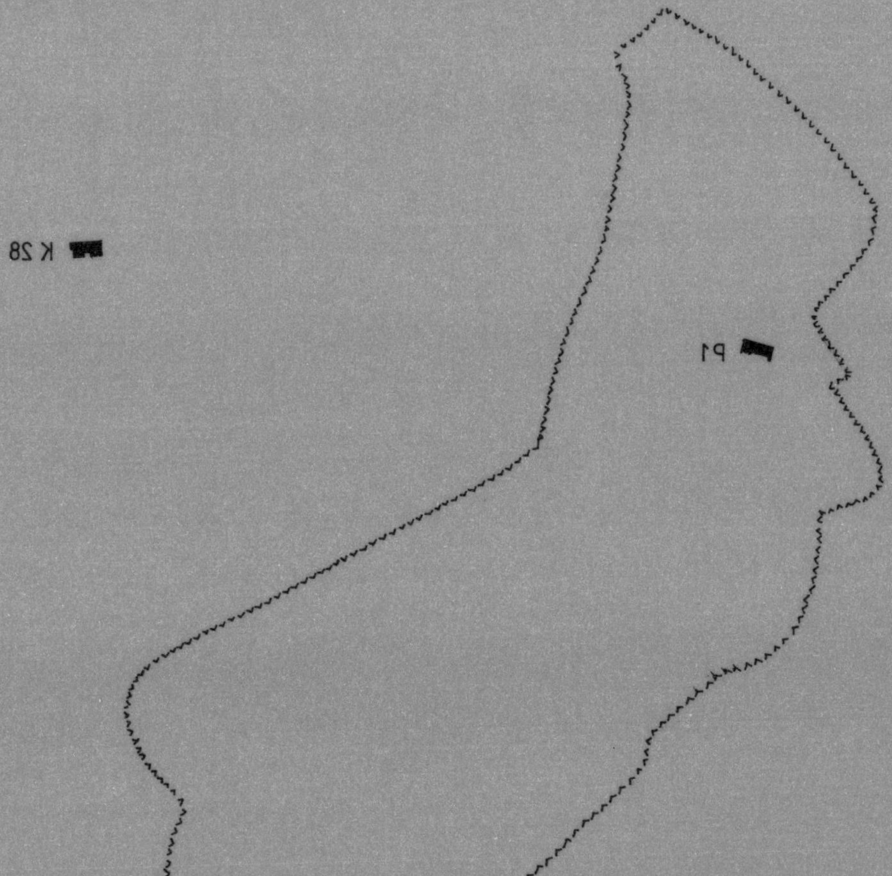

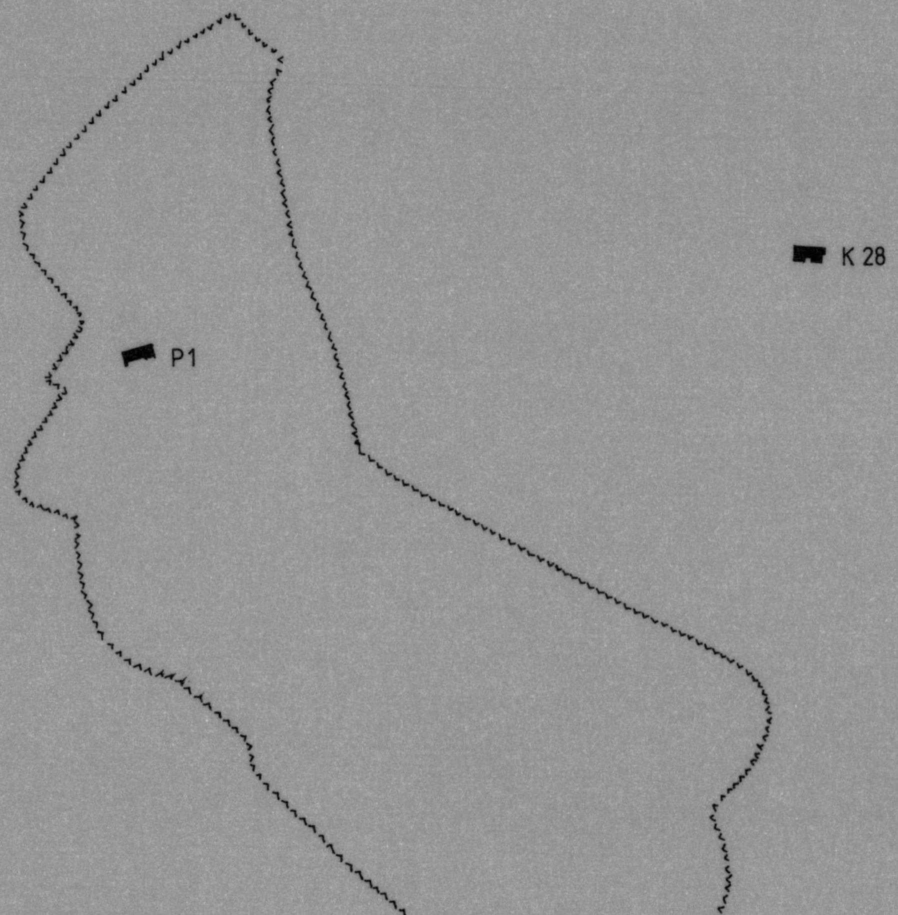
P1
K 28

TATTENHOE

TATTENHOE

The parish of Tattenhoe is the smallest medieval parish in Milton Keynes occupying the south west corner of the city. It does not appear in Domesday Book thus may at that time have been a part of Shenley. The village has gone, and it is in effect a deserted village, the church being the only surviving building at the centre. Close to the east end of the church there is a moat and a more substantial moat adjoining to the north. These may represent the house of the Staffords, relations of the Dukes of Buckingham, who acquired the manor of Tattenhoe in 1477 at the same time as Westbury Farm. Much building material and domestic debris can be seen in the fields around the church. The moats and associated ponds are scheduled ancient monuments and the site of a medieval post mill mound, 25m across, occurs on the boundary with Bletchley. Besides the church there are only two farmhouses in the parish. Its western boundary does not coincide with the boundary of Milton Keynes along the old bridle way to Calverton but lies a little to the west.

1 Church of St. Giles II*

A small building in a deserted setting. Stone with a tiled roof. The nave and chancel are in one, with only the size of windows to distinguish them. It is basically a C16 structure which originally belonged to Lavendon Abbey and shortly after transferred to Snelshall Priory. It is said to have been built with the remains of this latter Priory after its suppression, i.e. about 1540, which might account for the C15 south door and, internally the base of the font, probably C13–C14. It was reconsecrated in 1636 after repair by the Staffords, but, due to lack of sufficient people to maintain it, was frequently reported to be in poor condition. On the south side there are four probably C18 brick buttresses. The south door has a bracket moulding of early C15 date, but the north door has been removed, probably in 1636. It has cusped square headed windows, but those to the chancel with pointed heads and hoodmould. At the west end there is a bellcote of timber with one of the earliest bells in Milton Keynes, inscribed PETROS DEVESTON ME FECIT, pre 1347. Two mass dials can be traced, one on a south window jamb and another on the south west angle buttress.

Internally the building has a plaster ceiling of c.1960 and delicately coloured walls. The only medieval features are a piscina and two fine brackets for devotional figures on the east wall. The chancel screen was removed in 1883, at which time other fittings, the door and probably the pulpit and lectern were introduced. The three box pews, one for each of the farms, were probably installed earlier in the C19, whilst the painted altar table is C17. A simple and harmonious building.

In the graveyard there are some C19 monuments of the Clarke family. Outside the enclosure there are a series of water features and moats which were formerly more extensive.

2 Tattenhoe Hall Farm II

Farmhouse built in brick c.1840–50 probably incorporating the core of an earlier building which appears on the 1801 Selby survey. Two parallel blocks gabled at the ends with part-external stacks, the main elevation facing south, of three bays, with 12-pane sashes with concealed boxes and radial brick lintels. At the centre is a door, panelled with segmental re-entrant corners the top panels glazed, all within a four-centred brick arch. This unusual feature gives warning of the fine panelled Gothic style doors in the central stair hallway internally. Early C19 stair. The four roof trusses have struts, collars and carpenter's marks. Two rear extensions, joined by a recent glazed porch entrance.

Facing the rear of the house across the large yard is a five-bay brick barn of the C19.

P1

P2

P3

3 Tattenhoe Bare Farm II

Farmhouse of the late C18–C19, of brick, roughcast to the main south elevation. Three bays, two bays deep, and two storeys. The elevation has a central moulded doorcase and 20-pane sashes with wedge lintels and curiously heavy keystones. Large gable stacks. The house is extended to the west by a three-bay contemporary two-storey farm building.

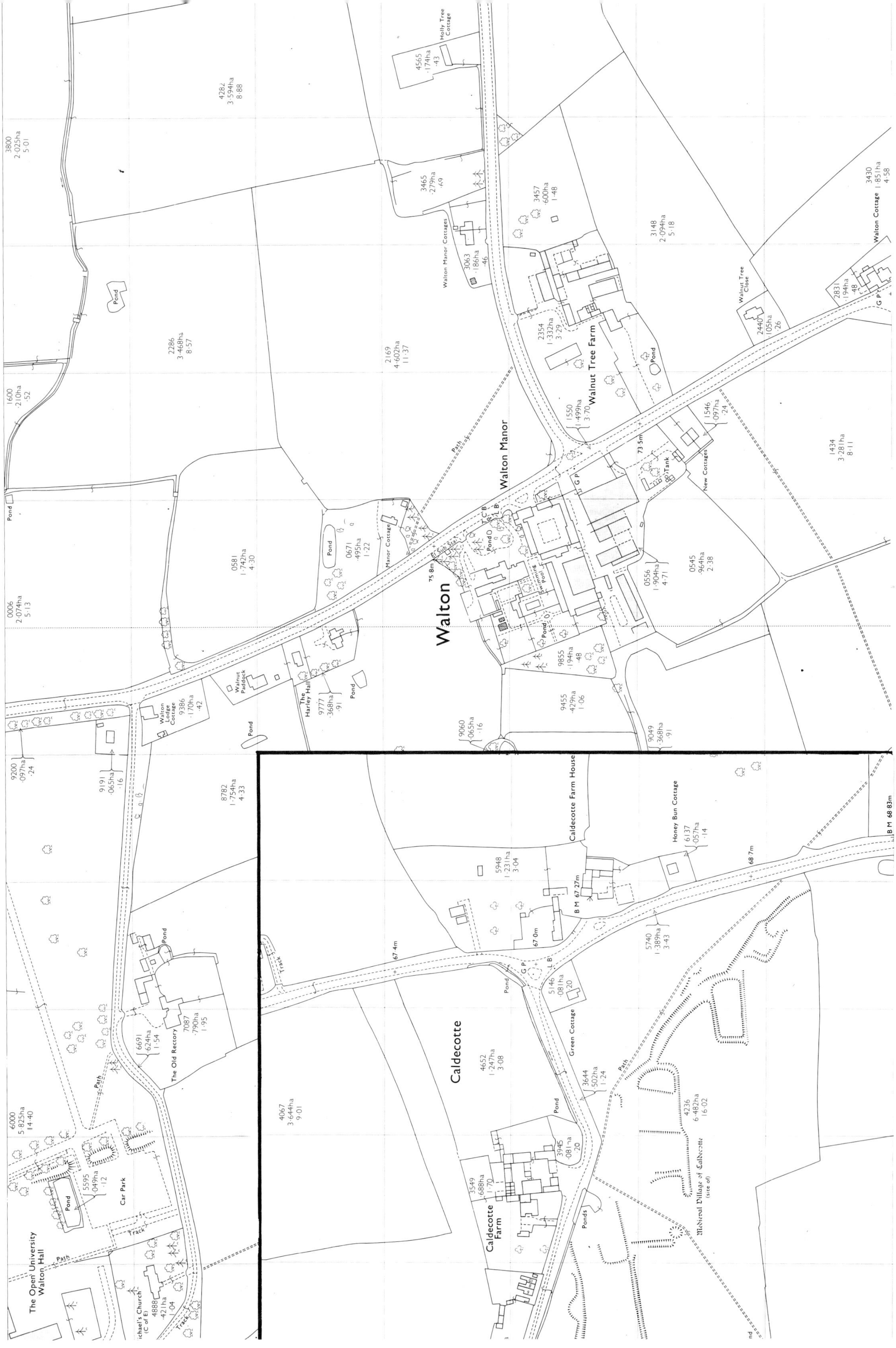
Walton
Walton Manor
Walnut Tree Farm
Walnut Tree Close
Walton Cottage
Walton Manor Cottages
Holly Tree Cottage
New Cottages
Manor Cottage
Walnut Paddock
The Harley Hall
Walton Lodge Cottage
The Old Rectory
The Open University Walton Hall
Car Park
Caldecotte
Caldecotte Farm
Caldecotte Farm House
Honey Bun Cottage
Green Cottage
Pond
Ponds
Path
Track
Swimming Pool
Tank

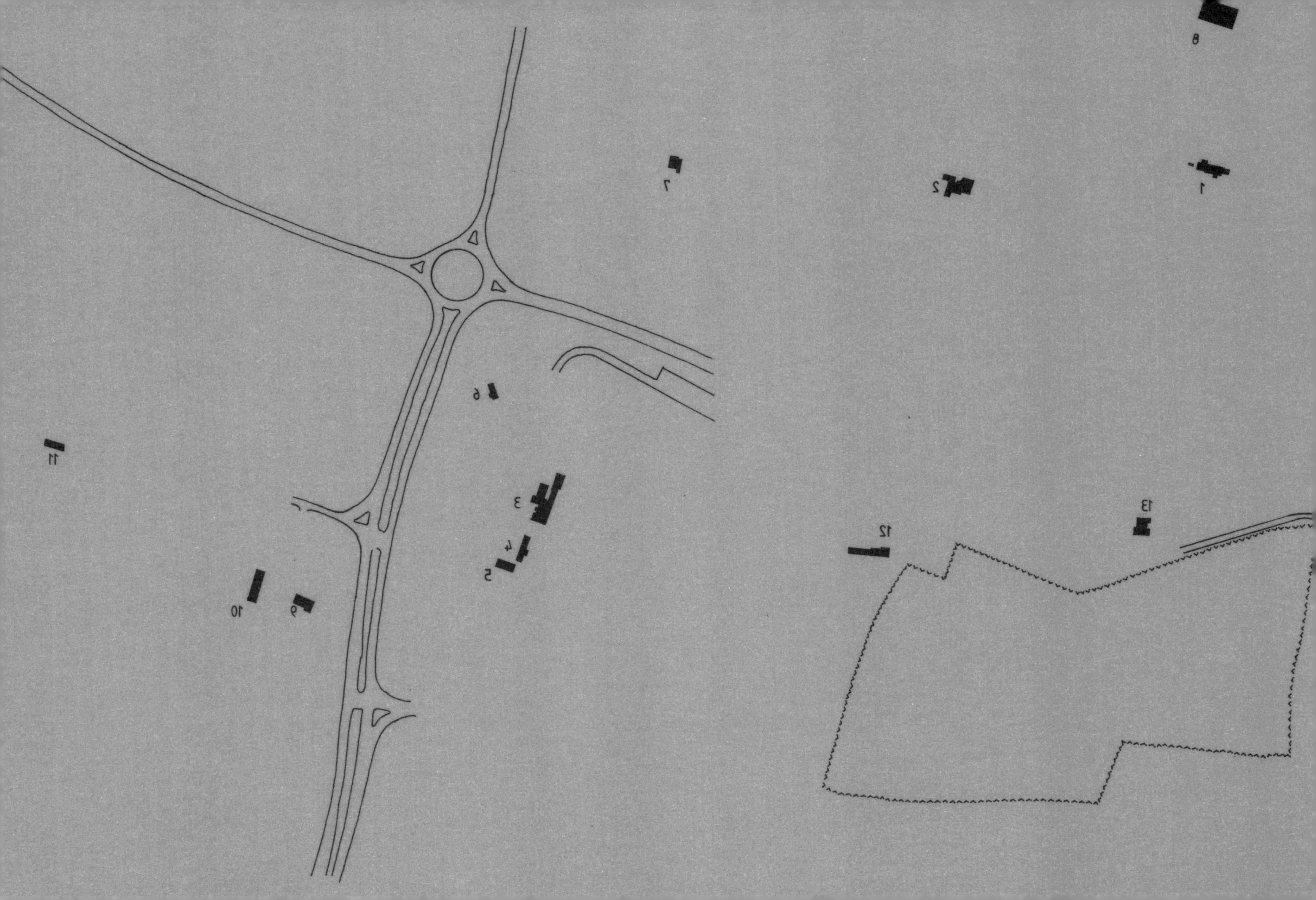
1
2
3
4
5
6
7
8
9
10
11
12
13

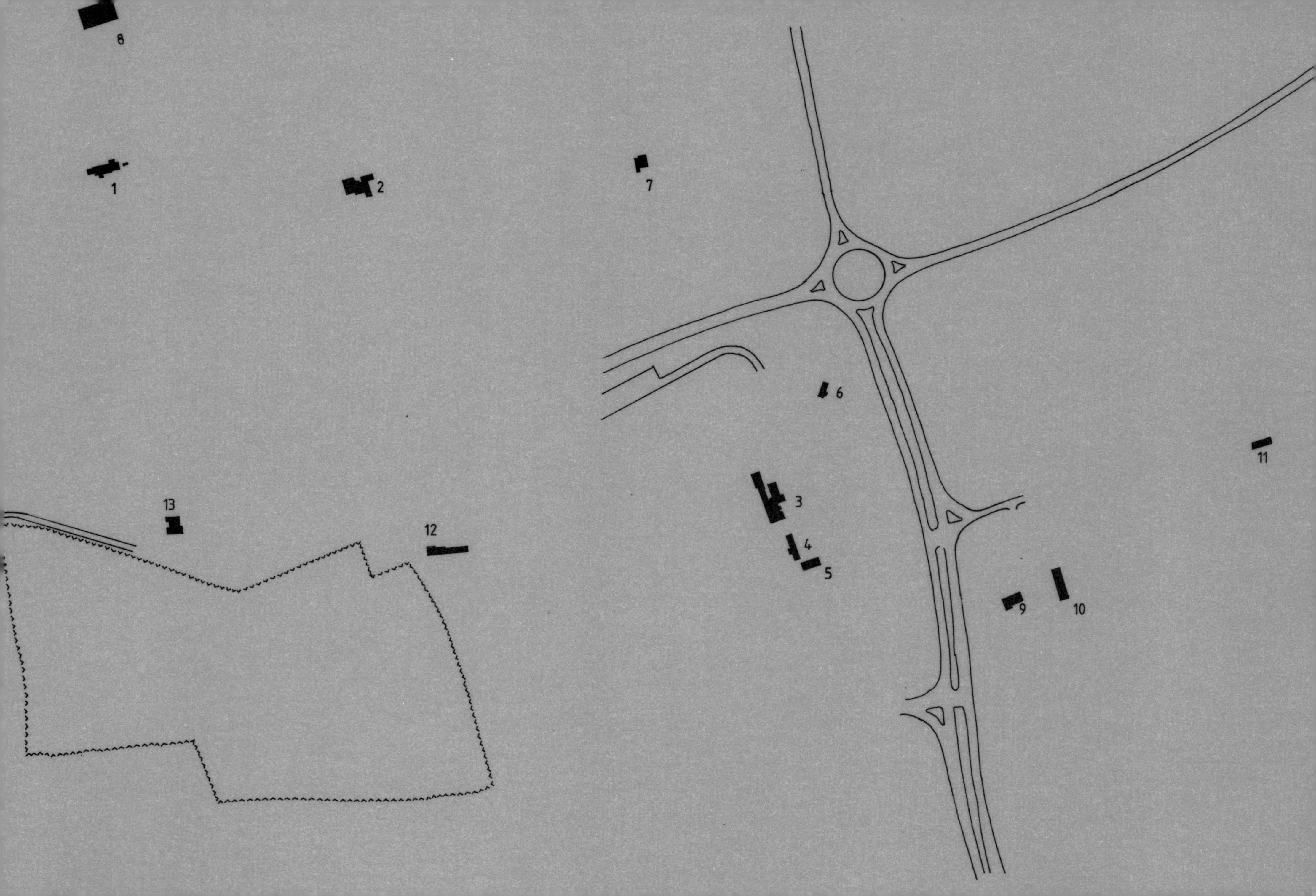

8
1
2
7
6
11
13
12
3
4
5
9
10

Q

WALTON and CALDECOTTE

WALTON AND CALDECOTTE

Walton is one of the smallest parishes in north Buckinghamshire, and although the name (in Anglo Saxon, the settlement of the natives) suggests it is a place of great antiquity, it did not develop to much more than a small village in the Middle Ages and later. Here, the part of Bow Brickhill parish included within Milton Keynes called Caldecotte has also been included with Walton for convenience. At the present time Walton is the land of the Open University and Hoescht Chemicals. Its early origin can be demonstrated by an imperfectly known Roman site under Groveway. The medieval village lay somewhat to the north around the parish church, now within the grounds of the Open University, but in later times development had moved to the south around the manor, where, surprisingly a small village green still survives with a Jubilee Oak planted in 1897. Walton is of special interest to the student of vernacular buildings in that it is a village of timber framed houses where the framing differs from other villages in Milton Keynes by the use of, not squared panels as elsewhere, but a closer set vertical studding and a heavier internal framework. Why this is so is not yet clear, as this is not present in other surrounding villages, and the implication is that the buildings here have survived from an earlier period in history, the fifteenth century rather than the sixteenth.

1 Church of St. Michael — II

Parish church. A simple building with a large squat tower, nave, chancel and south porch, all of local limestone with an admixture of Brickhill ironstone, and with tiled roofs. It is nearly all of the late C13 to C14, restored in 1861. The windows all have hood moulds with a variety of carved head terminals. The nave has a late medieval four-bay roof and a stair to the former rood screen with a tiny trefoiled light externally, and the porch is an addition of the C15–C16. The tower, with its diagonal buttresses carries two C17 bells. Excavations carried out in 1975–6 indicated that the walls may be of C12 origin. They also located two C17 brick vaults under the chancel and, within the nave, a bellfounder's pit, indicating that the bells had been cast actually on site in the medieval period. Internally, there are some interesting features. In the chancel there is a handsome wall monument in the form of an aedicule with columns and a broken pediment, and within, roundels with busts of Bartholomew and Katherine Beale, erected by their sons in 1672. One son, Charles married Mary, a pupil of Lely and who died in 1697. There are also a number of tablets to the Pinfold family, whose finest monument, to Sir Thomas Pinfold, King's Advocate and Chancellor of Peterborough, appears in the south wall of the nave. This tomb is of c.1701 and is by the famous sculptor, Joseph Nollekins. It has a portrait medallion on a tall black marble pyramid, book of law, and scrolls. There is also a brass in rhyming English and Latin, to Elizabeth Pyxe, dated 1617.

Q1

NL

In the churchyard, east of the chancel, lies the chest tomb of a later Charles Pinfold, died 1760 with a swept casket top and engraved panels surrounding the drapery. The obelisk on top is now so swathed in ivy as to be difficult to make out. There are also some good C18 headstones with their tops carved in low relief.

2 The Old Rectory — II

Parsonage house, now part of the University. In origin a timber framed building probably of the C16, to which various extensions have been added in the C18 and the main building re-windowed. It has a C19 wing on the east side and various other contemporary additions in brick of c.1860–70, now whitewashed.

Q2

3 Manor Farmhouse II

Farmhouse, now offices. An impressive C16 Manor house of the Gilpin, and later, the Pinfold families. It started as a main south range with a northern bay wing and a stair in the angle of the two. This was built out in 1701 by Sir Thomas Pinfold and further extensions were made to the north side in the C19. The construction is in heavy timber framing, clad now with roughcasting. A major stack on the south side has brick diagonal shafts. The interior has, in the main west room of the south range, a stone fireplace with a depressed head and moulded jambs. The stair is late C17 but altered. The house was extensively converted to luxury offices in the early 1970s.

Q3

4 Stables II

The farm buildings of the Manor were apparently rebuilt in the early–mid C19 and now form a well-kept yard laid out on regular lines with a gabled pitching door and clock as a centrepiece.

Q4

5 Barn II

A late C16–early C17 barn, six bays, timber framed with a tiled roof. An unusually complete barn owing its survival to it having been used regularly with the Manor. It may have originally been two, a wheat barn and a barley barn. The studding is comparatively close, with a bressumer rail and corner braces, and it has opposed cart entrances. Queen post roof trusses with angle braces to the tie beams.

Q5

6 Manor Cottage II

Cottage, now the social club for Messrs Hoescht. C16, timber framed with brick noggings. Storey height studding with corner braces to the internal trusses. Thatched roof. It is of two bays, with a central large brick stack, and lean-to structures both ends. A winding stair is set into the back wall, probably replacing the original stair by the stack. Chamfered spine beams, the room behind the stack with heavy floor joists. There are windbraces to the central queen-post truss.

Q6

7 Walton Lodge Cottage II

Mid to late C19 pair of cottages, now one house, slightly in the cottage ornée tradition, forming lodge to Walton Hall. Rubble stonework with a timber framed gable with ornate bargeboards. The roof has serrated ridges and the windows have patterned cast-iron frames. The cottage ornée, a romantic concept of the rustic cottage introduced in the late C18 to early C19 when the country peasantry was becoming of interest to the growing urban population, is a style only met with elsewhere in Milton Keynes at the station in Fenny Stratford.

8 Walton Hall II

An elegant house of stuccoed brick, built in 1830 for Charles Pinfold to replace the Manor House as the family seat, as here it was possible to lay out 60 acres of parkland away from the home farm. Two storeys and basement, three bays, with a projecting Tuscan tetrastyle portico with tryglyph frieze. The ground floor sash windows are set within a shallow arch. The front has end pilasters and a moulded cornice. Internally the building has a spacious entrance hall leading to a stair hall at the rear. Either side are two large reception rooms with the service rooms in an annex at the rear, and on the first floor, five bedrooms. It is a fine example of a small but dignified Regency country house. The hall screen, staircase, doors and fireplaces are original. It is now the University Vice-Chancellor's offices.

Q8

9 Walnut Tree Farmhouse **II**

A farmhouse of the C16 or C17, timber framed, the framing of storey height close studding without braces, replaced with brick on the ground floor. Tiled roof of c.1880–1900, on the original double purlin structure the upper purlin clasped. 'L'-plan, built up as a main three-bay block with cross passage and stack between bays two and three, to which has been added, in the C18, a rear passage leading to a wing room on the south west corner, extending the polite end of the building, and downgrading the older part to a kitchen and dairy. Inside there are moulded ceiling beams and a large central stack with inglenook fireplace. Up to the later C19 the village was famous for its walnut trees, of which some four mature trees remain. From these this farm takes its name.

Q9

10 Barn **NL**

To the east of the farmhouse lies the yards, the east side of which has a fine four-bay timber framed barn of vertical studding raised on a stone sill wall. Once central bressamur. It is also probably of the late C16–early C17 as the original house.

Q10

11 Holly Tree Cottage **NL**

A C17 cottage, originally one storey and attic, and later raised to two storeys. Vertical timber studding survives on the north side. It is of two bays with lobby entry plan.

CALDECOTTE

Milton Keynes boundaries as drawn in 1978 took in a strip of the northern part of the old parish of Bow Brickhill. This part included the nearly deserted village of Caldecotte. Here we find two farms, and some farmworkers' houses, most of which were of little interest and some have since been demolished.

Q11

12 Old Caldecotte Farmhouse **II**

A C17 farmhouse of interest in that it has remained more or less unaltered since the end of the C17. It is 10 bays long, one room wide, including a barn attached to its eastern end. The core building is timber framed with lath and daub infilling, mostly replaced in brick. It started as a two bays lobby entry plan, possible late C16, to which was added three further bays in the C17 and a hay barn later that century. Internally it has two inglenooks to the large central stack opposite the door, and a large dairy, and with a built-in Victorian dresser. The building was extended by one bay in brick to the west, and at the east the contemporary barn, also timber framed and weatherboarded, attached almost in the manner of a longhouse. The roof is thatched, and during repairs in 1976 the thatcher found traces of lime plastering of the thatch, an ancient precaution against fire. Internally it has chamfered spine beams.

Q12

13 Caldecotte Farmhouse **NL**

An early C19 two-storey farmhouse of three bays, built of yellow brick with a slate roof. Twenty-pane sash windows, replaced with casement windows and a French window on the ground floor.

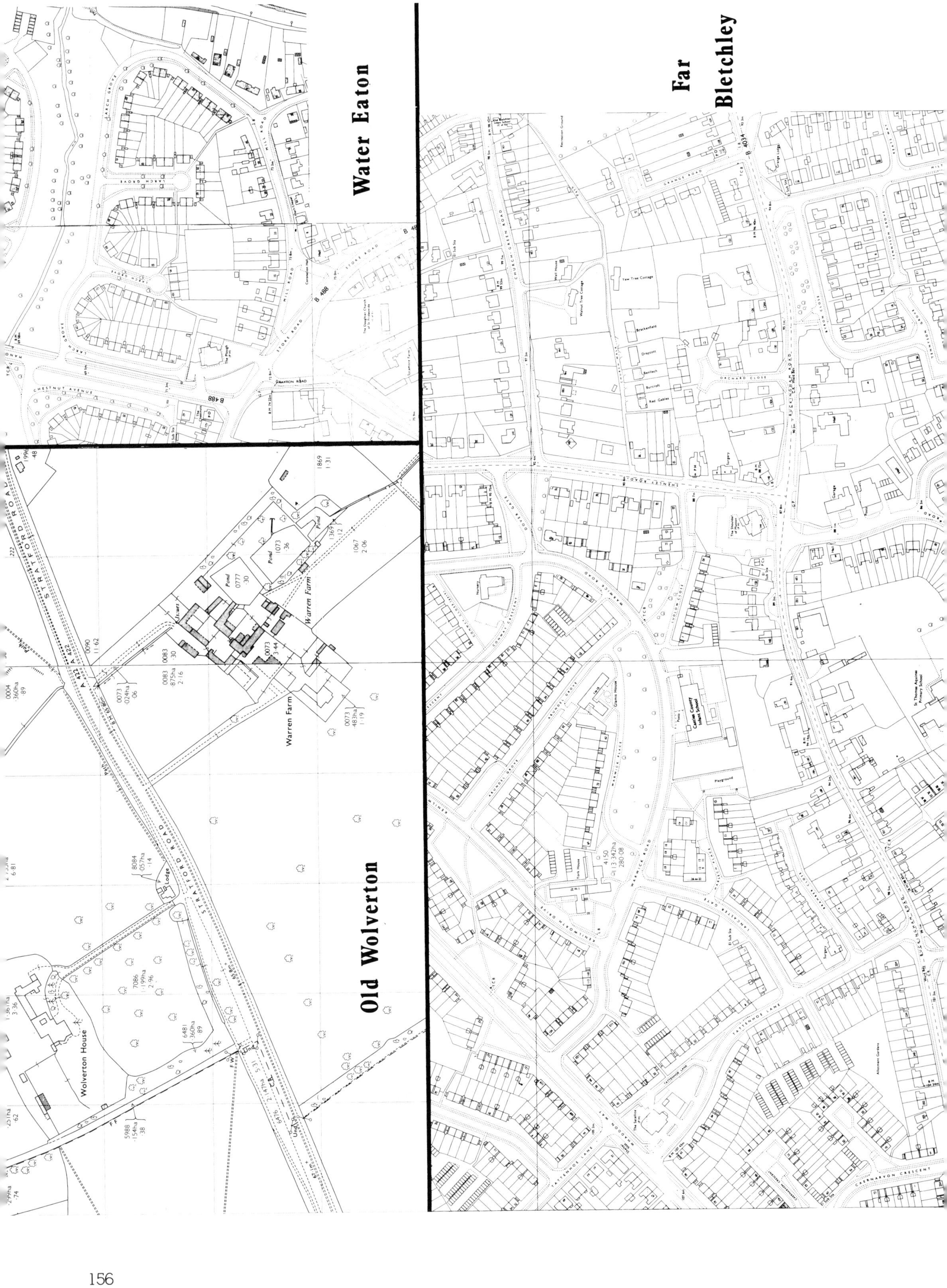
Water Eaton
Far Bletchley
Old Wolverton
Warren Farm
Wolverton House
STRATFORD ROAD
Pond

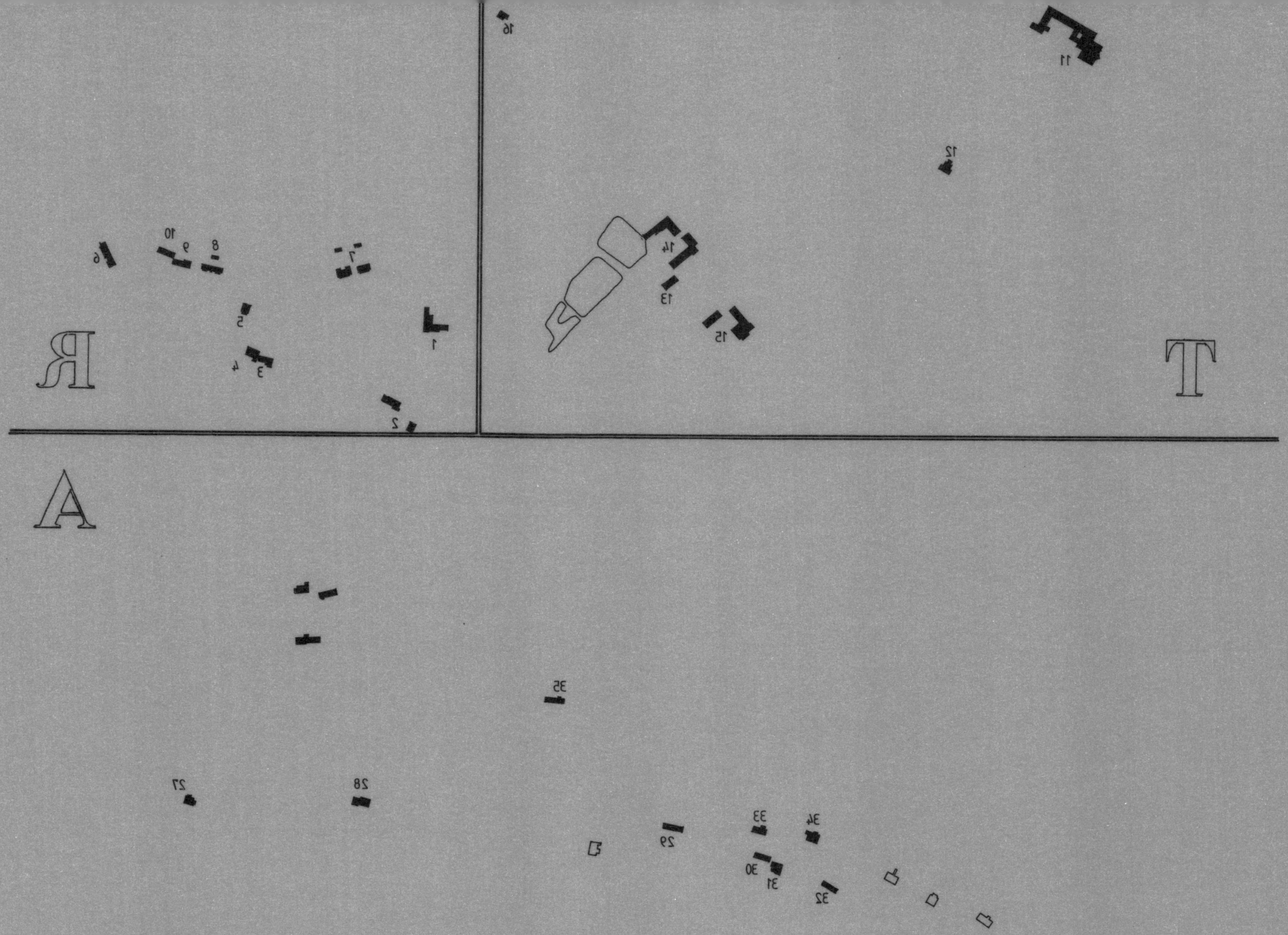
A
1
2
3
4
5
7
8
9
10
11
12
13
14
15
16
27
28
29
30
31
32
33
34
35

R
A
T
1
2
3
4
5
6
7
8
9
10
11
12
13
14
15
16
27
28
29
30
31
32
33
34
35

WATER EATON

WATER EATON

Water Eaton was, at one time, the principal manor of Bletchley and must have been a place of significance in that it was granted a charter for a market in the reign of King John. It has now become no more than a small settlement lost in the southern post-war suburbs of Bletchley. It is another riverside settlement, the first south of Fenny Stratford on the old road to Leighton Buzzard, and a minor cross roads provided trackways to the Shenleys to the north-west, and to the Brickhills across the river. Today the village centres on Mill Road, with a number of buff brick buildings of the early C19 interspersed between timber framed cottages. A collection of red-brick houses of the late C19–early C20 lend some coherence to the place as the centre. An unusual and fascinating survival relating to Water Eaton are the Compotus Rolls, detailed farm accounts of the demesne farm of Lord de Grey from autumn 1394 to autumn 1395. 174 acres were used as arable, wheat, barley and peas being the crops grown, but they show the transition taking place to increased animal husbandry. They are translated in Record of Bucks, XII, No. 4 of 1930. Brickmaking was first established in Water Eaton at Slad Farm in 1933. The industry has been operated by Fletton Ltd. since 1933.

DRAYTON ROAD

1 Home Farmhouse II

Farmhouse, now a women's hostel, c.1730 probably for Browne Willis. A very seemly early Georgian design using red and vitrified blue bricks with tiled roof, five bays, with a central panelled door and pedimented doorcase, and 12-pane sash windows. It has a central stair hall and gable end stacks to the reception rooms. Internally it was restored and converted in 1974 after much vandalism. It had, surprisingly, wattle and daub partitions, probably one of the last instances of the use of this elementary building construction. The rear extension was built for the Linnell family in 1846, and inscribed bricks with the date and initials JL, ML, AL, and SL can be seen. In the 1813 Enclosure Award the property was allocated 12 acres, rising to 141 acres in 1921. The Linnells, who had acquired it in 1768 then also held Water Eaton Mill.

R1

2 Sycamore Farmhouse II

Farmhouse, now offices, and remarkably similar to Home Farmhouse and probably also of c.1730. Vitrified bricks with red dressings, of six bays, with the entrance in a flat canopied doorcase with a pretty fanlight in the fourth bay. Slated roof and gable stacks. A day centre occupies a former barn, built in the mid-C19 with pale diaper brickwork, a vertical pattern being produced with Flemish bond. Perforated brick gables.

R4

STOKE ROAD

3 No. 5 II

A mid-C18 brick house of three bays, two storeys, with a central door and hallway, retaining its original 16-pane sashes. Dentilled eaves and gable stacks.

4 No. 7, Veterinary Centre II

Formerly the George Inn. To the rear, a small timber framed house of two bays, one storey and loft, with a central collar beam truss and clasped purlins. It appears to have continued as a third bay beyond the major stack which has been rebuilt in the C19 by the front block at right angles. It now has an amusing porch with C19 glass. It was, apparently, originally longer as both end walls have been rebuilt.

R5

LARCH GROVE

5 Methodist Chapel NL

Chapel, 1830, buff brick, now rendered and colourwashed. Two bays end on to the road and later C19 enclosed porch. The side windows have 'Y' glazing bars to their arched heads, and a window over the porch has painted glass of 1930.

6 No. 8 II

A C17 house, probably of a smallholder. Colourwashed roughcast on timber framing. Two bays, two storeys, lobby entry plan. Half-hipped thatched roof. The framing is exposed internally and it has one opened inglenook fireplace, the other still bricked up. Chamfered spine beams with faceted ogee stops. Corner braces and straight windbraces on the upper floor. It is a building unusual for this area for it is in a Dorset–Wilts vernacular style.

R6

MILL ROAD

7 Nos. 1, 3, 5 and 7 II

Two pairs of semi-detached estate cottages for the Duncombe Estate. C.1830–40, buff brick with dark blue tiled roofs, each cottage 'L'-plan with entrance in the re-entrant front corner with an open timber porch. Cogged gables to front and side with diamond iron lattice glazing under segmental coloured brick arches. The large central stack with offsetting head survives on block 1–3.

At the bottom of the garden is a long single storey structure containing a bakehouse at the centre, flanked by coal houses and earth closets at the back. The bakehouse has an external oven, which must have been used in common.

R7

8 Nos. 29, 31 and 33 II

Three cottages in a terrace for the Duncombe estate, similar in design to Nos. 1–7, c.1830–40. Windows have been altered in the recessed centre cottage.

9 Nos. 37 and 39 II

A pair of C17 timber framed cottages of one storey and attic bedrooms and a thatched roof, the framing replaced with brick on the front. C19 segmental headed windows. Three flush dormers. Internally, a blocked inglenook fireplace.

R10

10 No. 41, The Homestead II

Timber framed C17 cottage, once three cottages, and probably built as two. 3½ bays, the right bay with corner braces, and a stack in the centre half-bay. Stone plinth and thatched roof.

11 Canal Bridge II

Accommodation bridge No. 93, 1775–1800, pale red brick with elliptical arch of three rings of blue bricks, and with cast iron bars protecting the arrises from tow ropes on the towpath side. Two course string at roadway level, and rounded copings terminating in stone capped piers.

R13

12 (Water Eaton Wharf)

Of the wharf there is now little sign, the last two diaper brick cottages having been demolished ahead of redevelopment in the 1970s.

13 Water Eaton Millhouse and Mill II

A C19 brick mill of three storeys on a millstream from the River Ouzel. Three storeys, the end bay over the race. No wheel survives, but the building is still used as a grain store. It occupies the site of earlier mills. Attached is a range of outbuildings ending in the mill house, a mid-C19 three-bay building of two storeys.

R11

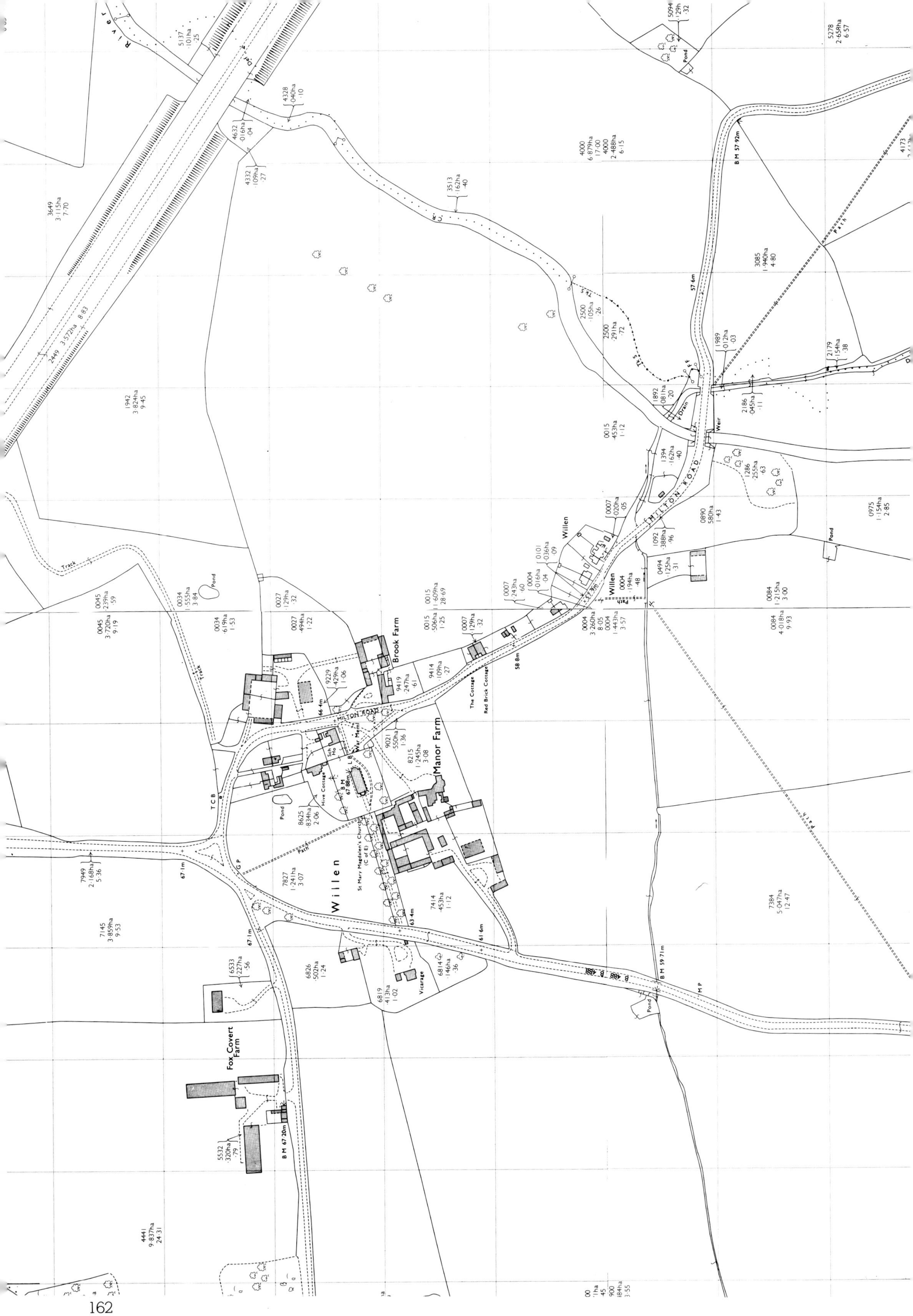

Willen
Manor Farm
Brook Farm
Fox Covert Farm
MILTON ROAD
St Mary Magdalen's Church (C of E)
Vicarage
Hive Cottage
War Meml
Sch Ho
The Cottage
Red Brick Cottage
Pond
Track
Path
Weir
Drain

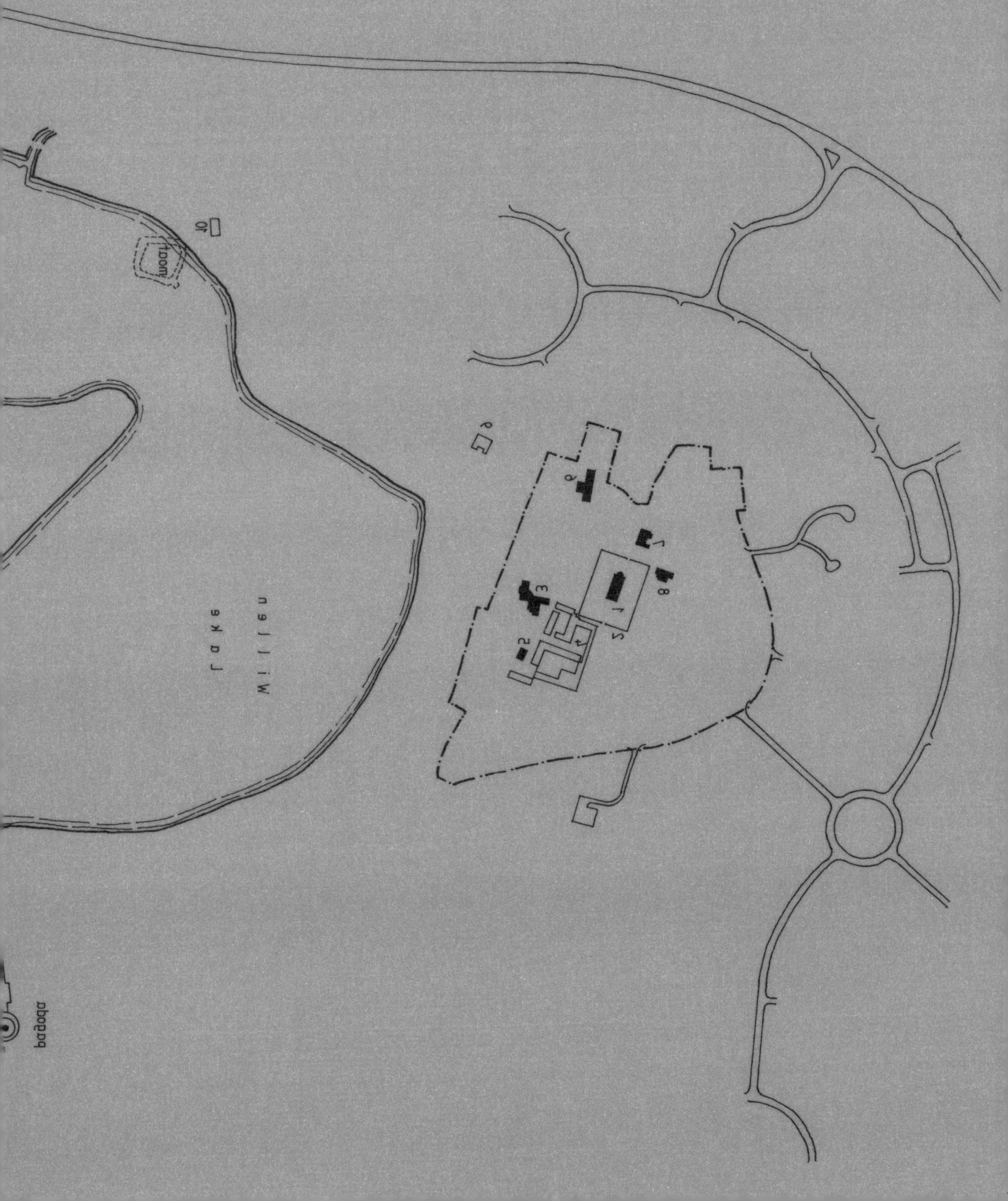
Lake
Willen
moat
pagoda
10

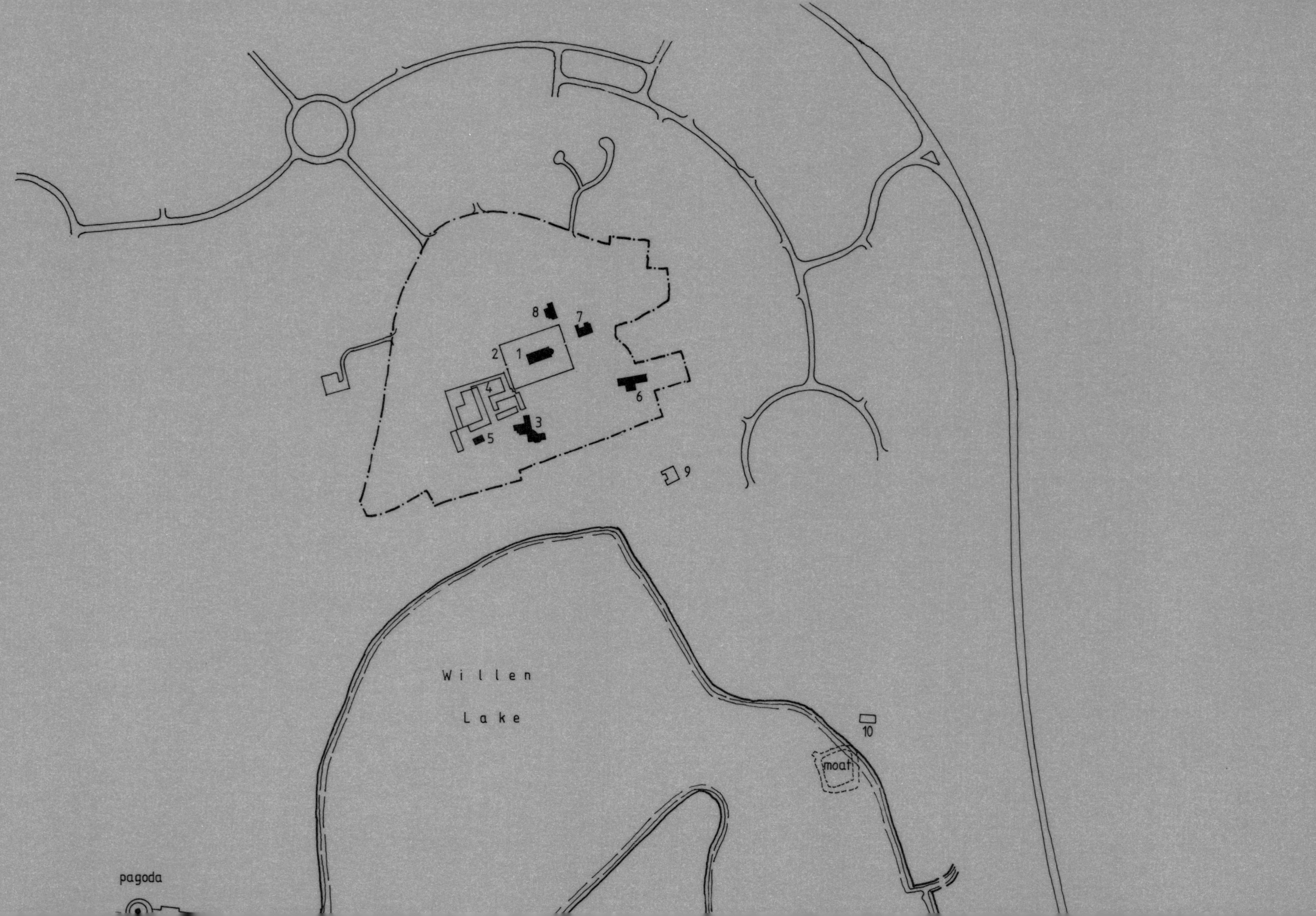

1
2
3
4
5
6
7
8
9
10
Willen
Lake
moat
pagoda

WILLEN

WILLEN

Willen is one of the smaller villages of Milton Keynes and is not separately mentioned in the Domesday survey. The population of the parish for 1567 has been estimated at 48, and on the eve of Milton Keynes, 40, thus until recently has remained virtually static. The parish was at one time accounted with Caldecotte near Newport Pagnell. It had a moated site, excavated in the early 1970s and producing Roman material but no early medieval house. Enclosure of common land took place early, starting c.1511 and continued by the Nicholls family, lords of the manor, who appear again at Woughton, and was completed by Act of Parliament of 1660. The Nicholls stood on neutral ground during the Civil War.

1 Church of St. Mary Magdalene **I**

Anglican parish church, built 1678–80 by Robert Hooke, mathematician, scientist and amateur architect, colleague of Sir Christopher Wren, for Dr. Richard Busby. The main builder was a Richard Atterbury of Newport, who was well known in the area, and also built the Almshouses at Linford. The church is on the site of a two-cell Norman building with a double arched bellcote, which had apparently fallen into decay by the later C17. Mellow red brick with limestone quoins and dressings and a copper, replacing a lead roof. Nave and apsidal chancel, and west tower. The entrance is in a recessed entrance under the tower, and steps counterbalancing the curve, similar to Wren's slightly earlier church of St. Mary le Bow, London (1670–83). The tower is of three stages, with a segmental headed and round-headed window in the top stage, with corner pilasters, and a stone pineapple parapet, all rather naive and delightful. The nave has large round headed leaded windows, the Victorian glass happily removed in 1979 and sold to Japan. The eastern chancel was square but this was replaced in 1861 by T. H. Lewis with the present apsidal chancel in a manner that could not but have met the approval of Hooke and Wren. The building is extended to the west to provide a room each side of the tower and entrance for a vestry and a library, the roofs tied by simple curves and pineapple finials to the tower. Internally the entrance vestibule leads through double wood doors to the splendour of the nave, barrel vaulted and with wall stucco decoration in frames embellished with floral scrolls, now all painted chastely white. The decoration of the apse, although Victorian, is as equally sensitive as the exterior. The pews, reading desk and pulpit are complete of 1680 and are not too flamboyant as behoves a country church. The open rails in front of the organ are believed to be the original altar rails. The font is a delicate essay in black and white marbles, and has a fruitwood cover by Baites, whom Wren employed in St. Anne and St. Agnes, London. All the details of the church repay study, as do the building accounts which have been preserved in the archives of Westminster Abbey. These show that Hooke provided at least two schemes for Busby's approval, one with shallow gabled transepts. He visited a number of times, and stayed at the Swan, Newport Pagnell while the church was being built. It cost the extravagantly large sum of £5,000 at the end of the works. It is one of the architectural treasures of Milton Keynes.

S1

S1a

2 Churchyard Walls and Gate Piers II

The church lies in a square graveyard enclosed by a brick wall with specially made brick copings, and sweeping up to tall gate piers on the east and west sides: these have stone cornices surmounted by ball finials, all late C17, the stone cappings at the east having been recently and unforgivably incorrectly replaced.

3 Willen Hospice formerly Manor Farm II

In 1632 Manor farmhouse came into the ownership of Roger Nicholls, Councillor of Law, whose successor sold to Colonel Robert Hampden, who had held Charles I prisoner in the Isle of Wight. Later, in 1671 it was bought by Dr. Richard Busby, the famous headmaster of Westminster School, grammarian and classical scholar notorious for his beatings. Amongst his pupils were Christopher Wren and Robert Hooke, who is remembered today by schoolchildren for his Hooke's Law of elasticity. Busby lived in retirement at Willen until his death in 1695, and provided for the replacement of the medieval church. Earliest records show that the house was originally timber framed. However, the present building has stone cellars of indeterminate date, over which is built an imposing four by two bays house of the early C19, being itself an extension of a late C18 building now containing the kitchens. It appears that this building was partly demolished on its south side and rebuilt before the main block was added shortly afterwards. A later C19 canted bay window on the south side has recently been rebuilt.

There are two wells, one over 60ft deep.

4 Outbuildings to former Manor Farm NL

Manor Farm had a large number of outbuildings on its western side, extending as far as shelter sheds against the lime-tree alley leading to the church. The earliest of these was a barn, timber framed and probably of the C18, and some other C18 fragments built into the general rebuilding which took place in the first half of the C19.

5 Granary II

One building is listed, this is a large granary on staddles, mushroom-like supports to prevent vermin entering the building. This is timber framed and weatherboarded with a shallow pitched roof, also of early C19 date.

6 Brook Farmhouse II

Farmhouse probably of the late C17 or early C18, of brick and stone with a tiled roof. It is of five bays with a wing to the south of 1899 replacing an earlier extension on this side. Attached to the east gable is a former kitchen and dairy, C19. It has a large stone stack at the centre, raised through the roof in early brick. It may have originally been two buildings as the roofs were of different pitches in 1822.

Brook Farm has a series of outbuildings including a stone barn of the early-mid C19 and, further north, another range of stables and a timber framed barn, also C19, and still having jowled posts. **NL**

S2

S3

S5

S6

7 The Old School II

A small and delightful village school dating from 1847 for 24 children, of brick with a tiled roof. It has a gabled porch with the datestone, and a gable to the schoolroom on the left. The windows have diamond panes.

8 Hive Cottage NL

Cottage, late C18, with a large central stack, much refurbished in the 1980s.

9 Broughton Road NL

The 1822 survey of the parish shows a number of cottages standing on the north-east side of the road, where the present house, from The Cottage to Kitsend now are. The pale red brick, rather like a Yorkshire stock, is visible, particularly in Nos. 10 and 12 with its central stack. This probably represents the construction of the first decades of that century, and Hollytrees House and No. 15 may incorporate the cottage newly erected by the tenant in 1817.

10 (Willen Mill)

The mill at Willen, which first appears in Domesday Book, was a timber framed and weatherboarded building with a half-hipped thatched roof, lying astride the millrace. Being in the ownership of Dr. Busby in the late C17 the documents of its part rebuilding and repair have been preserved in the archives of Westminster Abbey, although the mill has disappeared.

S7

River Great Ouse
Manor Farm
Manor Cottages
Canal Cottage
The Galleon (P H)
Timber Yard
Overflow
Towing Path
Motte & Bailey
Old Wolverton
Holy Trinity Church (C of E)
Vicarage
Medieval Village (site of)
Wolverton Park
Rose Cottage
Allotment Gardens
SLATED ROW
TRINITY ROAD
MANOR ROAD
LONGVILLE
CAXTON ROAD
STRATFORD ROAD
Playing Field
Shelter
Clinic
Pond
Ponds
Cattle Grid
Track
Sinks
Issues
Pipe Line
Tunnel
Drain
Path
A 422

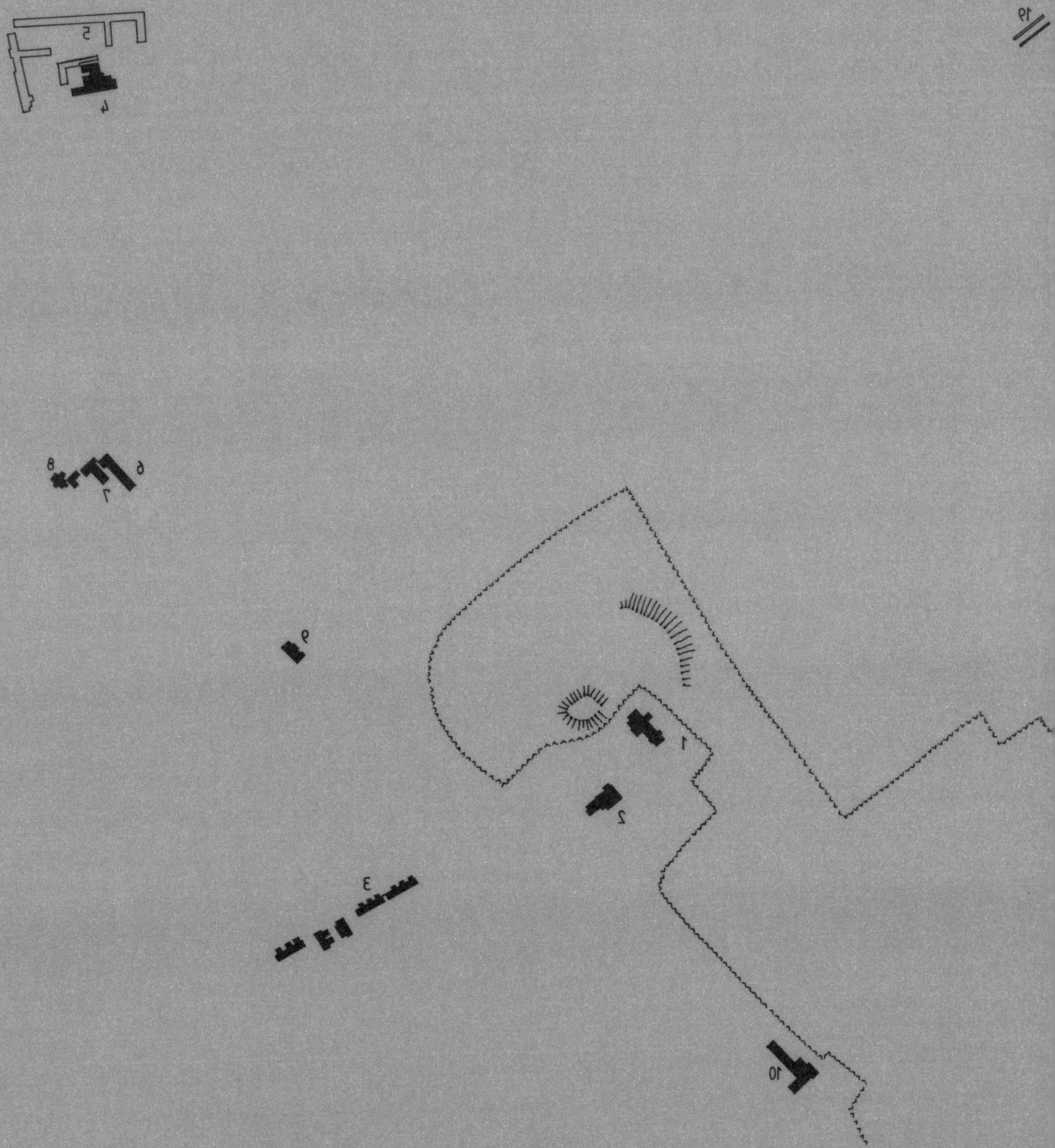

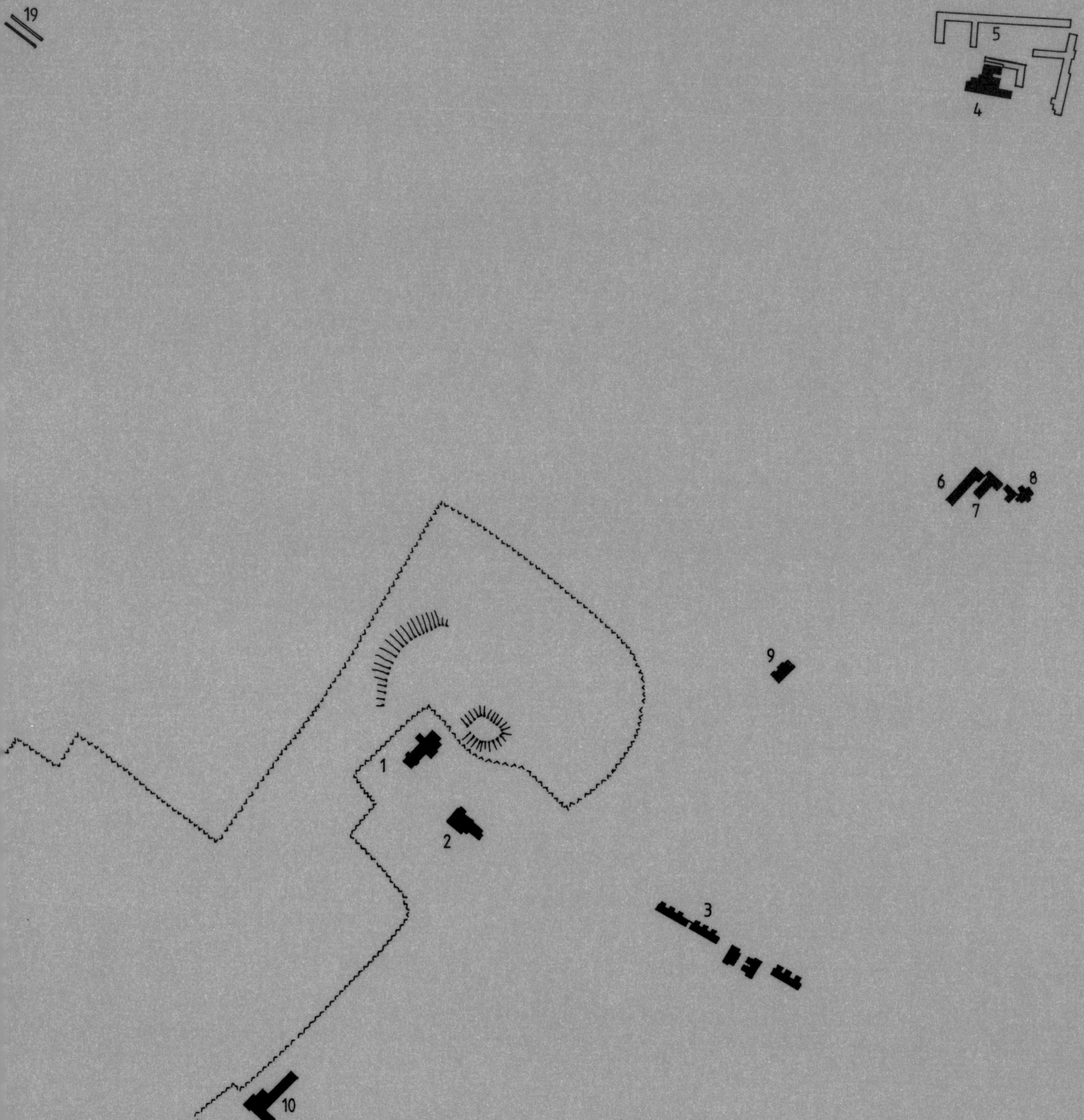
19
5
4
6
8
7
9
1
2
3
10

WOLVERTON

WOLVERTON

Wolverton appears in Domesday Book as Wluerintone, a parish with two mills on the River Ouse, which forms its northern boundary against Northamptonshire. The centre was established on a bluff where a small motte and bailey castle was erected close to the church, part of the moat being filled in when it was built. The motte can still be seen. The village associated with this early settlement lay to the west of the church on lower ground, and today it is still possible to see the ancient roadways and building platforms of the village, one of the best preserved archaeological sites in Milton Keynes. The Longueville family was established here in the medieval period, Sir John of Wolverton being granted a right by the Bishop of Lincoln to establish an oratory in his house. By 1342 the barony became extinct, but the family continued here: in 1501 the Longuevilles had a deer park in the parish, which was 20 acres in 1713 and a low park of 30 acres. Part of their Elizabethan mansion can still be seen in a later building, and in 1720 their house, which had recently been sold to the famous physician Dr. John Radcliffe, was described as a fine seat. The Radcliffe Estate, which included the whole of Wolverton, was left in trust for the benefit of University College, Oxford. It is the same family that donated their name to the famous hospital and the Radcliffe Camera, part of the Bodleian Library. The enclosures of the parish took place in 1654. Religious houses also held land, the Prior of Bradwell having the eastern Mead Mill, and the alien priory of Chicksands held a grange, probably on the site of Manor Farm.

Wolverton parish originally extended as far as Watling Street to the west, the east side of that settlement known as Stony Stratford being within Wolverton. To the east it runs to Stantonbury. To the south the parish extends up on to the colder glacial deposits, where at one point, near Brick Kiln Farm, clay was dug in the C19 for brickmaking.

OLD WOLVERTON

1 Church of All Saints B

The parish church, built 1809–14, by Henry Hakewill, and said to incorporate the tower of the medieval parish church. The original church consisted of a nave, south aisle, chancel and central tower. The new work is of Attlebury stone, with Bilston (Staffs) stone for finer work, brought to Wolverton wharf by canal. Pavings are of Kingsthorpe stone and it has lead roofs. It comprises nave and transepts, chancel with a south vestry, and a west tower. It is remarkable in a national context for being one of the earliest and unschooled examples of the Romanesque Revival style which the builder called Saxon, and which did not reach general acceptance and popularity until the 1840s. Decoration is restrained to that around the west door; the rest is notable for its simplicity and smooth surfaces, its wide spaced corbel table and corner turrets copying those of Peterborough Cathedral, to the gables. The east window is a huge rose window.

Internally there is a fine wall monument of 1685 to Sir Thomas Longueville, resting on a sarcophagus. The interior was a significant example of stencilled decoration by Bell of Bell and Almand, 1877, much of which has been needlessly obliterated during the re-ordering process carried out in about 1974. Edward Swinfen Harris of Stony Stratford inserted the ceiling and carried out various works between 1870 and 1898.

In the graveyard there are two chest tombs earlier than the building, both with recessed corner balusters: one of the Ratcliffe family 1790–1808 and the other to Edward Cook who died 1794, and his wife. It has good lettering.

T1

T1a

2 Longueville Court (formerly the Rectory and c.1840, The Vicarage House) II

House of the early–mid C18 incorporating the doorway and string course from the Elizabethan Manor House of 1584, built by Henry and his wife Elizabeth Cotton. This doorway has handsome Corinthian columns and a broken pediment enclosing the Longueville arms. The string course has metopes and rosettes. The house was rebuilt in 1729, of ashlar limestone with a slate roof, three storeys and five bays wide. The windows are 12-pane sashes with moulded boxes and keyed lintels. To the left is a large C19 bay window. Moulded eaves. The building has a double pile plan with tripartite windows to the rear. Internally it has a doorcase from the original house, and a section of dog-tooth ornament from the medieval church. Something is known of the 1584 house. It has a great hall and parlour with 14 large escutcheons painted with the family arms, and painted glass in its transomed front windows. It was of nine bays, three storeys with a hipped roof and five dormers to the attics. The porch was also of three storeys, with columns in rank of orders, those surviving being from the top storey.

T2

3 Slated Row NL

A small development of c.1820 on land owned by the Radcliffe Trust, comprising eight semi-detached limestone rubble cottages with simple casement windows and blind lunettes in the gables. The cottages were extended in brick c.1880, some partly over the road.

T3

4 Manor Farm II

Farmhouse, early C19, largely a rebuild of a C17 house on the same site, squared limestone with a tiled roof. The front is of three bays, extended both ends, and having a shorter block to the rear. Two storeys, with extensive cellars and attics. The central door in a simple portico leads to a wide stair hall and from this rises a late C17–early C18 stair with turned balusters and ball knobs. C17 doors in the attics. Fine early C19 cast iron fireplace on the first floor and the kitchen at the rear has a large faggot oven. Front shutters drop into a wall cavity on sash cords, a curious early C19 arrangement which is not uncommon. A room at the west end is claimed to be haunted.

The garden walls and gate pier are early–mid C19. II

T4

5 Farm Buildings II

The farm buildings were laid out in the mid C19 on model farm principles. There are two yards divided by a stone wall. The buildings are of high quality finishes with a square brick building at the east end. A small yard, still pitched with stone, has stables and tack rooms close to the house. This interesting layout has recently been prejudiced by a modern open structure dominating the eastern yard.

Manor Farm is said to be near the site of a grange of the monastery of Clattercote, Oxfordshire, of the Order of Gilbertines, a curious monastic community founded in England. The property was later transferred to Chicksands Abbey, Beds. A field north of the house was long known as The Grange. The area north of the drive is the High Park, that beyond the church being the Low Park.

T5

6 Nos. 1–3 Manor Farm Cottages

An C18 range of stone farm cottages of stone with tiled roofs. NL

7 Nos. 4 and 5 Manor Farm Cottages II

Stone cottages of the early–mid C18, now one house. The stone quoins have the dates 1745 and 1754. Internally there is an inglenook fireplace and simple stopped chamfered spine beam.

8 Nos. 6, 8 and 10 Manor Farm Cottages II

A group of stone built cottages placed near the former driveway to Manor Farm. They are of the early–mid C18.

9 The Galleon P.H., formerly The Locomotive Inn NL

Public house early C19 built to serve the canal wharf. Three bays, the centre bay slightly set forward and gabled, and containing the entrance under a segmental arch. Sash windows.

T9

STRATFORD ROAD, OLD WOLVERTON (North side)

10 Wolverton Park II

House of c.1720. Limestone rubble with patterned tiled roof. Probably part demolished in the later C18 to erect a three bay, two storey and attic house to the north. This block received a brick rear wing with cogged eaves c.1840–60 and a link to a former free-standing barn, converted to a stable and carriage house, with a pigeon loft over the door. A central porch and bay window with colonettes were added later. The approach to Wolverton is through fine gate piers.

Internally the house has a fine staircase with heavy turned balusters. In 1742 the piece of land behind the house was known as Kiln Close.

The house became the residence of the superintendent of Wolverton Works. J. E. McConnell lived here up to his retirement in 1861.

T10

11 Wolverton House II

Boarding house for the Radcliffe School. Mid C17, much remodelled c.1820. Rubble limestone with tile and slate roofs, but the front and side link block in ashlar work. Double pile plan with through hall to stair. Tripartite ground floor windows within arched recesses. Gabled shallow porch. It has three round headed dormers to attic rooms. The west side linking block has a very fine two-storey bow window with 15-pane sashes and swept lead roofs, extended as a cast iron verandah. To the east, a late C19 block with intersecting glazing bars in pointed arched windows. The interior has reeded architraves to the doors, all early C19. In the grounds, the stable ranges to the east have been much altered to offices. To the west a stone walled garden is faced internally with brick. The lodge at the end of the drive is later C19 with scalloped bargeboards.

The stable block to the east is early C19. II

T11

12 A small lodge was erected c.1820 at the end of the driveway. NL

STRATFORD ROAD, OLD WOLVERTON (South side)

13 Warren Old Farmhouse II

Farmhouse. C18. Previously known as Wolverton House Farm. Limestone rubble with a tiled roof. Three storeys one side, two to the garden front, which has a gabled porch and three-light windows with monolithic wedge lintels. Gable stacks, the major one for the original kitchen to the south, the kitchen being in the basement with an inglenook and a bread oven.

T13

14 Farm Buildings to Warren Farm II

The farm buildings remain one of the most complete ranges of farm buildings to survive in the area. They are in stone up to the mid C19, those added later, including pig sties, cattle shelters etc. of brick. There are two large barns, the one nearest the main entrance yard being listed.

15 Warren New Farmhouse NL

A new farmhouse of 1899 replacing the old one. English bond brickwork with slate roofs and perforated ridges. Rear wing of three bays. Moulded brick string courses and corbelled eaves. Paired sash windows, the upper sash with stepped margin glazing. Moulded bargeboards and stacks with diagonal shafts. The rear wing has service rooms and forms an open court with a contemporary stable and carriage house. The front garden is surrounded by a ha-ha.

T15

16 Warren Farm Cottage NL

A C17 or C18 stone cottage of two bays close to the Stratford Road. Re-roofed and provided with a large gable by E. Swinfen Harris in 1887. The gable is timber framed with brick noggings.

T16

17 Milestone by Warren Farm Cottage NL

Milestone erected by the Turnpike Trust on their new road in 1833. Of cast iron, triangular in section with a sloping top. The inscription reads BUCKINGHAM 9, STRATFORD 1, AND NEWPORT 5, STRATFORD WOLVERTON 1.

The 1833 turnpike gate and cottage stood nine chains east of the track to Wolverton Mill.

T17

18 Wolverton Mill II

Mill house and watermill, of four periods from the later C18 to the late C19. The main building is 'L' plan, of three storeys with a south wing of two storeys spanning the millstream. This was extended to the south by one bay and again to form the present façade. This has timber casement windows and a round headed door with raised stone quoins, early C19. Later, the two-storey section of the mill was raised to three storeys and the north front of the mill extended to cover a second millstream. A further open shelter on cast iron columns, and with a brick square chimney covering steam machinery. The mill wheel in the second race, which appears to have replaced the original one, was breast shot and has quatrefoil vents. Around the site are much worn Peak stones, and a French Burr lies in front of the mill.

The site is apparently that of Wolverton West Mill first recorded in the C11 and has been continuously used for this purpose ever since. When the long and wide race was made is not known.

T18

19 Iron Trunk **Sched Mon & II**

Aqueduct, built 1809–11 by Reynolds & Co. of Ketley, east Shropshire at the cost of £3,667, for the Grand Junction Canal Company in order to carry their canal from London to Blisworth over the river Great Ouse. The cast-iron trunk is of two spans supported on a central masonry pier resting on the river bed. It has radial plates bolted over arches in the manner of stone construction, emphasising its newness as a constructional material. The aqueduct is 15ft wide, 6ft 6in deep and 101ft long and is 35ft above river level supported on brick and Hornton stone piers. It was a bold solution to a problem posed by the collapse of two of the three arches of the brick aqueduct built in 1803–5 completing the navigation. To the west of the trunk traces might be seen, particularly in winter, of the temporary solution to the river crossing built by Harrison and others in 1800, a system of five locks bringing the canal down to river level and a further flight raising it again to the wharf on the old Stratford Road pending the completion of the three-arched aqueduct. The abutments were rebuilt 1919–21.

20 The Grand Junction Canal was initially proposed in 1792 as a means of connecting the industrial Midlands with the Thames. The survey of its route through the Milton Keynes area was conducted by James Barnes, the company's first engineer, in 1795, and the engineering works were directed by William Jessop. There were wharves at Old Stratford, Wolverton (Galleon), Wolverton (Stantonbury end), Great Linford, Woolstone, Fenny Stratford and Water Eaton. Barnes recommended the aqueduct solution to the river crossing in 1799, but it was not until 1802, after the canal had opened, that Jessop received instructions for a brick aqueduct. After the collapse of the brick aqueduct in 1808, a temporary wooden trough was built and used until the Iron Trunk was available.

T19

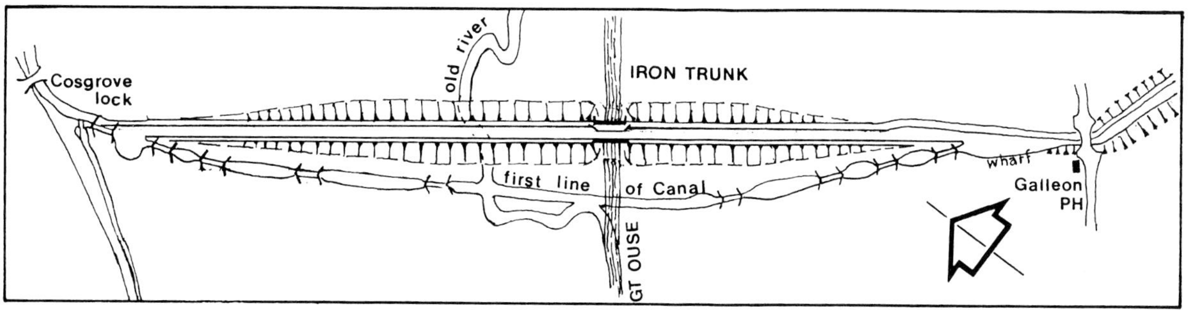

21 Parish School **NL**

A rock-faced limestone structure built 1857 by the Radcliffe Trust for 40 children. Now a private house.

22 McCorquodale's Printing Works **NL**

Factory originally established in 1878 as printers to the Railway Company employing wives and daughters of railway employees, later becoming the premier manufacturer of post office stationery and banknotes. The main building is of 1884, and was extended along the Stratford Road as the envelope department in 1905, and again, in response to a contract for stamped postal stationery, in 1910. Further buildings were built on the south side of the road in 1912, and the main offices removed to a new building in 1926. The wall, with its continuous brick arcading, some still bearing traces of the camouflage of the 1939–45 war, makes more effort towards public acceptability than that of the Works itself, and remains one of the most memorable images of Wolverton.

T22

Grand Union Canal
Steel Stock Holders
Steel Stock Holders
Wolverton Park Sports Ground
Wolverton Station
Bowling Green
Bowling Green
Tennis Court
The Limes
The Hawthorns
The Firs
Yew Tree House
Works
St George's Way
Glyn Square
Ledsam Street
Creed Street
Works Training School
Milk Depot
St George the Martyr's Church (C of E)
Vicarage
Cinema
PO
Hall
Stratford Road
Radcliffe Street
Church Street
Buckingham Street
Market Sq
Bedford
Moon Street
Cambridge Street
Windsor St
Jersey Rd
Anson Rd
Aylesbury Street
Wolverton County Infants School
Wolverton County Junior School
Wolverton County Infants School
Printing Works
Printing Works
Library
Bank
Hotel
Warehouse
Allotment Gardens
Allotment Gardens
Gantry
Tanks
Carriage & Wagon Repair Works
Heating & Ventilation Engineering Works
Food Processing Works
Assembly Works
Scrap Yard
Pump House
Towing Path
Old Wolverton Road
WOLVERTON
Plastics Factory
Transport Repair Depot
Grand Union Canal
Tennis Court
El Sub Sta
46 Chains
409

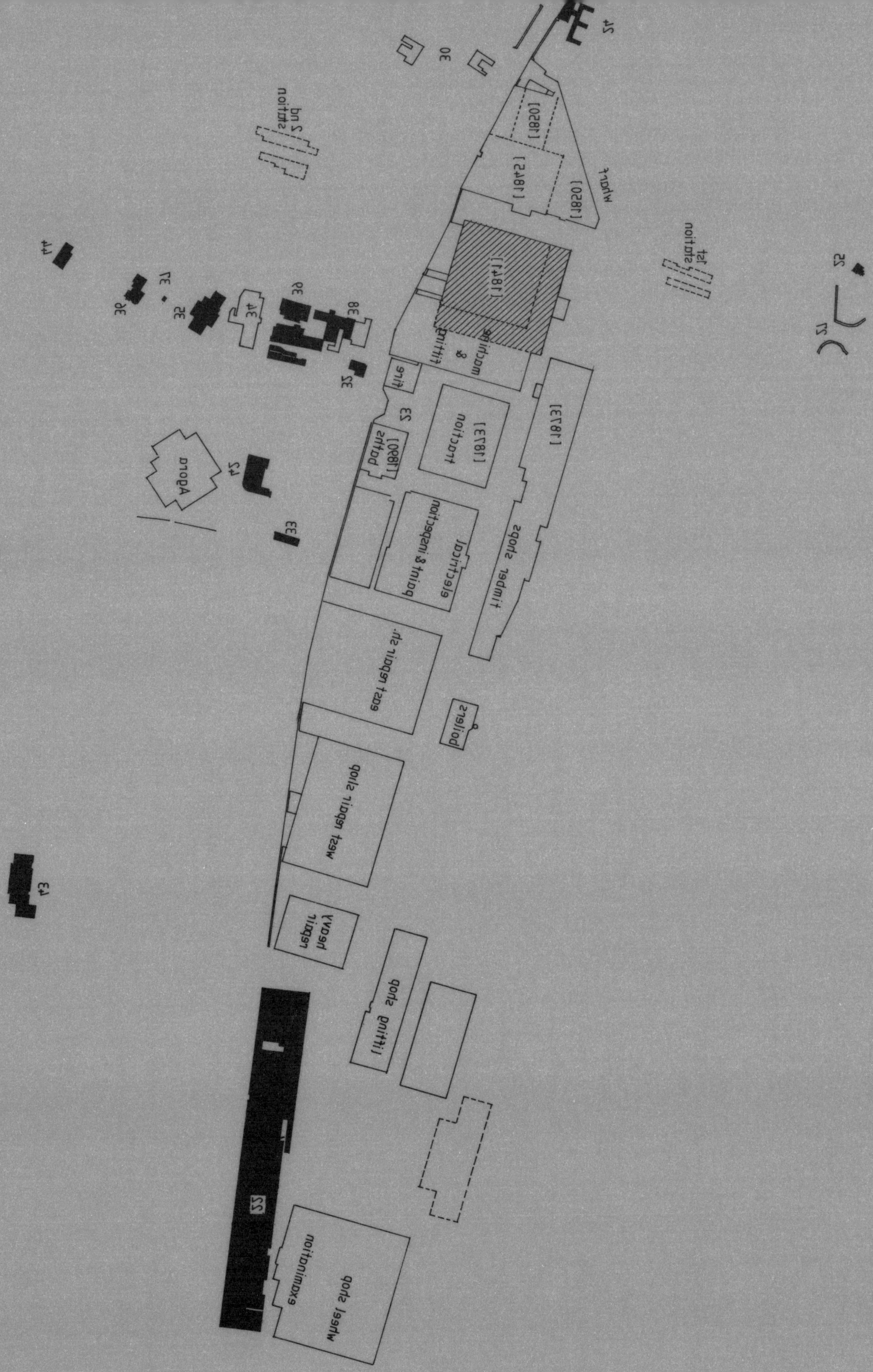

wheel shop
examination
22
fitting shop
heavy repair
west repair shop
boilers
east repair sh.
timber shops
electrical
paint & inspection
[1873]
traction
[1873]
[1890]
baths
23
fire
machine
&
fitting
[1841]
[1845]
[1850]
[1850]
wharf
1st
station
2nd
station
30
42
21
52
32
38
39
34
35
36
37
41
47
Agora
33
43

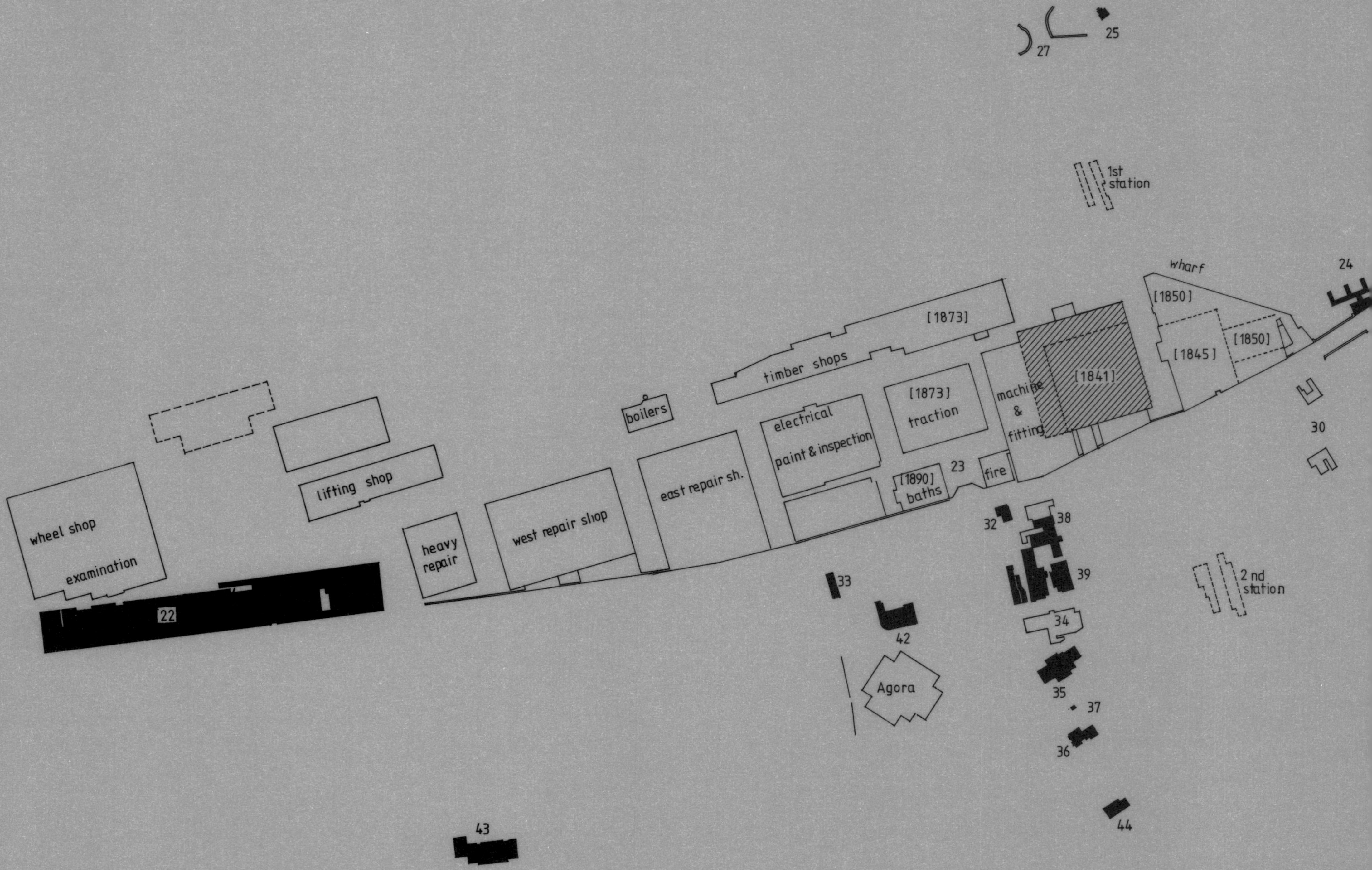

25
27
1st station
wharf
24
[1850]
[1845]
[1850]
[1841]
[1873]
timber shops
machine & fitting
30
[1873] traction
electrical
paint & inspection
boilers
23
fire
[1890] baths
east repair sh.
lifting shop
wheel shop
examination
heavy repair
west repair shop
22
32
38
39
33
42
Agora
34
35
37
36
2 nd station
43
44

T23

23 The Railway Works NL

A maintenance and repair works for rolling stock for the London and Birmingham Railway Company was established at Wolverton, conveniently half way between London Euston and Birmingham Curzon Street, in 1838. The Company, which was originally founded in 1833, became the London and North West Railway Co. in 1846 and remained so until amalgamated as the London Midland and Scottish Railway in 1923, and British Railways in 1948. It has been British Rail Engineering Ltd. since 1969, and is now exclusively concerned with the repair of carriages.

The works were originally established in 1838 on land purchased from the Radcliffe Charity in the bend of the Grand Junction Canal south of the old Stony Stratford to Newport road. A deciding factor must have been the availability of wharfage at this point. The original layout was in the form of a large open square, west of the line, and consisted of a great lifting and boiler shop, 100 yds × 115 yds in size with various specialist shops around on two floors; iron-founding, smithing, boiler shop and wheels shop. This was all hemmed in by industrial housing for the workers. To the east of the line, there was a warehouse and a loading bay for horse-drawn carriages to mount the rail trucks. In 1838 the first station was built to the north, beyond the canal.

Manufacture of locomotives started in a small way in 1845, but on amalgamation, Wolverton became the headquarters for the L & N.W.R. Southern Division under its Locomotive Superintendent J. E. McConnell. Under instructions to become self-supporting, the works expanded rapidly, building a loco shop east of the line in 1846, and extended in 1850. In 1858 the works began its expansion to the west and further erecting and boiler shops were added. In 1864 the decision was taken to centralise the building of carriages at Wolverton, a decision which heralded a major reorganisation of space within the works, and the erection of further shops for bodywork and a sawmill. After the retirement of James McConnell in 1861, locomotive construction was run down, and ceased altogether in 1877. Meanwhile the private Newport Pagnell branch line had been laid into the works in 1867, to be taken over by the L. & N.W.R. in 1875. 1878 brought another great reorganisation: the main line was looped around to the east and quadrupled, necessitating the building of a third, the present, station and a new gas works, followed by an iron foundry and brass shop, and the enclosure of the works behind a high brick wall in 1882 which is now so marked a feature of the town. After a serious fire that same year a new body shop was built together with a bogie shop, and further development included a fitting shop in 1904. By 1906 the works had reached the apogee of its development, its early housing had been rolled back again and again. The works now covered some 80 acres of land.

The Company's housing was initially laid out on a grid of streets close around the first square. As the works expanded so this land rapidly became insufficient, and for a time the Company was unable to expand except on to land acquired in Stantonbury parish, now New Bradwell, where they initially built terrace cottages for workers. The intransigence of the Radcliffe Trustees, the owners of the land in Wolverton, was however overcome in 1858 and the Company acquired land to the south of the Stratford Road for further housing, whilst the original houses were replaced bit by bit as further land for the works became essential. House building was begun by Mr. Aveline for the Company along Stratford Road in 1860, and continued as required until the completion of Buckingham Street in 1878. Thereafter private enterprise continued to supply the housing needs of Wolverton except for special needs, such as The Beeches, Green Lane, built for two managers in 1894.

The map indicates dates of erection of the more significant of the remaining buildings in the works. All are of red brick and strictly utilitarian in design. Architecturally the most ambitious is the original square, now the brake shop, of a number of parallel naves supported on cast iron columns and with basic Doric pilasters at its external corners.

RAILWAY STRUCTURES

24 Wolverton Station NL

Originally known as Wolverton Station Hill. Built 1878 on the by-pass line and on the diverted Stratford Road. The building is carried on blue brick arches, and is of timber, symmetrical and gabled, and with a timber covered walkway to the lines, dividing and descending by steps to the platforms. It is a modest station compared with its predecessor, the second station, which lay on the original line to the west, and which had elegant refreshment and waiting rooms, and conveniences which being the first stop from London, were well appreciated by the travelling public of Victorian days. Amongst many provisions supplied to the earlier station, were 182,000 Banbury Cakes which were consumed annually, as well as much liquid refreshments.

25 Park Lodge NL

The recreation ground to the north, between the canal and the loop line, was opened in 1885 to replace the former recreation field on Stacey Hill Farm. The lodge, built c.1885–90 is a part brick part timber framed house at the northern end between the high embankments.

26 Wolverton Viaduct NL

A viaduct carrying the railway over the Ouse valley. Built 1838 by Robert Stephenson at the cost of £30,000. Six tall blue brick arches 57ft high and 60ft span carry the line for 660ft. It was widened on the east side in 1878–82 to take two extra lines.

27 Skew Bridge, Old Wolverton Road NL

Bridge, 1838, by Robert Stephenson, the chief civil engineer to the London and Birmingham Railway Company. Blue engineering bricks with high flank walls. The bridge crosses the old turnpike road at an angle, hence rings were set out on the skew on formwork for the bricklayers to follow.

28 Stratford Road Bridge and Canal Bridge NL

Both bridges, built in 1834–5 for the railway company, use cast iron girders by the Butterley Co., and are interesting examples of railway construction, although now difficult to appreciate.

29 Blue Bridge NL

To the south of Wolverton, an accommodation bridge for Stacey Hill Farm, built 1834–5, of local bluish limestone and engineering bricks. Two oval spans on a central pier. Again the bridge had to be lengthened in 1878–82 to take the two extra lines added then.

STRATFORD ROAD (South side)

30 (Staff Houses)

Immediately west of the canal lay two pairs of semi-detached villas of the 1850–60 period, called after trees, The Firs, The Hawthorns, The Limes and Yew Tree House. These were erected for senior staff and had a flight of steps up to the recessed entrance and large and elegant front and back rooms.

31 (Market Hall)

The original market hall lay immediately south of the road. It was burnt out in 1906 and replaced with a gas filter shop.

32 The Royal Engineer P.H. NL

One of the original public houses of the town, built 1841–2, now much altered in the present century.

T24

T25

T26

T29

The North Western Hotel, mid C19, and the Crauford Arms, built 1907 are the other major public houses along the Stratford Road.

33 Church of St. Francis de Sales NL

Roman Catholic church, built 1865–7 to serve the needs of immigrant railway workers, and still the senior RC parish church north of Aylesbury. A small building with open trusses and a sacristry attached with access either side of the high altar. Four high stained glass windows. St. Francis de Sales was a French bishop 1567–1622 whose writings and exemplary conduct appealed to such diverse persons as James I and John Wesley.

CHURCH STREET (South side)

Church Street was laid out by Mr. Charles Aveline at the same time as Ratcliffe Street and the Stratford Road in the 1860s and was developed from the eastern end as far as Nos. 97/108 by 1881, and beyond Windsor Street by 1898. For much of its length it is in a similar but not repetitive late Victorian villa style. No. 122 is notable for its elaborate moulded brickwork. Beyond Windsor Street, development took place later than 1900 and included the Wolverton West Primitive Methodist Church of 1907, the foundation stones of which were apparently never formally laid, and the Wolverton Industrial and Provident Society's Branch No. 2, of 1912.

T33a

34 (Science and Arts Institute)

Wolverton's single greatest loss, the Science and Arts Institute, stood where the Agora car park now is situated. It was erected for the Railway company in 1861–64, possibly to the design of G. E. Street, and was extended in 1880 and again in 1891. It was first called the New Mechanics Institute, and was intended to become the cultural and educational focus of the community, reflecting the time when large employers felt a patron's responsibility towards their employees and their families. A similar building had been erected by the Great Western Company at Swindon. The building contained a large hall and library, with a steeply pitched roof and a rose window in the gable in the Gothic style. It was damaged by fire in 1970 and demolished shortly afterwards.

T34

35 Church of Wolverton St. George the Martyr B

Anglican parish church of Wolverton Station, as the new town was called at the time. Built July 1843 to May 1844 by architects Thomas H. Wyatt and David Brandon. It was altered in 1870 by E. S. Harris and further extended in 1895–6 by J. Oldrid Scott, the builder at this stage being Henry Martin. The cost was met by the Dr. John Radcliffe Trust, Sir Robert Peel, son of the ex-prime minister being one of the Trustees. It is of limestone rubble with red Hollington sandstone dressings and an ironstone west window of 1884. It consists of a wide nave with two-bay aisles (part of Scott's later work but allowed for in the original design), gabled externally in the form of double transepts, and choir and clergy vestries added 1896 and 1900 respectively. Dressings are in Farleigh Down stone. A north-east tower is set on the north side of the chancel. The design is in the Early English style, respected by those who altered it. Internally the nave has seven close spaced timber trusses of industrial character and probably made in the Works. The chancel of two bays has a transverse arch to the sanctuary, marking its lengthening in 1903. Mosaic panels are set in the east wall. The chancel screen is an interesting curvilinear design. The font is a limestone bowl on five columns, the cover in the form of a crown, supplied in 1897. The glass is by Powell of Whitefriars, and the organ by Walker & Co.

T35

36 St. George's Vicarage II

Vicarage, 1844 by Wyatt and Brandon, built alongside the church. Limestone rubble with tiled roof. The entrance porch faces the church. The building was altered by E. Swinfen Harris in 1889–90 and provided with a new dormer, bargeboards and a bay window, and at the rear, a large extension and bedroom.

37 Gazebo in the grounds of the Vicarage II

This small structure of the later C19 contains some interesting masonry of the Tudor period, including four doorheads and two with shields, and a sundial plate dated 16??. It is possible that these came from the Longueville Manor house at Old Wolverton.

T36

CHURCH STREET (North side)

39 St. George's Church Hall — II

T39

Sunday Schools and Church Institute, on the corner of Creed Street, c.1902, by C. M. Oldrid Scott, the builder Henry Martin of Northampton. Two-coloured brick with tiled roof. It has a large hall with a stage on the upper floor approached by steps from outside, thus the services remain below. A relief figure of St. George, who was martyred in the C3–C4 AD, is set over the doors. The gable was designed as an open pediment with lunette windows, the side windows being leaded. It is an interesting building in the late Arts and Crafts tradition. A club room was attached to one end in 1910.

40 Methodist Church — II

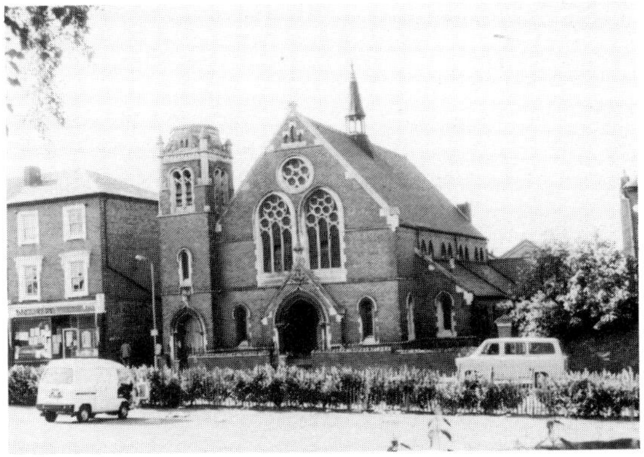

T40

Free Methodist chapel, now the Christian Foundation. Built 1892 by Ewen Harper of Birmingham, the builder H. C. Burden. It replaced an earlier Methodist Chapel of 1869 which had become too small for the flourishing congregation, which was the strongest of the non-conformist groups in Wolverton, and founded as early as 1839. Red brick with stone dressings. A shallow gabled and crocketed south porch with carved geometric windows and a roundel in the gable. The tower on the left, also with a door, has had its strange openwork spire removed, but the nave has a tiled bellcote. Nave and aisles, and a large school room to the rear.

41 Nos. 6 and 8 — NL

A pair of shops, now bakehouse and adjacent shop. c.1838–40. Three storeys, four bays, brick with stone architraves and bracketed cornices to the upper windows. The original bakehouse did not stand here, but on the corner of Church Street and Radcliffe Street.

42 Queen Victoria — NL

T42

The Victoria Hotel on the corner of Radcliffe Street has now become a public house and restaurant. Built c.1860 of red brick with yellow brick dressings. It is of three storeys with tall moulded doorcases with handsome modillion canopies and etched glass surviving in some of the ground floor windows. Brick modillion eaves and striped chimneys. The Radcliffe Street elevation shows a contemporary two-storey rear wing. The hanging sign is similar to, and is perhaps a copy of, that at the Cock, Stony Stratford.

CREED STREET (West side)

38 The British Endowed and Infants Schools — NL

Erected by the London & North Western Railway Co. in 1839 and much extended in 1857. It became the Market Halls after that building was burnt down and has now been partly demolished and the remainder converted into offices for a travel firm.

AYLESBURY STREET

43 Wyvern School — NL

T43

Infants and Junior School, c.1912. Brick with stone lacings and dressings. Three storeys with a symmetrical north front and square domed corner turrets and a central bell tower. Venetian windows to the upper floor. An interesting example of a style of architecture fashionable for schools at this particular time.

The front garden has a rare specimen, a mature Judas tree.

GREEN LANE

Green Lane formed the southern boundary of the railway settlement for many years.

44 The Elms

A private house built in 1907 for Dr. John O. Harvey, medical officer and surgeon to the Railway company, by Edward Swinfen Harris. Brick with tiled and slated roof. The entrance is at the side of a front stair tower with Westmorland slate dome. The entrance hall has twin stone arches and the house is fitted out with good quality joinery including window lockers. It is Harris's most mature work having a studied simplicity of design derived from the more advanced thinking of the Domestic Revival movement of the last years of the C19. It was divided into two dwellings after neglect and fire, and an extensive range of stables and outbuildings west of the house were demolished c.1980.

45 Water Tower

C.1890. A brick built tower crowned with an interesting wrought iron sectional tank providing a head for the town's water supply. The substructure is used for storage.

Water was provided from a spring in the farthest south east corner of the parish near the Bancroft Roman villa, and was pumped to the tower from whence it flowed by gravity to the works and housing. A second tower of similar design was added at the back of Osborne Street c.1910.

STACEY AVENUE

47 Nos. 2 and 4 NL

Cottages built as farm workers' dwellings for Stacey Hill Farm, now engulfed in the C19 expansion of the town.

48 Stacey Hill Farm II

Built c.1840–50 to replace Stacey Bushes Farm. Brick, in a late Regency style, three bays. External porch with arched windows leading to a through hall, and linking to a cross passage at the rear. Twelve-pane sashes with fine glazing bars and concealed boxes. Hipped slate roof with central lead flat. A wide rear wing is extended to the north containing the milk house, and other service rooms, continuing as beast houses.

49 Farm Buildings to Stacey Hill Farm II

To the west of the rear range is the farm yard divided into a north and south yards by a walled roadway. On the north side, a fine c.1840 timber framed barn with weatherboarding and slated roof. On the west side of the south yard is a range of brick farm buildings, ending with a two-storey granary with an external stair to the upper floor of cantilevered stone steps and landing. The buildings are interested for the planning of a new farm layout of the period.

50 Stonebridge House Farm

Farmhouse of the C18, stone, with a tiled roof. Four bays, with 12-pane sash windows and three hipped dormers. Stone doorcase and pilasters and an entablature. Glazed door leading to a wide hall with parlour on each side. Service rooms have been added to the back, described in 1855 as including a wine cellar, an ale house, a small ale cellar and a brewhouse. These are in fact fairly normal appointments, and do not signify especially bibulous occupants.

The farm buildings were described as newly erected in 1855. They are arranged around three yards and include pig sties, bullock sheds, a barn and granaries. It appears to have been a largely arable and livestock fattening farm, with little provision for dairy products.

T44

T48

T46

WATLING STREET

46 Brickkiln Farm Buildings II

Brickkiln Farm is named from its proximity to the brick kilns which operated in the C18 and C19, all traces of which have now disappeared. The farmhouse was rebuilt in this century and is of not historic interest. However, a fine range of farm buildings survive, with one inner yard, and two outer yards to the south-east surrounded by shelter sheds. The stable block on the south west has lunette windows, and round iron glazed windows above to the loft, with an external brick stair. The main barn is of three bays, with patterned tiling on the north side and an extension to the south-west with a dovehouse in the gable. The north-east range has a timber building with half-hipped roof.

The brickworks lay 440yds south-east of the buildings and consisted in c.1840 of a rectangular muffle kiln with drying sheds and clay pits. They were operated at least from 1825, and later by Richard Bailey and after, George Gibbs.

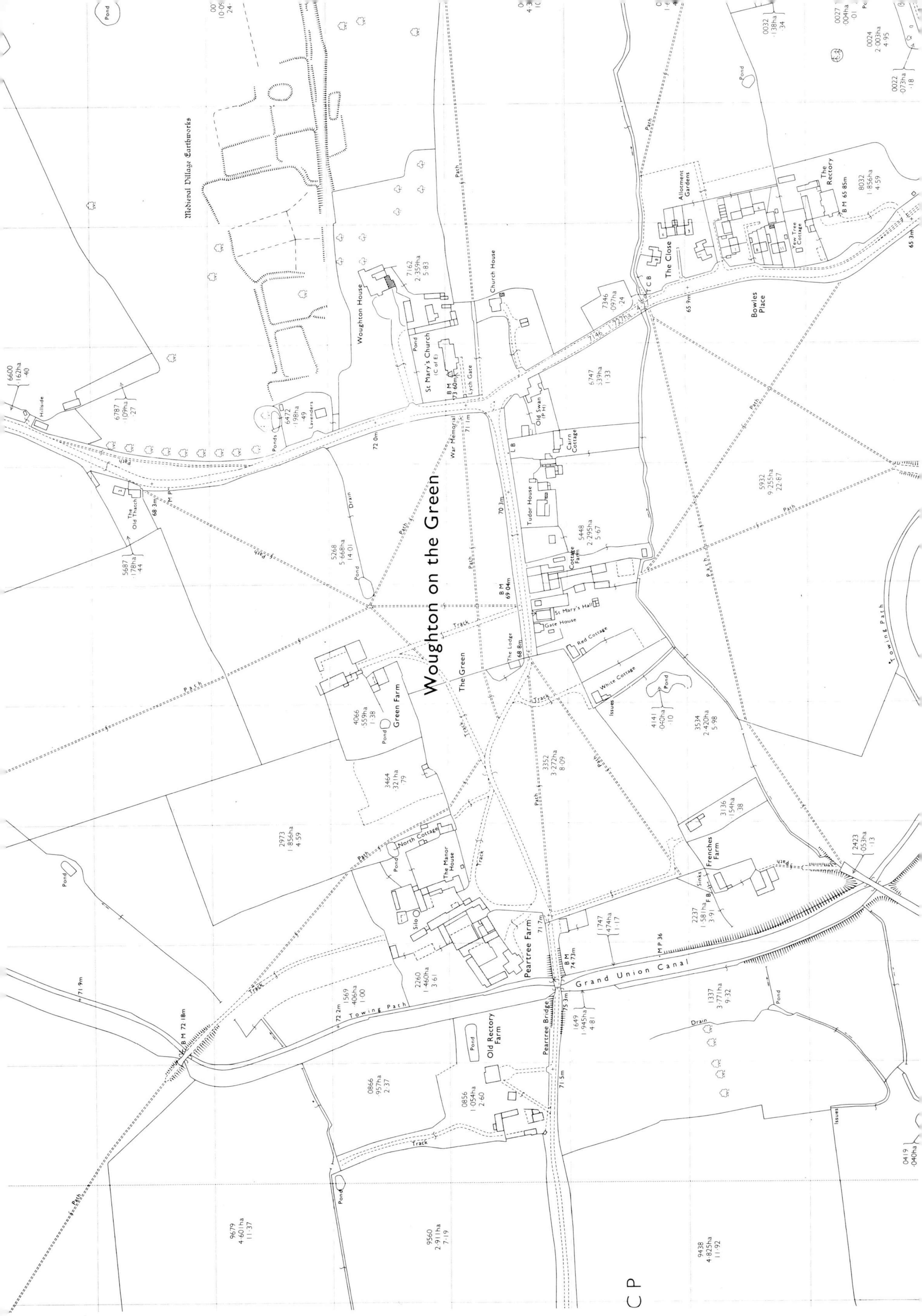
Woughton on the Green
Medieval Village Earthworks
Woughton House
St Mary's Church (C of E)
Church House
Lych Gate
War Memorial
The Green
Green Farm
North Cottage
The Manor House
Silo
Peartree Farm
Peartree Bridge
Old Rectory Farm
Grand Union Canal
Towing Path
Frenches Farm
White Cottage
Red Cottage
Gate House
St Mary's Hall
Cottage Farm
Tudor House
Cairn Cottage
Old Swan (P H)
The Lodge
Bowles Place
The Close
Allotment Gardens
The Rectory
Yew Tree Cottage
Hillside
The Old Thatch
Lavenders
Ponds
CP

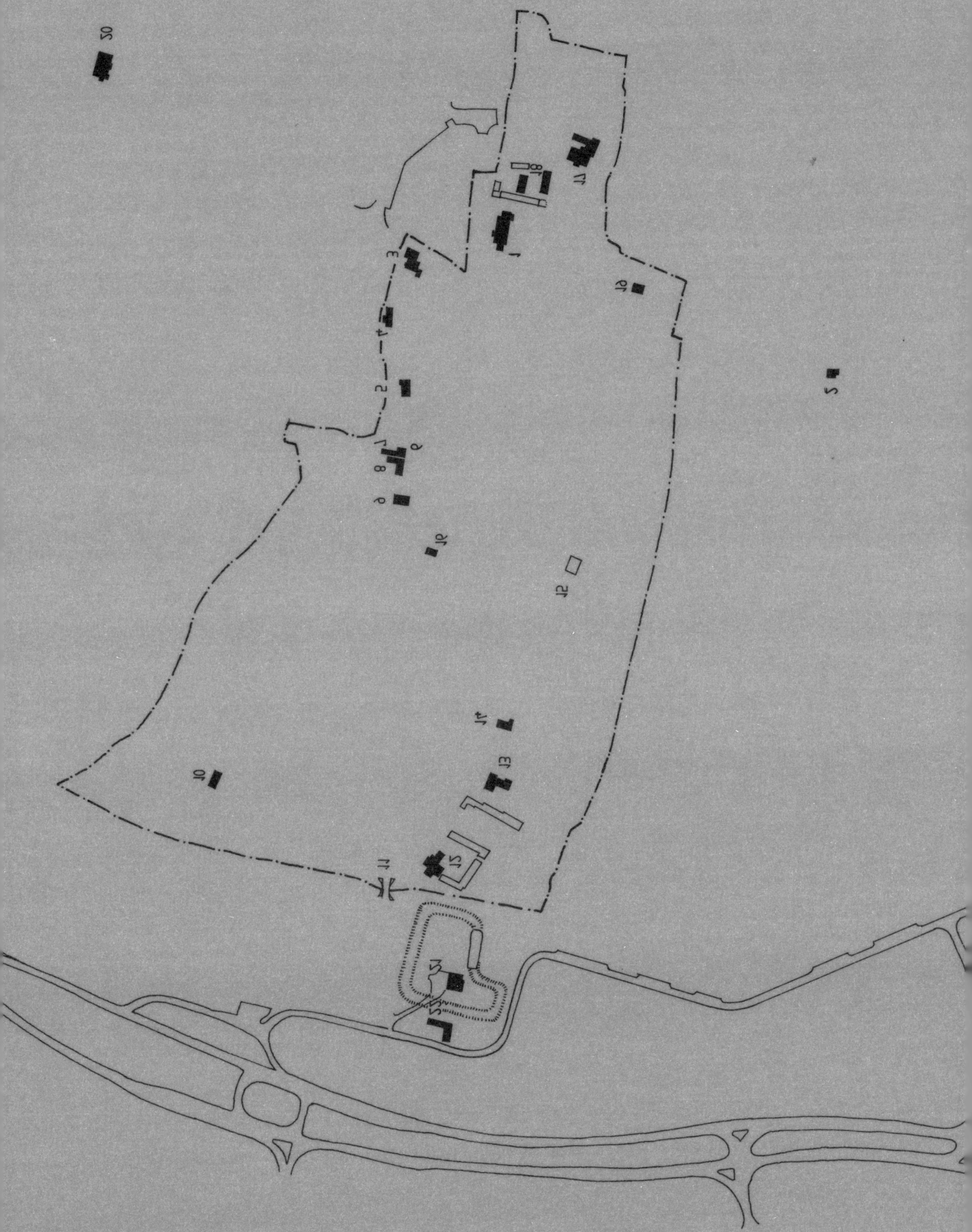

1
2
3
4
5
6
7
8
9
10
11
12
13
14
15
16
17
18
19
20
21
22

V

WOUGHTON ON THE GREEN

WOUGHTON ON THE GREEN

Woughton on the Green is one of the string of villages situated at about 1 mile intervals along the west bank of the river Ousel. In Saxon times there was an east–west route across the valley at this point, giving access to the higher boulder clay topped lands of the outfields to the west, and to the water meadows to the east, Monxton bridge, and the road to Walton. The Domesday population has been estimated 120, larger than on the eve of Milton Keynes, and continued to increase up to the time of the Black Death. The initial settlement seems to have begun around small paddocks and enclosures on the Green, and extended later along the trackway to the river. This remains conjectural in that it has not been tested by excavation. The early manor apparently stood at the western end of the Green, where a moat is still visible, and the church on the east margin. In the C17 there was, in common with most places, an economic revival which was reflected in much rebuilding and movement into the previously abandoned areas, as, for example, the establishment of a new farm at Pineham. The enclosures, which had already partially been effected by the Longuevilles in the C16, were completed by Parliament in 1769, creating further outlying farms at Bleak Hall and Coffee Hall, and the settlement of squatters on the margins of the wide droveways, as can be seen for instance, fossilised in the shape of the plots immediately north of the village. The Grand Junction Canal passed through the eastern end of the Green in 1800, bringing Hassel on his famous journey in 1819 when he described the village as 'a truly pictorial spot'.

NEWPORT ROAD (East side)

1 Church of The Assumption of St. Mary II*

Anglican parish church, C14, replacing an earlier two-cell building, the tower added C15, of limestone with some Brickhill ironstone, and a tiled roof. Restored 1865–7 by J. S. Wing, including substantial repairs and the replacement of the window tracery throughout, and further restored by J. Oldrid Scott in 1891, who also provided the chancel screen. There was work carried out in 1825, when the chancel was reroofed, and a gallery was inserted in the nave in 1832, later removed. It has a nave with south aisle and porch, a chancel and a three-stage crenellated west tower. Also a north vestry probably dating from the 1865 work. Two carved stones are built into the eastern porch buttress. The tower clock is dated 1897.

V1

Internally, the arcade has interesting quatrefoiled columns and arches of two chamfered orders. A splendid C14 canopy survives over the stair to the rood loft. In the chancel is a defaced monument to a priest, probably C14. There is a C13 font and a screen of 1896.

The church was re-ordered in 1974 when the pews removed and the nave carpeted, the axis being turned towards the north.

NEWPORT ROAD (West side)

2 No. 4, The Old Thatch II

An C18 cottage set on the common land of the old droveway, brick with a thatched roof. Two bays with off-centre entrance to right bay which includes the stair and a gable stack. A further external stack to the living room is on the half-hipped south gable and extensions were built in 1976.

V2

3 Ye Olde Swan Tavern II

Inn of the C17, timber framed, originally 'L' plan and two storeys, with a central stack to the east-west block. The framing is of storey height, studding with tension braces and clasped purlin roof. The entrance is at the junction of the north wing. The doors and windows are mostly renewed and there have been various recent extensions. The interior has chamfered ceiling beams with stopped ends to the forward parlour, and a large fireplace to the tap-room. The parlour has an C18 corner cupboard. There were C19 extensions to the west and south. A sign reading 'dairy' over one window was placed there to avoid the window tax, a dairy not being a taxable room.

The inn is associated in legend with Dick Turpin, being one of the places he is supposed to have reversed his horse's shoes to foil his pursuers. With the churchyard wall, the Jubilee Oak, and lychgate of 1906, it forms one of the more picturesque corners of old Milton Keynes. In the car park there is a mid-C19 diaper brick barn with loft over, all that remains of various outbuildings of that period.

V3

THE GREEN Sched Mon

The Green has not always been exactly in the form it now is. Before the Canal it extended further to the west and continued up to the Newport Road on the west, interrupted by the construction of Clarkson's Farm. The irregularities in the ground indicate that it once had a number of trackways and enclosures and perhaps temporary buildings. It is a scheduled ancient monument. The outlying section of the Green to the west of the canal was subjected to archaeological investigation c.1973. It was demonstrated that there had been a variety of houses here during the later middle ages.

THE GREEN (South side)

4 No. 1, Cairn Cottage II

C17 timber framed cottage with a thatched roof, the framing originally infilled with wattle and daub. Two bays, and one storey with an attic, and with a tiled extension on both sides. Internally it has heavy timbers on the first floor and exposed wall studs. Rethatched after a fire in 1984. It was once the village post office.

V4

5 No. 3, Tudor Cottage II

An interesting house possibly of the C16 to early C17, timber framed with storey height studs and tension bracing. Lobby entry plan, with the original major living room in two narrow structural bays to the left of the entrance, and two bays to the right, both jettied. The second of these two bays appears on plan as if added subsequent to the original construction and provided with a gable stack. The roof is half hipped. Internally the house has chamfered spine beams and a large stone fireplace to the eastern room.

V5

6 No. 5, Cottage Farm II

A brick cottage of the early C19 with a slate roof. Two bays, with central stack and windows. The upper floor was rebuilt later in the C19 and has cogged eaves. To its rear is:

7 Woodbine Cottage II

An early C19 cottage of yellow diapered brickwork formed from the rear single bay wing of No. 5, to which is added a further bay to form a separate dwelling.

V6

8 No. 6, Appletree Cottage II

Of two builds in the late C17 or early C18, the left a two-storey cottage, timber framed with a brick facade, and to the right, a taller one-bay structure, also timber-framed with a half-hipped roof, which originally extended over the driveway to its side. The framing of the taller section has storey height framing with tension braces to both floors.

9 Village Hall NL

A Wesleyan Methodist brick chapel erected 1867, which bears a benchmark. Between Appletree Cottage and the hall is a garage built c.1900 for Sir Ferriman Bowles' use when he called to collect the rents.

V8

The south side of the Green itself had, before recent development, indications of former building plots of the C17 or earlier.

10 No. 18, Frenches Farm II

Probably a C17 farm or smallholding, completely altered in the C18 and again in the 1970's. Brick, with a slate roof, and central stack. It has two lattice paned windows to the gable, and once had a timber framed barn.

THE GREEN (North side)

11 Pear Tree Bridge NL

Canal bridge. c.1790–1800, a simple brick arch with splayed parapets almost totally rebuilt c.1974–5.

V12

12 Pear Tree Farm NL

A C17 farm, rebuilt in about 1825 by Robert Nixon of Woburn. The original building was of three bays with a forward wing parlour, a kitchen to the rear, and a timber framed stable on the east end. The farmyard to the east contained two barns for barley and wheat, pig sties and a stone stable.

The present building is of brick, with brick dentils as a wall string and the gable verges, and it has cross timber windows. The front garden has an unusual limestone wall, and the farm buildings, now detached and of the C19 have, against the green, a brick milking parlour.

V13

13 The Manor II

Not the original Manor House, but an important farm, the rear timber framed section of the C16 and a front block refaced in brick in the C18. It was altered again c.1840–60 by the addition of a pedimented doorcase and gable in a slightly projecting central bay, and later in the C19, canted bay windows were added to the ground floor rooms. The rear wing is extended by a stone and tile outbuilding. The roofs are tiled and hipped. Internally there is a central stair hall leading to the early rear wing with a large lateral stack. The left front room has a fine C16 stone fireplace partly of Totternhoe stone, with mouldings and faceted spandrels, and a C17 stair in the hall with turned balusters. To the rear were clay pits for brickmaking, a brickmaker, John Eastment recorded as living west of the Green in 1728.

14 North Cottage II

A C17 cottage of two storeys and attic, gable on to the green. Lobby entry plan with a C17 stair behind the stack. It may have originally been timber framed and enclosed in brickwork in the early C18, with a brick plat band. Half hipped tiled roof. Accounts suggest it was at least in part rebuilt in the C18.

15 (Clarkson's Farmhouse)

A two-storey brick farmhouse of the early C19 possibly incorporating earlier work. It had a lobby entry plan with a rear range containing a dairy, kitchen and cellar, and to the rear, a harness house. It was demolished under mysterious circumstances c.1970.

16 The Lodge NL

Lodge c.1820–40, at entrance to the Green. Regency style, stucco with a low-pitched slate roof and wide eaves. The house was extended in c.1980.

17 Woughton House Hotel II

Small private mansion, now a hotel and restaurant. c.1840 extended to the rear, and remodelled in 1876 by W. J. Levi. Red and yellow banded brick, since white-washed. Two storeys, five bays with central projecting flat roofed porch with a round door opening. The windows have segmental heads and built-in blind boxes. The front wall is raised as a parapet to conceal the shallow pitched slate roof, and has ball finials. The added block to the rear is in a similar style. Until recently it had a lean-to conservatory on the south side with a vine of local repute.

The building occupies the site of one of the two manor houses of Woughton, probably the one owned by the Longuevilles at least up to the Civil war.

18 Outbuildings to Woughton House II

Against the driveway is a yard with early C19 carriage house, stables and various farm buildings of an earlier period, including, until 1983 a C17 timber framed and slated corn barn originally with wattle and daub infilling replaced with weatherboarding. The stables accommodated ten horses, and it had piggeries, a chaff house and a straw barn. The carriage house, which has lunette windows and a loft, is now a bar.

Woughton House, in recent times, had a modest park of some 43 acres, and embraced the remains of the medieval village sunken roadway passing down to the ancient Monxton Bridge over the Ouzel.

19 Lavenders NL

This house replaced an earlier timber framed building on the same site.

20 The Rectory NL

Parsonage house of 1867 by Richard Sheppard of Newport Pagnell, for the Rev. Maurice Farrell. Brick, originally with central hall and dining room and wing on west containing sitting room and study, the services being to the east. Sash windows with brick two-centred relieving arches and half-hipped roof. Major extensions to the rear forming a bayed breakfast room were made by Rev. Frederick F. Field in 1897, including reorganising the entrance through the sitting room and adding a large bay with verandah over to the former study.

V14

V15

V17

21 Old Rectory II

Former parsonage house, now Interaction. Occupying site of former manor house and surrounded by a moat the east arm of which was utilised in 1800 for the construction of the canal. It is a brick building, of two storeys, probably of the early C18, and 'L' plan, extended to a square and provided with a new frontage in c.1832. This is of four bays with a central rendered portico and flat entablature. Sash windows, and the roof lowered in pitch and slated, replacing the patterned clay tiles still remaining on the rear. Restored 1974 and the waterlogged cellar filled in. The building which the bishop recorded as being empty and ruinous in 1517–31, has a series of fascinating glebe terriers of 1612, 1619, 1639, 1674, 1680, 1693, 1706, 1707, 1745 and 1832, all but the last recording a five bay house of 14 rooms, timber-framed in the earlier documents, comprising a hall, two parlours, a study, kitchen and buttery, and bed chambers over. The kitchen and service rooms still had earth floors in 1707. The property also had, outside the moat, three barns, a hay house, a milk house and other outbuildings. It was known as the Old Brewery in 1881.

V21

22 Outbuildings to the Old Rectory NL

A number of C19 barns and cattle shelters existed to the west of the house until drastically altered in the 1970's. On the south side of Pear Tree Lane stood, until the late 1970's, a four-bay hovel, of brick with a pantile roof. Traditional pantiled are rare in the Milton Keynes area, not having penetrated further west than Bedfordshire since their original introduction in the C18 until modern times.

23 (Coffee Hall)

All that remained of Coffee Hall farm in the 1970's were ruinous buildings around a farmyard. The barn, on the north side, had a red brick plinth and timber framed superstructure.

24 (Bleak Hall)

A timber framed barn of the late C17–early C18 survived at Bleak Hall Farm until the mid 1970's. It was of two bays, with tension braces, and curved struts to principal rafters.

PLACE NAMES IN MILTON KEYNES

Milton Keynes' historic past is echoed throughout the city, as in the roads, grid squares and Central Milton Keynes. The names and their origins are listed below:

GRID SQUARES

Ashland: Field name from 1781.

Bancroft: Of Roman origin, remains of a Roman villa were excavated between 1972–8.

Beanhill: Field name from 1781. The theme for the grid square is old names associated with foods and grasses, i.e. Beanfare (land on which beans were grown), Wastel (white bread formerly made of very fine flour).

Blakelands: From A. Saxon 'bleak ir desolute'. Theme is field names in industrial areas and the Industrial Revolution in the housing areas, i.e. Minton Close, Bessemer Court.

Bleak Hall: Characters and places from Charles Dickens' 'Bleak House', i.e. Chesney Wold, Summerson Road.

Bletchley: From A. Saxon 'Blecca's Lea'. Many streets named after famous battles, i.e. Waterloo Court, Bosworth Close.

Blue Bridge: Theme is game of bridge and associated moves, i.e. Van Der Bilt Court (inventor of bridge), Culbertsons Avenue (international system).

Bolbeck Park: Hugh de Bolebec was the Norman holder of the manor of Linford in 1066. Names all based on Norman history and associates of William I, i.e. Orne Gardens (river in Normandy), Redvers Gate (after Baron Richard de Redvers).

Bradville: Local name attached to this area. Names associated with history of the parish, i.e. Abbey Way (old road leading to Bradwell Abbey).

Bradwell: Village and parish name from A. Saxon 'wella' — a spring. Names associated with history of parish, i.e. Atterbrook (John atte Brook de Wiston, Vicar 1361).

Bradwell Common: Existing name of district. Theme is London and Buckinghamshire Commons.

Broughton: Village and parish name.

Coffee Hall: Taken from farm formerly located on the old lane from Woughton to Denbigh Hall. Theme is names of London coffee houses.

Conniburrow: From Connie Burrough Hill, 1641. Theme is British wild flowers, i.e. Marjoram Place, Bramble Avenue.

Crownhill: From Crown Hill, field name, 1693. Theme is deceased rock stars, i.e. Fury Court, Presley Way.

Downs Barn: From Downs Barn, 1829. Area was referred to as 'Horse Ground' on a C17 map. Theme is horses, i.e. Cantle Avenue (part of saddle), Farrier Place.

Downhead Park: From field name 'Down Head Furlong'. Theme is the Cotswolds, i.e. Daylesford Court (Cotswold village).

Eaglestone: Field name provided by last owner of Peartree Farm, Woughton. Theme is mixture of birds of prey, i.e. Kite Hill and developers' names, i.e. Buckingham Gate.

Elfield Park: Probably from A. Saxon 'Hela' — 'heel of parish'.

Emerson Valley: Theme is Belvoire Valley, Vale of the White Horse (Wiltshire) and Taunton Deane.

Fishermead: From field name 'Fishers Mead'. Theme is Cornish fishing, i.e. Bossiney Place (near Tintagel), Perran Avenue (Perran Bay near Perranporth).

Fox Milne: Name given to Milton Keynes Water Mill in 1313 and 1418.

Fullers Slade: A5 intersection in this field was known as Fulwell Slade. Theme is wool and sheep, i.e. Weavers Hill, Shepherds.

Furzton: From Hodge Furze, 1742 field name. Theme is Exmoor high points and villages.

Giffard Park: Walter Giffard (Lord of Longueville, Normandy) and son Walter (1st Earl of Buckingham) and Commissioner of Domesday Survey of 1069 both owned land in Great Linford. Theme is places of interest in Thames and Chilterns.

Great Holm: From field name Great Holme, 1769. Theme is Royal residences for grid roads and stately homes for remainder.

Great Linford: Mentioned as Linforda (944 A.D.). Precise origin is uncertain but it probably referred to a tree close to a ford, i.e. 'Hlyn' = maple, 'Lind' = lime tree.

Greenleys: From A. Saxon 'land under grass or pasture'. Theme at Greenleys and Hodge Lea is medieval manorial occupations, i.e. Cotman Close (cottager), Bounds Croft (serf).

Heelands: Means 'highlands'. Names are associated with North West Yorkshire, i.e. Deepdale, Gordale, Mossdale.

Hodge Lea: Adapted from A. Saxon 'Hodge Furze'. Area was cleared by the Longuevilles for sheep shearing.

Kents Hill: Field name.

Kiln Farm: Farm name. Theme is brickmaking, i.e. Brick Close, Potters Lane.

Kingsmead: Ancient field name.

Kingston: Name of existing bridge north of Wavendon.

Knowlhill: From field name, Knowle Hill, 1769.

Leadenhall: Name of a C17 London coffee house.

Linford Wood: Theme is open land in England and Wales.

Loughton: Village and parish name from A. Saxon 'Luha's tun'.

Neath Hill: Dates back to at least 1641. Road names identify ancient crafts and trades associated with City Livery companies in London, i.e. Coachmaker Court, Glazier Drive.
Netherfield: Field name from 1781.
Newlands: Farm name.
Northfield: Field name—'The Great North Field', 1685.
Oldbrook: Field name, 1850. Theme is game of cricket, grid layout is based on cricket field.
Peartree Bridge: Ancient bridge. Names are from local history.
Pennyland: Field name. Theme is old coins, i.e. Bodle Close (2 Scots pence), Carolus Creek (23/-).
Pineham: Farm name.
Redmoor: Field name, formerly much larger area. Railway runs through part of original field. Theme is Peterborough fens.
Rooksley: Field name, 1790. Theme is types of engines that ran along adjacent railway.
Simpson: Village and parish name from A. Saxon 'Sigewine's Tun'.
Springfield: Name originates from 1923 name for field in Little Woolstone. Road names are associated with historical rivers/wells in London.
Stacey Bushes: Formerly common land — 'Stumpy Bushes'. Theme is trees and shrubs on high and low land.
Stantonbury: Parish name — Stanton — with suffix derived from Barre family, lords of the manor in late Norman times. Theme is local field names and history.
Stonebridge: Farm name. Presumably near a 'stone bridge' over Bradwell Brook.
Stony Stratford: Probably derived from 'Stone Street', a common local name, for Watling Street, and the 'ford' over the river Ouse. Name was 'Stani Stratford' in late C12 and early C13.
Tattenhoe: Norman manor and parish.
Tilbrook: Land between Walton Road and the railway belonged to Tilbrook Farm, Bow Brickhill.
Tinkers Bridge: Taken from bridge over canal at Woughton. Road names associated with Grand Union Canal.
Tongwell: Farm name. Theme is American companies and states.
Two Mile Ash: Ash tree on Watling Street was used as a marker for travellers. Theme is English topography and golf courses.
Walnut Tree: Farm name, 1600.
Walton: Village and parish name from A. Saxon 'Walla's tun'.
Walton Hall: Walton Hall (c. 1750) is a former mansion house and home of the Pinfold family.
Wavendon: From A. Saxon 'Wafa's dun'.
Willen Park: Adjacent to Willen Road in Ouzel Valley.
Winterhill: Field name from 'Winter Hill Furlong'. Theme is British mountains and industrial.
Wolverton: From A. Saxon 'Wulf'heres ton'.
Woolstone: Village and parish name from A. Saxon 'Weitfraige's Tun'. Names are based on local history.
Woughton: Village and parish name from A. Saxon 'Wulha's tun'.
Woughton Park: Theme is the Grand Union Canal.
Wymbush: Taken from Michael Wymbis, C13 City of London founder who made two of the bells in Bradwell church. Also Nicholas Wymbyss, Rector of Hanslope 1419, Rector of Olney 1434–1455 and later Canon of York and Archdeacon of Nottinghamshire. Theme is the printing world.

CENTRAL MILTON KEYNES

The names used for the roads in Central Milton Keynes have two main sources of origin, the area's general historical background and the association the area has with the ancient Secklow Hundred, a group of families which met in Saxon times on the highest local point, probably on or near Bradwell Common. The modern view is that the meetings were held on the mound behind the new CMK Library.

Midsummer, Avebury and Silbury Boulevard all take their names from the Midsummer Solstice. The first is so named because the road itself is aligned to within a few degrees of the line of the midsummer sunrise, and the second two are so-called because of the traditional links with the summer solstice of the Avebury stone circle and the man-made Silbury Hill, both in Wiltshire.

Secklow Gate—originates from 'Seggeslawa', 'Seckly' or 'Sigelai', the name given in Saxon and Norman times to the meeting place of the Secklow Hundred. 'Secklow' originally meant 'Warrior's Hill'.
Saxon Gate/Street—the modern V7 passes within a few metres of the original Secklow Hundred meeting place.
Witan Gate—the Witan was the Saxon assembly equivalent to our modern Parliament.
Grafton Gate—like Grafton Street (V6) it is named after the Dukes of Grafton who lived at Grafton Regis.
Elder Gate—Saxon community leaders were called Elders as a sign of respect. From this we get the modern term 'aldermen'.
Middleton Hall—'Milton' is derived from the original Saxon name Middleton.
Queen's Court—so named after the visit in 1979 of HM The Queen.
Acorn Walk—from the main charge of the shield.
Borough Walk—the arms being the Borough arms.
Crown Walk—a mural crown encircles the base of the oak tree on the shield.
Deer Walk—two bucks support the shield.
Eagle Walk—the crest contains a gold-coloured Roman eagle.
Field Walk—the field is the basic background to the shield.
Gold Oak Walk—both the oak tree on the shield and the oak branches of the crest are coloured gold.
Milton Keynes is, more than anything perhaps, a city of variety and contrasts, and although many may think that has come about since the inception of the new city, it is in fact a tradition established many centuries ago by the city's diverse and numerous forefathers.

Many of the names we associate so easily today with residential, commercial and recreational areas in fact owe their existence to a time when deer still roamed in Linford Wood (C13), when the C17 watermill at Caldecotte still functioned and when trams were installed in Wolverton (late C19).

The name 'Milton Keynes' itself dates back to Saxon times when it was referred to as 'Middle Tun'. The village of Middleton, as it later became known, was owned by the de Cahaignes family, hence 'Milton Keynes'.

Detailed below is a list of the grid squares within the designated area with a short account of the origin of each name.

GRID ROADS

V1 Snelshall Street	— name originates from the nearby site of Snelshall Priory.
V2 Tattenhoe Street	— the road passes the village of Tattenhoe.
V3 Fulmer Street	— Fulmer is the name of an ancient pond at Shenley Brook End.
V4 Watling Street	— the original name for the Roman-built highway.
V5 Great Monks Street	— associated with nearby Bradwell Abbey.
V6 Grafton Street	— after the Dukes of Grafton of Grafton Regis.
V7 Saxon Street	— this runs through Secklow Corner, the site of the meeting place of the Secklow Hundred in Saxon times.
V8 Marlborough Street	— the road begins at Stantonbury which itself is associated with Sarah Jennings, Duchess of Marlborough.
V9 Overstreet	— was once a track or field near Downs Barn in the C17.
V10 Brickhill Street	— leads to the three Brickhills, Great, Little and Bow.
H1 Ridgeway	— an ancient Roman track and name.
H2 Millers Way	— passes Bradwell Windmill.
H3 Monks Way	— passes Bradwell Abbey.
H4 Dansteed Way	— from Dunstead, an ancient site and field name.
H5 Portway	— an important C13 track.
H6 Childs Way	— an C18 track or field name in east Loughton.
H7 Chaffron	— C18 track through Woughton.
H8 Standing Way	— C18 track through Woughton.
H9 Groveway	— an existing C18 name.
H10 Bletcham Way	— an C18 track through Woughton.

A11. Rectory Cottages, Bletchley

A11. Interior Roof

A12. Freefolk Cottage, Bletchley

B3. Brookfield Cottages, Old Bradwell

B3. Brookfield Cottages after renovations

B10. Home Farm, Old Bradwell

C1. Bradwell Abbey Farm

C2. Chapel of Our Lady of Bradwell

C2a. Wall Paintings of Pilgrims

E21–E23. Fenny Lock and Pump House

E15–E16. Fenny Stratford Station

E45. St Martin's Church

E45. St Martin's Church, Interior

E47. The Chantry House

F3. Linford Manor

F3. Ballroom Ceiling

F4. The Pavilions

F6. Almshouses, Linford Manor

F1. Pritchard Monument, Church of St Andrew, Great Linford

F18. Cricket Store, Great Linford

F24. No 6 The Wharf, Great Linford

G3. Holy Trinity Church, New Rosebery Music Room, Great Woolstone

G5. The Rectory, Great Woolstone

G17. Church Farm, Little Woolstone

G17. Church Farm before restoration

G19. Tower of Holy Trinity Church

H1. Church of All Saints, Loughton

H20. Beckett House, Loughton

K3. White Cottage, Shenley Church End

K9. Stafford Almshouses, Shenley Church End

K24. Westbury Farm, Shenley Brook End

J20. The Old Rectory, Milton Keynes

L13. Simpson Village

M5. Bradwell Windmill

M5. Restoration of Cap of Windmill

N9 and N121. Market Square, Stony Stratford

N117 and N118. Market Square, Stony Stratford

N97. No 101 Horsefair Green, Stony Stratford

N13. No 25 High Street, Stony Stratford

N17. The Old George, High Street, Stony Stratford